Lotus

# Illustrated DICTIONARY of MANAGEMENT

*Complied and Edited by:*

***Oliver Lindwig***

Lotus PRESS
4735/22, Prakash Deep Building
Ansari Road, Daryaganj,
New Delhi - 110002

Lotus *Illustrated*

# DICTIONARY *of* MANAGEMENT



***ISBN 81 89093 44 4***

*Published by:*

**Lotus Press Publishers & Distributors**
Unit No. 220, 2nd Floor, 4735/22,
Prakash Deep Building, Ansari Road, Darya Ganj,
New Delhi- 110002, Ph.: 32903912, 23280047, 09811838000
• E-mail : lotuspress1984@gmail.com www.lotuspress.co.in

*Printed at :* Lotus Press Publishers & Distributors, New Delhi

# PREFACE

Traditionally, the term 'management' refers to the activities (and often the group of people) involved in the four general functions: planning, organising, leading and coordinating of resources. Note that the four functions recur throughout the organisation and are highly integrated. Emerging trends in management include assertions that leading is different than managing and that the nature of how the four functions are carried out must change to accommodate a 'new paradigm' in management. This topic in the library helps the reader accomplish broad understanding of management (including traditional and emerging views) and the areas of knowledge and skills required to carry out the major functions of management.

In this dictionary we have tried to discuss each and every aspect related to management. We have tried to explain all the key terms of management in great details with the help of the examples. These examples will help in clear understanding of these terms. We have tried to keep the language of the dictionary as simple as possible. This dictionary also contains pictures related to management terms. These pictures will make your knowledge of the subject clearer. It is a dictionary for all those people who are in any way related to the field of management. It will not only prove helpful for the management students but will be of great advantage to people who are actually working in the field of management.

## ■ 'best in class' principle

apart from the traditional financial analysis the SRI Unternehmensanalyse looks for the best companies from selected industries ('best in class' principle), which correspond to the ecological and social criteria.

## ■ 'what if' analysis

the capability of 'asking' the software package what the effect will be of changing some of the input data or independent variables.

## ■ 3pl, third-party logistics

describes businesses that provide one or many of a variety of logistics-related services. Types of services would include public warehousing, contract warehousing, transportation management, distribution management, freight consolidation. A 3PL provider may take over all receiving, storage, value added, shipping and transportation responsibilities for a client and conduct them in the 3PL's warehouse using the 3PL's equipment and employees or may manage one or all of these functions in the client's facility using the client's equipment or any combination of the above. Another term, 4PL is sometimes used to describe businesses that manage a variety of logistics related services for clients by using 3PLs.

## ■ ABC classification

a method for prioritising items based on the product of the annual demand and the unit cost. The high 'annual money volume' items are classified as 'A' item. The low annual money volume items are classified as 'C' items. Based on pareto's law, the ABC classification system drives us to manage 'A' items more carefully. This means that these item should be ordered more often, counted more often, located closer to the door and be forecasted more carefully. Conversely, 'C' items are not very important from an investment point of view and therefore should be ordered rarely and not counted often. Some firms use other methods for defining the ABC classification — such as the stock out cost or the medical criticality of the item. This has nothing to do with Activity Based Costing. See **pareto's law.**

## ■ ABC stratification

method used to categorise inventory into groups based upon certain activity characteristics. Examples of ABC stratifications would include ABC by velocity (times sold), ABC by sales money, ABC by quantity sold / consumed, ABC by average inventory investment, ABC by margin. ABC stratifications are used to develop inventory planning policies, set count frequencies for cycle counting, slot inventory for optimised order picking and other inventory management activities.

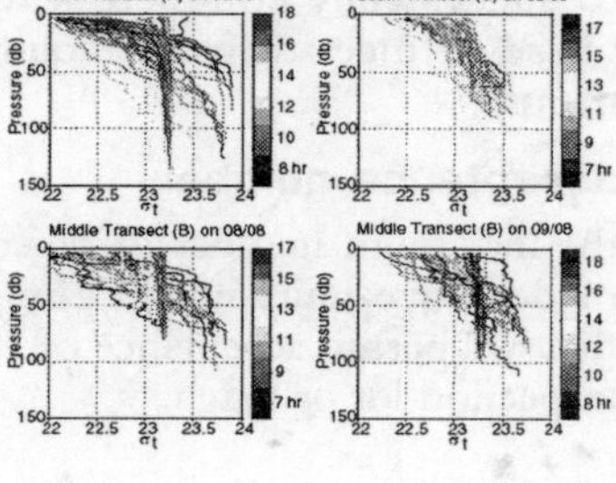

## ABC, activity based costing

usually refers to costing method that breaks down overhead costs into specific activities (cost drivers) in order to more accurately distribute the costs in product costing. Has also been applied to customer and vendor management.

## acceptability criteria

a limit or limits placed upon the degree of non-conformance permitted in material or products expressed in definitive operational terms. Also known as acceptance criteria.

## Acceptable Quality Level (AQL)

when deciding whether or not to accept a batch, a sample of *n* parts is taken from the batch and a decision is made to accept the batch if the number or percent of defects is better than the AQL. See **acceptance sampling.**

## acceptance

an action by an authorised representative of the acquirer by which the acquirer assumes ownership of products as a partial or complete performance of contract.

## acceptance criteria

the criteria a product must meet to successfully complete a test phase or meet delivery requirements.

## acceptance number

the maximum number of defects or defective units in the sample that will permit acceptance of the inspection lot or batch.

## acceptance review

a control gate at which the buyer determines that the item presented for acceptance complies with its specification. Acceptance reviews occur at all levels in the system hierarchy. The verification results are presented as evidence of specification compliance.

## acceptance sampling

acceptance sampling plans are used to make accept/reject decisions for each lot. With attribute sampling plans, these decisions are based on a count of the number of defects and defectives, with variable sampling plans these decisions are based on measurements. Plans requiring only a single sample set are known as single sampling plans, double and multiple sampling plans may require additional samples sets. For example, an attribute single sampling plan with a sample size n=50 and an accept number a=1 requires that a sample of 50 units be inspected. If the number of defectives in that sample is one or zero, the lot is accepted. Otherwise it is rejected. Ideally, when a sampling plan is used, all bad lots will be rejected and all good lots accepted. However, because accept/reject decisions are based on a sample of the lot, there is always a chance of making an incorrect decision. So what protection does a sampling plan offer? The behaviour of a sampling plan can be described by its operating characteristic (OC) curve, which plots percent defectives versus the corresponding probabilities of acceptance. See **inspection.**

### ■ acceptance test

formal testing conducted to determine whether or not a system satisfies its acceptance criteria and to enable the acquirer to determine whether or not to accept the system.

### ■ Acceptance Test Procedure (ATP)

detailed step-by- step instructions for the set-up, operation and evaluation of tests. The procedure includes the approach to sampling and statistical quality control.

### ■ access

a users ability to communicate with a system.

### ■ accommodate concerns

1. make room for opinions
2. make an allowance for a preference
3. tolerate a different point of view.

### ■ account

a listing or statement of fiscal, corporate or project cost data.

### ■ accountability

responsibility for the progress of a project or the progress of the firm.

### ■ accountability matrix

a structure that relates the project organisation structure to the work breakdown structure to help ensure that each element of the project's scope of work is assigned to a responsible individual..

### ■ accreditation

certification by a duly recognised body of the facilities, capability, objectivity, competence and integrity of an agency, service or operational group or individual to provide the specific service(s) or operation(s) needed.

***Accreditation Certificate***

| | |
|---|---|
| **Company** | Taitron Components Inc |
| **Address** | 28040 W Harrison P'Way<br>Valencia<br>CA 91355<br>USA |
| **Scope of Activities** | Distributor of Discrete Semi-Conductors. Opto-Electronic Devices |
| **Assessment Standard** | ISO 9001:2000 |
| **Certifying Body** | Professional Quality Assessments |

*Certified* that the above referenced organisation has been registered on the ASCB(E) list of accredited assessed and certificated suppliers in accordance with our terms and conditions.

Signed — Accreditation Mark

Expiry Date of this certificate

**21-Feb-03**

Certificate Number

**4011900**

### ■ accrual accounting

a system of accounting in which expenses are recognised when incurred and revenues are recognised when they are known, regardless of the time when actual payment of cash is made or received.

### ■ accrued cost

a cost that is incurred all at once at a certain time in a project or gradually, for instance, over the entire time a task is being worked on.

### ■ accuracy

degree of exactness, usually expressed as a range when used in connection with cost and time estimates.

**acquirer**

an organisation that procures products for itself or another organisation.

**acquisition**

obtaining under contract supplies and services to meet the needs of a project.

**acquisition control**

a system for acquiring project equipment, material and services in a uniform and orderly fashion.

**acquisition evaluation**

review and analysis of responses to determine supplier's ability to perform the work as requested. This activity may include an evaluation of supplier's financial resources, ability to comply with technical criteria and delivery schedules, satisfactory record of performance and eligibility for award.

**acquisition methods**

the various ways by which goods or services are acquired from suppliers.

**acquisition negotiations**

contracting without formal advertising. This method offers flexible procedures, permits bargaining and provides an opportunity to prospective suppliers to revise their offers before the award.

**acquisition plan**

the document that describes the approach for acquisition. It defines competitive or sole source, schedule, funding, manpower, facilities, risk, etc.

**acquisition process**

the process of acquiring personnel/goods/services for new or existing work within the general definitions of contracts requiring an offer and acceptance, consideration, lawful subject matter and competent parties.

**acquisition programme**

a directed, funded effort designed to provide a new, improved or continuing system in response to a validated operational need.

**action item**

something agreed to be done as a result of a discussion at a meeting and usually recorded in the minutes of that meeting.

**action item status**

a list of problem issues, including a description, point of contact and dates of action and resolution.

**action plan**

a description of what needs to be done, when and by whom.

**active item**

any inventory item that has been used or sold within a given period (say last year). It is common for some retailers to have 200,000 items in their item master, but only 20,000 'active' items.

**activity**

an element of work performed during the course of a project. An activity normally has an expected duration, expected cost and expected resource requirements. Activities are often subdivided into tasks.

## Activity Based Cost (ABC)

Activity-Based Costing (ABC) is an information system that maintains and processes data on a firm's activities and products. It identifies the activities performed, traces cost to these activities and then uses various cost drivers to trace the cost of activities to products. These cost drivers, such as the number of persons performing work or the number of set-ups required per product reflect the consumption of activities by the products. By costing the various activities performed, it is easy to see how•you might easily pinpoint changes in resource requirements for each activity if you changed your process or procedure. If you operated under a traditional costing system, pinpointing changes in resource requirements would be virtually impossible because it accumulated cost under budgetary line items (such as salaries) or functions (such as engineering). Activity-Base Management (ABM) is merely the use of the activity-based costing tool by process owners to control and improve their operations. Because process analysis is conducted in the building of an activity-based cost model, management knows its business much better and can consequently evaluate value added and non-value added activities. Because all of the costs for processes are known, outsourcing and privatisation questions can easily be evaluated. Because a certain volume of work produces a certain outcome, 'what if' analysis can be conducted to determine what resources are required if operations are scaled back or expanded. The potential of the activity-based costing tool to assist management in daily operational decisions is powerful.

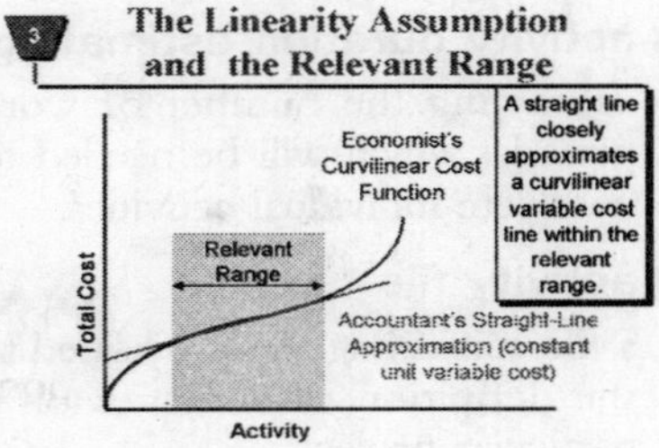


## activity calendar

in computer scheduling, the calendar that defines the working and non-working patterns for an activity. The activity calendar is normally overridden by the project calendar.

## activity code

a set of numeric or alpha-numeric characters that uniquely identifies a particular activity. Typically developed by numbering the activities and tasks in the WBS.

## activity definition

the process of identifying the specific activities that must be performed in order to produce the various project deliverables.

## activity description

a short phrase or label used in a project network diagram. The activity description normally describes the scope of work of the activity.

**■ activity duration**

the best estimate of the time necessary for the accomplishment of the work involved in an activity, considering the nature of the work and resources needed for it.

**■ activity duration estimating**

estimating the number of work periods, which will be needed to complete individual activities.

**■ activity file**

a file containing all data related to the definition of activities on a particular project.

**■ activity id**

a unique code identifying each activity in a project.

**■ activity list**

list of project activities.

**■ Activity on Arrow (AOA)**

a network diagram showing sequence of activities, in which each activity is represented by an arrow, with a circle representing a node or event at each end.

**■ Activity on Node (AON)**

a network where activities are represented by a box or a node linked by dependencies.

**■ activity properties**

a description of the attributes of the activity such as start and finish times, resources required and anticipated cost, etc.

**■ activity status**

the state of completion of an activity. A planned activity has not yet started. A started activity is in progress. A finished activity is complete.

**■ actual**

information that shows what has actually occurred. For example, the actual start date for a task is the day on which the task actually started and its actual cost is the amount spent up to the present.

**■ Actual Cost Of Work Performed (ACWP)**

total costs incurred (direct and indirect) in accomplishing work during a given time period.

**■ actual costs**

the costs actually incurred and recorded for work performed.

**■ actual dates**

the dates that activities really started and finished as opposed to planned or projected dates.

**■ actual direct costs**

those costs specifically identified with a contract or project, based upon the contractor's cost identification and accumulation system.

**■ actual expenditures**

see **actual costs**.

**■ actual finish**

date on which an activity was completed.

**■ Actual Finish Date (AF)**

the calendar date that work actually ended on an activity. It must be prior to or equal to the data date. The remaining duration of this activity is zero.

■ **Actual Start Date (AS)**

the date work actually started on an activity.

■ **added value**

the addition of some worthwhile quality or performance improvement as a result of some action taken, which may or may not have been part of the original understanding, agreement or contract.

■ **address**

to provide words on a topic which may have little or no meaning.

■ **adequate public facilities**

adequate public facilities ordinances prevent new construction until municipal services, including water, sewer, roads and schools, are available to serve that development.

■ **ad-hoc query**

any spontaneous or unplanned question or query. It is a query that consists of dynamically constructed SQL and is one capability in a data-driven DSS.

■ **administrative change**

a unilateral contract modification, in writing, that does not affect the substantive rights of the parties (e.g., a change in the billing office).

■ **administrative closure**

generating, gathering and disseminating information to formalise project completion.

■ **Advanced Planning And Scheduling (APS)**

a manufacturing planning and scheduling system that is often used to supplement 'infinite planning' systems based on MRP (ERP) logic. An APS can create detailed schedules for orders, whereas traditional MRP systems create very crude plans based on fixed planned lead times. Currently, the two best known APS software vendors include i2 Technologies and Manugistics.

■ **affect the production**

1. to reduce output.
2. a reduction in output that is not desired.

■ **AFV**

■ **see investment trust regulation.**

■ **agency**

a legal relationship by which one party is empowered to act on behalf of another party.

■ **agency management**

a term that refers to those people who are responsible for the business operations of an agency.

■ **agenda**

a list of things to be done or discussed, typically at a meeting.

■ **aggregate inventory management**

inventories with thousands or even hundreds of thousands of items are difficult to manage at an item level. Aggregate inventory management tools allow managers to group items and manage each group with policies, key performance indicators, targets and reports. For example, a particular group of items might share carrying charge parameters, turnover goals and have a fixed space allocation.

## ■ aggregate or aggregated data

data that results from applying a process to combine data elements. Data that is summarised.

## ■ aggregate planning (aggregate plan)

the process of translating the annual business and marketing plans into a production plan. In academic circles, the result of the aggregate planning process is called the 'aggregate plan', whereas in APICS circles it is known as the 'production plan'. Aggregate planning is particularly difficult for firms with seasonal products. An aggregate measure is particularly useful if the production plan includes many dissimilar products. Costs relevant to the aggregate planning decisions include: inventory carrying costs, capacity change costs (hiring, training, firing, facility expansion or contraction, equipment expansion or reduction) and possibly the opportunity costs of lost sales.

## ■ aggregation

summation of parts. Typically used in reference to estimating.

## ■ aggressive quote

a low bid to produce a good or provide a service.

## ■ agio

The agio is the proportional difference between current market prices and the payment-settled inventory value plus last payment (proportionate).

## ■ agreement, legal

a legal document that sets out the terms of a contract between two parties.

## ■ AIAG

Automotive Industry Action Group.

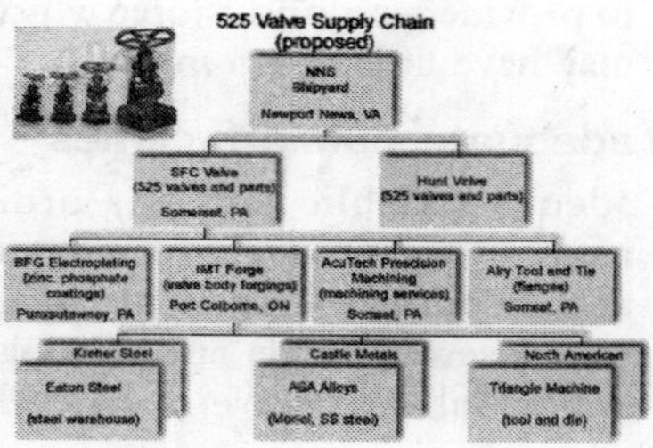


## ■ alerts

a notification from an event that a trigger has exceeded a pre-defined threshold. Alerts can be used with data-driven DSS.

## ■ algorithm

a type of mathematical model used for running calculations, typically computerised. For example, different project management scheduling software programmes use different algorithms for calculating resource levelling.

## ■ alignment

the degree of agreement, conformance and consistency among

organisational purpose, vision and values. Structures, systems and processes and individual skills and behaviour.

## ■ allocated baseline

requirements allocated to lower level system elements that are controlled by formal change control.

## ■ allocated stock

a quantity of an item that has been reserved, but not yet withdrawn or issued from stock. Allocated inventory is not available for other purposes.

## ■ allocations

allocations in inventory management refer to actual demand created by sales orders or work orders against a specific item. The terminology and the actual processing that controls allocations will vary from one software system to another. A standard allocation is an aggregate quantity of demand against a specific item in a specific facility. Standard allocations do not specify that specific units will go to specific orders. A firm allocation is an allocation against specific units within a facility, such as an allocation against a specific location, lot or serial number. Firm allocations are also referred to as specific allocations, frozen allocations, hard allocations, hard commitments, holds, reserved inventory. Standard allocations simply show that there is demand while firm allocations reserve or hold the inventory for the specific order designated.

## ■ all-time demand

the total future requirements for an item. This is the sum of the demand until the product termination date or until the end of the world. This is used to determine the requirements for the final purchase or production run. This is sometimes called the 'all-time' or the 'lifetime' requirement. See **geometric decay.**

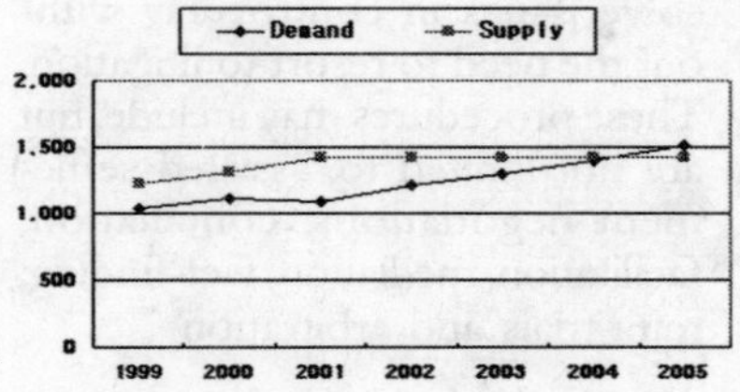


## ■ all-time order

the last order for a particular product in the last phase of its life cycle. This order should be large enough that the stock provided will satisfy all expected future demand for the product concerned. Sometime called a 'life-time' buy.

## ■ alternate resource

a resource that may be substituted in a task if the requested resource is not available.

## ■ alternative analysis

breaking down a complex situation for the purpose of generating and evaluating different solutions and approaches.

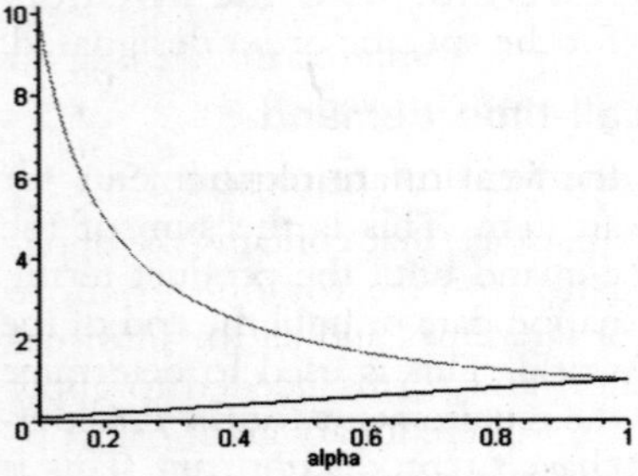


■ **Alternative Dispute Resolution (ADR)**

any procedure or combination of procedures voluntarily used to resolve issues in controversy without the need to resort to litigation. These procedures may include, but are not limited to, assisted settlement negotiations, conciliation, facilitation, mediation, fact-finding, mini-trials and arbitration.

■ **alternatives**

review of the means available and the impact of trade-offs to attain the objectives.

■ **alternatives analysis**

breaking down a complex scope situation for the purpose of generating and evaluating different solutions and approaches.

■ **ambush marketing**

to tie a firm's name to its competitors advertising.

■ **analogous cost estimating**

an estimating method, which determines the rough cost of a project by comparing it with an older, similar project for which actual costs are available. A variety of top-down estimating that is typically used in the early planning stages before a more accurate, bottoms-up approach can be generated.

■ **analysis**

the detailed study and examination of something, in order to discover more about it. Analysis typically includes discovering parts of the item being studied, as well as how they fit together. An example is the study of schedule variances for cause, impact, corrective action and results.

■ **annexation**

a change in existing community boundaries resulting from the incorporation of additional land.

■ **annual report/half-yearly report**

the fund line publishes an examined annual report for everyone of its administered investment trusts within four months after conclusion of the business year and within two months at expiration of the first half of the business year an unchecked half-yearly report. The annual report contains, among other things, data for annual account, the discharges and

**Activity-based Budget Allocation by Sector, 2000-2001**

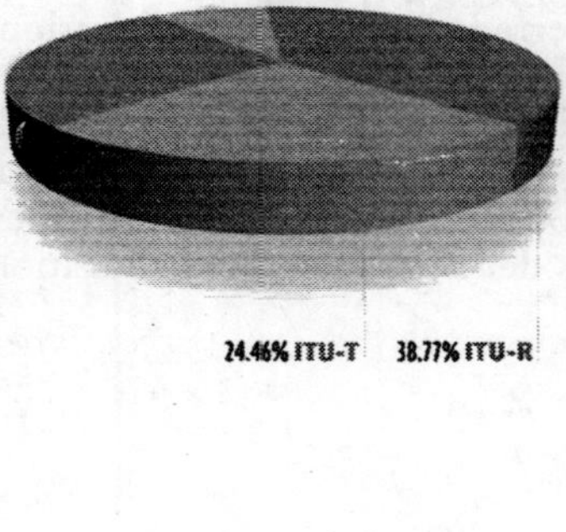

for the inventory of the fortune as well as the report of the revision place. The half-yearly report contains the most important half yearly results.

■ **anticipated award cost**

the most probable contract price at time of tender and award. It forms part of the forecast to complete.

■ **anticipation stock**

Inventory held in order to satisfy seasonal demand, cope with expected reduced capacity due to maintenance or anticipated strike or store seasonal supply for a level demand throughout the year.

■ **A-plant**

in this type of manufacturing process, we have many components that are 'assembled' into just a few end items.

■ **apparent low bidder**

the contractor who has submitted the lowest compliant bid for all or part of a project as described in a set of bid documents.

■ **application**

an act of putting to use (new techniques): an act of applying techniques.

■ **application area**

a category of projects that have a common element not present in all projects. Application areas are usually defined in terms of either the product of the project (i.e., by similar technologies or industry sectors) or the type of customer (e.g., internal vs. external, government vs. commercial). Application areas often overlap.

■ **application package**

a package that contains the application notice for one or more programmes and all the information and forms needed to apply for a discretionary grant or cooperative agreement.

■ **application programmers**

those programmers responsible for the development of computer programmes that perform a specific function.

■ **apportioned effort**

effort that is not itself readily divisible into short-span work packages but which is related and proportional to measured effort in other work packages. Project management overhead as an example.

■ **apportioned task**

a task that is dependent on or related to the performance of another task.

■ **appraisal**

an impartial evaluation of information concerning a system, service or product to determine either its value or its measure of effectiveness and efficiency for purposes of making recommendations.

■ **appraisal cost**

the expenses associated with the direct costs of measuring quality through inspection and testing.

**appropriation**
an allocation of funds to a project by the owner or sponsor after the project has been approved to proceed.

**approval**
written notification by an authorised representative of the acquirer that the developer's plans, design or other aspects of the project appear to be sound and can be used as the basis for further work. Such approval does not shift responsibility from the developer to meet contractual requirements.

**approval to proceed**
approval by an authorising committee or person at a project's initiation or prior to the beginning of the next stage.

**approve**
to accept as satisfactory. Approval implies that the item approved has the endorsement of the approving entity. The approval may still require confirmation by somebody else, as in levels of approval. In management use, the important distinction is between approved and authorised. See **authorisation.**

**approved changes**
changes that have been approved by higher authority.

**approved data**
that issue or version of data which has been identified by the developer/supplier as being the master issue or version of data subject to configuration management which has been submitted for acquirer approval and which has been approved by the acquirer..

**APS, Advanced Planning and Scheduling**
software system designed to integrate with ERP and MRP systems to enhance the short term production planning and scheduling systems that are notoriously inadequate in MRP systems. APS systems have extensive programming logic that allows them to be more effective in dealing with rapidly changing customer demands.

**AQL**
Acceptable Quality Level.

**arbitrage**
utilisation of local or international evaluation differences of same securities or related values, whereby these are bought on the market with the lower price and sold at the market with the higher price.

**arbitrary**
something done without apparent logic.

**arbitration**
a formalised system for dealing with grievances and administering corrective justice as part of collective bargaining agreements.

**architecture**
the organisational structure of a system HWCI or CSCI, identifying its components, their interfaces and a concept of execution among them.

**■ architecture**

the design and interconnection of the main components of a system.

**■ archive**

a repository for infrequently used or historic records.

**■ Area of Project Management Application (APMA)**

the environment in which a project takes place, with its own particular nomenclature and accepted practices e.g. facilities, products or systems development projects.

**■ areas of responsibility**

used to define the person or organisational entity responsible for specific policy areas, processes and procedures as identified.

**■ arrow**

the graphic presentation of an activity.

**■ Arrow Diagramming Method (ADM)**

a network diagramming technique in which activities are represented by arrows. The tail of the arrow represents the start and the head represents the finish of the activity (the length of the arrow does not represent the expected duration of the activity). Activities are connected at points called nodes (usually drawn as small circles) to illustrate the sequence in which the activities are expected to be performed.

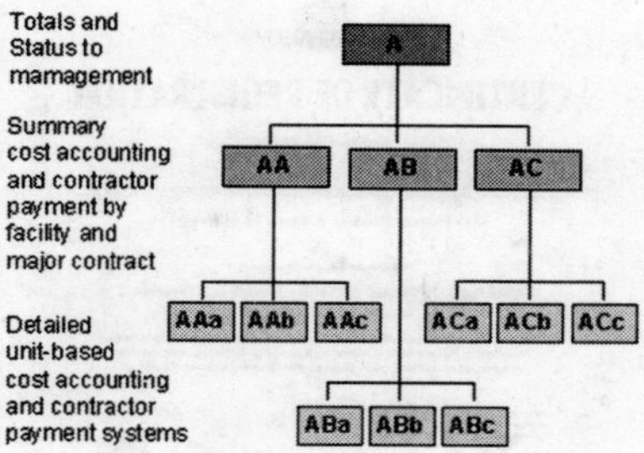


**■ arrows to fire**

points to mention and/or tactics to take.

**■ article**

the Prime system or equipment being acquired under a contract.

**■ artificial intelligence**

a broad term encompassing anything relating to making computers behave like humans.

**■ AS**

see **actual start date.**

**■ as late as possible**

an activity for which the project scheduler sets the start dates as late as possible without delaying the early dates of any successor.

**■ as soon as possible**

an activity for which the project scheduler sets the start date to be as soon as possible. This is the default activity type in most project management tools.

**■ AS9100**

quality system requirements for suppliers to the aerospace industry (previously known as AS9000).

CERTIFICATE OF REGISTRATION

Certificate No. 95-4854

Turbine Engine Components Technologies Corp.

8839 Pioneer Boulevard, Santa Fe Springs, CA

The Quality Management System is registered to:

ISO 9002:1994 and AS9100 - Revision A/Section 2

The Quality Management System is applicable to:

The machining and assembly of turbine and turbocharger hardware including impellers, integrally bladed rotors, high precision diffusers, small quantity compressor blades and vanes plus complex titanium airframe hardware.

Authorized Signatory

Intertek Testing Services
Systems Certification

## ■ asap

see **as soon as possible.**

## ■ Advanced Shipment Notification (ASN)

advanced shipment notifications are used to notify a customer of a shipment. ASNs will often include PO numbers, SKU numbers, lot numbers, quantity, pallet or container number, carton number. ASNs may be paper-based, however, electronic notification is preferred. Advanced shipment notification systems are usually combined with bar-coded compliance labelling which allows the customer to receive the shipment into inventory through the use of bar-code scanners and automated data collection systems.

## ■ as-needed

delivery or consumption of resources or information just as and when required.

## ■ as-of date

the date that a piece of information, such as a status report, is reporting up to.

## ■ Application Service Provider (ASP)

a recent twist in software marketing in which the software licenses are owned by the ASP and reside on their system while the client rents the rights to use the software. The ASP may be the software manufacturer or a third party business. The benefits of using an ASP are lower upfront costs, quicker implementations and the reduction of the need for internal IS personnel and mainframe/server hardware. It is hoped that ASPs will allow small to midsize businesses greater access to technology than was previously available.

## ■ as-performed schedule

the final project schedule which depicts actual completion (finish) dates, actual durations and start dates.

## ■ ASRS, Automated Storage and Retrieval Systems

a system of rows of rack, each row having a dedicated retrieval unit that moves vertically and horizontally along the rack picking and putting away loads.

## ■ Assemble-To-Order (ATO)

a customer interface strategy that responds to a customer order by putting together standard components and modules for the customer. Customer lead time is sum of the assembly, packing and shipping time. This approach allows for a large variety of final products within a relatively short customer lead-time.

**■ assembly**

a number of parts or subassemblies or any combination thereof joined together to perform a specific function and capable of disassembly.

**■ assessment**

1. an evaluation process including a document review, an on-site audit and an analysis and report.
2. a determination of value, usually in money terms, of an asset, situation or condition that requires some action.

**■ assumptions**

factors that, for planning purposes, are considered to be true, real or certain. Assumptions affect all aspects of project planning and are part of the progressive elaboration of the project. Project teams frequently identify, document and validate assumptions as part of their planning process. Assumptions generally involve a degree of risk.

**■ assumptions analysis**

a technique to explores the assumptions' accuracy and identifies risks to the project from inaccuracy, inconsistency or incompleteness of assumptions.

**■ assurance**

to examine with the intent to verify.

**■ at some juncture**

some unspecified point in time in the future.

**■ at this point**

now.

**■ ate allocation**

depending upon fund the distribution of the plants on the different plant instruments (obligations, shares and real estates), industries, markets and currencies.

**■ atlas test specification**

an atlas test specification is dedicated to defining the test requirements for the Unit-Under-Test in a manner, which is independent of the test equipment used for its implementation. It is derived from the System/Subsystem Specification or CIDS/PIDS and shall contain the absolute values of the functional design performance parameters. The actual implementation may use manual test equipment, automatic test equipment or a combination of both. The acceptance test procedure shall be derived from this specification suitably adjusted to remove the uncertainties of the target test equipment being used.

**■ attribute**

a term used by quality professionals that deals with a binomial state of being.

**■ attributes**

qualitative data that can be counted for recording and analysis. Examples include characteristics such as the presence of a required label and the installation of all required fasteners.

**■ attrition**

the loss of a resource due to causes beyond the control of the project manager.

**audit**

an onsite verification activity used to determine the effective implementation of a supplier's documented quality system.

**audit client**

organisation or person requesting an audit.

**audit conclusion**

outcome of an audit provided by the audit team after consideration of the audit objectives and all audit findings.

**audit criteria**

set of policies, procedures or requirements used as a reference (while conducting an audit).

**audit evidence**

records, statements of fact or other information which are relevant to the audit criteria and verifiable.

**audit findings**

results of the evaluation of the collected audit evidence against audit criteria.

**audit programmed**

set of one or more audits planned for a specific time frame and directed towards a specific purpose.

**audit resolution process**

the process by which the department determines whether costs in an audit report are actually allowable or unallowable. If costs are identified as being unallowable, the department initiates action to have grantees return unallowable expenditures.

**audit team**

one or more auditors conducting an audit.

**auditee**

organisation being audited.

**auditing**

auditing records the sequence of activities that occur on any given file or body of content within a content management system. This sequence of events - an audit trail - can be used by content contributors, managers and auditors alike to determine how and why content was changed.

**auditor**

person with the competence to conduct an audit.

**authentication**

the procedure (essentially approval) used by the approval authority in verifying that specification content is acceptable. Authentication does not imply acceptance or responsibility for the specified item to perform successfully.

**authorisation**

the power granted by management to specified individuals allowing them to approve transactions, procedures or total systems.

**authority**

the power to make and enforce a decision.

**authorise**

to give final approval. A person who can authorise something is vested with authority to give final endorsement which requires no further approval.

**authorised un-priced work**

the effort for which contract cost adjustments has not been agreed to, but for which authorisation to proceed has been granted.

**authorised work**

an effort that has been approved by higher authority and may or may not be definitive.

**autonomation**

stopping a line automatically when a defective part is detected.

**autonomous maintenance**

a TPM principle of having each worker responsible for both maintaining and operating a machine. Maintenance activities include cleaning, lubricating, adjusting, inspecting and repair. See **total productive maintenance.**

**availability**

the ability of an item to perform its designated function when required for use.

**Available-to-Promise (ATP)**

The uncommitted portion of a company's inventory and planned production, maintained in the master schedule to support customer order promising. The ATP quantity is the uncommitted inventory balance in the first period and is normally calculated for each period in which an MPS receipt is scheduled. In the first period, ATP includes on-hand inventory less customer orders that are due and overdue.

**average cost method**

cost averaging. Favourable utilisation of exchange rate fluctuations. It sets on the advantage of regular payments, with same monthly deposits the investor acquires more with low issue prices and with higher issue prices of fewer portions. The investor thereby on a long-term basis achieves a more favourable average cost price than with the regular purchase of a given number of items of portions in the same period.

**average or mean**

the most common expression of the centring of a distribution. It is calculated by totalling the observed values and dividing by the number of observations.

**Average Outgoing Quality (AOQ)**

the average quality of outgoing product including all accepted lots, plus all rejected lots after the rejected lots have been effectively 100 percent inspected and all defectives replaced by non-defectives.

**Average Outgoing Quality Limit (AOQL)**

the maximum of the average outgoing qualities for all possible incoming qualities for a given sampling plan.

**average sample size curve**

the curves that show the average sample sizes which may be expected to occur under the various sampling plans for a given process quality.

## ■ avoidable costs

avoidable costs include any expense that is not incurred if a new investment is made that would make the expense unnecessary. For example, if a conveyor belt is broken and must be fixed to operate the facility, there is a cost to fix the conveyor as well as the option to purchase a new one. If a new conveyor is purchased, there is no need for the repair expense and hence, it was avoided.

## ■ avoidance

keeping away from. Typically used as a risk reduction strategy by adopting a workaround.

## ■ award

the notification to a bidder of acceptance of a bid.

## ■ award fee

a contract fee provision used to motivate a contractor to respond to issues that are assigned and measured periodically. The contract specifies award fee periods, usually six to nine months long. The award fee criteria are negotiated prior to the start of the award fee period, providing the buyer flexibility to change the incentive emphasis as the project evolves. The determination is made unilaterally by the buyer and is not subject to the legal disputes clause provisions.

## ■ award letter

a letter sent in response to an offer that accepts that offer.

## ■ B2b

Business-to-business. A business selling to other businesses.

## ■ B2c

Business-to-consumer. A business selling directly to consumers.

## ■ back charge

the cost of corrective action taken by the purchaser, chargeable to the supplier under the terms of the contract.

## ■ backflush

method for issuing (reducing on-hand quantities) materials to a manufacturing order. With backflushing, the material is issued automatically when production is posted against an operation. The backflushing programme will use the quantity completed to calculate through the bill of material the quantities of the components used and reduce on-hand balances by this amount. There are usually options during the backflush process to report scrap. In operations using backflushing it is advisable to set up specific machine locations and have materials transferred from storage locations to machine locations when they are physically picked for production. The backflush operation will then issue the material from the machine locations.

## ■ backflushing

A means of reducing the number of inventory transactions by relieving (reducing) the inventory count for parts only when the final product is shipped. For example, instead of counting the number of letter 'A's that issued to assembly, we simply count the number of keyboards that we ship and reduce the letter 'A' inventory count accordingly. Backflushing gives us an imprecise inventory count because of the delay — but it can reduce the transaction cost significantly. A concept of measurement used to periodically explode an end item's BOM to calculate how many of each part went into the final product(s). This eliminates much of the shop-floor data collection activity, which is required if each part must be tracked and accounted for during production.

### ■ backorder

a customer demand for which no stock is available and where the customer is prepared to wait for the item to arrive in stock. If a firm cannot immediately satisfy a customer order, the customer is asked to wait. This order is called a 'backorder' and is usually filled as soon as the items become available. If a product is not available, it is said to be 'on backorder'. In a sense, when we 'backorder' demand, we are 'inventorying' the demand. The set of backorders for a firm is often called the 'order backlog'.

### ■ backward loading (back loading)

a planning method that plans backwards from the due date to determine the start date. The word 'loading' implies that we are not creating a detailed schedule. Backward loading might fill up a time 'bucket' (say a half-day) until the capacity is fully utilised. See **backward scheduling.**

### ■ backward pass

the calculation of late finish dates and late start dates for the uncompleted portions of all network activities. Determined by working backwards through the network logic from the project's end date. The end date may be calculated in a forward pass or set by the customer or sponsor.

### ■ backward scheduling

a scheduling method that plans backwards from the due date (or time) to determine the start date (or time). Unlike backward loading, backward scheduling creates a detailed schedule for each operation based on the planned available capacity.

### ■ balanced matrix

an organisational matrix where functions and projects have the same priority.

### ■ balanced scorecard

a reporting tools that shows senior management key performance metrics so that they can assess how well the firm is achieving the strategy. Typical 'boxes' include owners (financial metrics), operations (internal non-financial metrics such as cycle time and quality), customers (customer satisfaction/loyalty), employees (employee satisfaction) and suppliers (on-time delivery, quality, etc.). The balanced scorecard includes measures of performance that are lagging (return on capital, profit), medium-term indicators (like customer satisfaction indices) and leading indicators (such as adoption rates for or revenue from, new products).

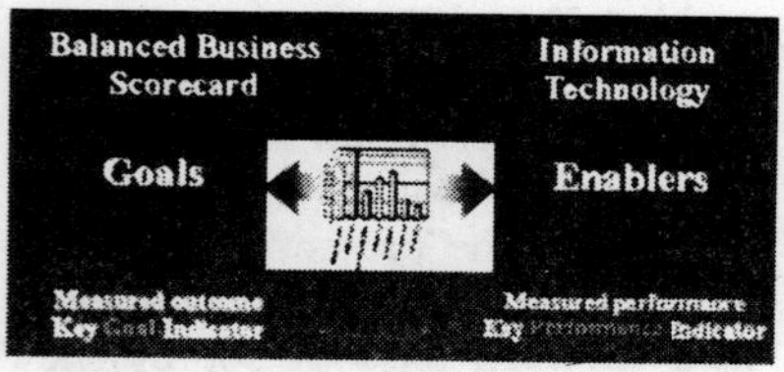


■ **balanced score-card**

developed by Kaplan and Norton as a tool to measure intellectual capital. Designed to focus managers' attention to those factors that help the business strategy, it adds alongside financial measures, measures for customers, internal processes and innovation.

■ **Balanced Scorecard System (BCS)**

method of measuring performance of a firm beyond the typical financial measures. Links corporate goals and direct performance measures in a framework specific to a firm and is one method of measuring the impact of knowledge management.

■ **band aid**

A quick temporary fix which when the fix works, is frequently ignored because of the higher expense to permanently fix the problem

■ **bandwidth**

1. capacity.
2. maximum amount.

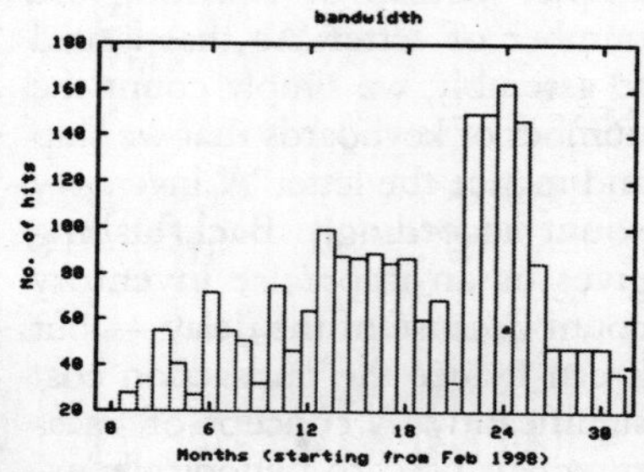


■ **bank**

a planned accumulation of work in progress to permit reasonable fluctuations in performance during times of coordination or associated operation.

■ **bank-internal special estate**

a fortune administered by the bank separated, for which no public advertisement may be made.

■ **bar chart**

a graphic display of schedule-related information. In the typical bar chart, activities or other project elements are listed down the left side of the chart, dates are shown across the top and activity durations are shown as date-placed horizontal bars.

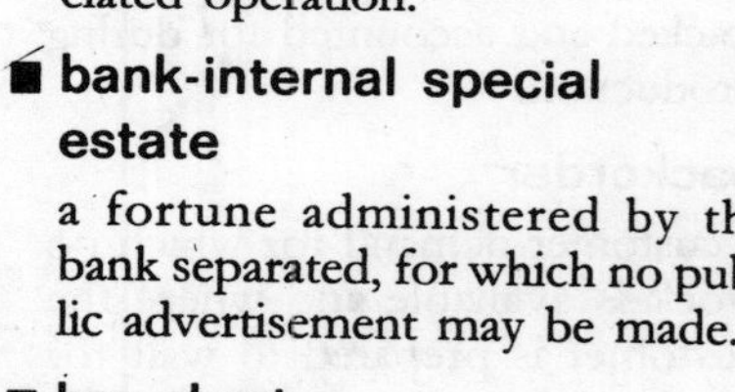

■ **bar code**

information encoded into a pattern of parallel bars and spaces that can be read by a scanner. The encoded information is a unique serialisation that can be correlated with other information from a database. Bar codes are particularly well suited for tracking products through a process.

7 012345 678908

■ **bar net yield**

see **payment net yield.**

■ **barriers**

obstacles in the way of progress, mutual understanding, negotiated settlements, etc.

■ **base lining**

obtaining data on the current process that provides the metrics against which to compare improvements and to use in benchmarking.

■ **base value**

financial value (security, currency, index, raw material etc.), which is appropriate for an option or a future to reason.

■ **baseline**

the original plan for a project, a work package or an activity, plus or minus approved changes. Usually used with a modifier (e.g., cost baseline, schedule baseline performance measurement baseline).

■ **baseline - budget**

a reference base that includes the time phased budget, total funding, time phased funding profile and management reserve.

■ **baseline - cost estimate**

the estimated cost to perform all work defined by the project baseline based on the defined conditions, for example, without overtime.

■ **Baseline at Completion (BAC)**

total completed cost of work as originally planned.

■ **baseline concept**

management's project management plan for a project fixed prior to commencement.

■ **baseline cost**

the amount of money an activity was intended to cost when the baseline plan was established.

■ **baseline management**

the planning organising and control of baseline documentation.

■ **baseline plan**

the original plan (for a project, a work package or an activity), plus or minus approved changes. Usually used with a modifier, e.g., cost baseline, schedule baseline, performance measurement baseline, etc.

■ **baseline review**

a customer review conducted to determine with a limited sampling that a contractor is continuing to use the previously accepted performance system and is properly implementing a baseline on the contract or option under review.

**■ baseline schedule**

a fixed project schedule that is the standard by which project performance is measured. The current schedule is frozen after formal approval until it is formally modified through the change control process as the result of a significant change. When formally changed, the current baseline becomes invalid and should not be compared with the new schedule.

**■ basis of estimate**

the justifications for arriving at a particular cost estimate, including estimating methods, approach taken, prices used, assumptions made, etc.

**■ batch picking**

order picking method where orders are grouped into small batches, an order picker will pick all orders within the batch in one pass. Batch picking is usually associated with pickers with multi-tiered picking carts moving up and down aisles picking batches of usually 4 to 12 orders, however, batch picking is also very common when working with automated material handling equipment such as carousels.

**■ bathtub curve**

a 'U' shaped curve used for reliability theory that shows a typical hazard function with products more likely to fail either very early in their useful life or very late in their useful life.

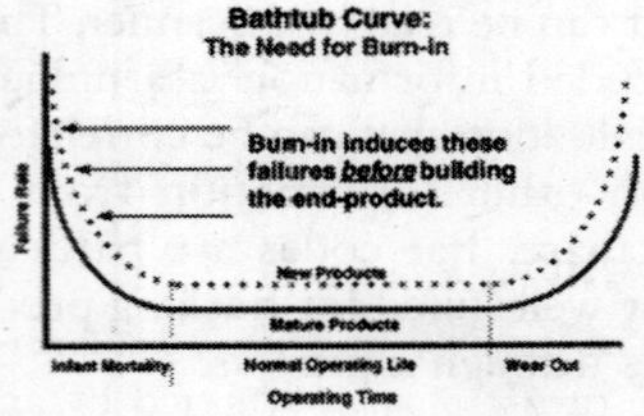


**■ bearish on**

1. against.
2. to assert a belief that something will decrease.

**■ because it keeps them from overproducing**

producing before the output is needed. Blocking avoids 'over-production' and keeps the total work-in-process inventory down to a reasonable level. Blocking for a bottleneck process is bad because it causes the system to lose valuable capacity.

**■ believe in**

behind an idea or in favour of something.

**■ bench mark**

index, which serves an investment trust as basis for a compromise for the performance. Also reference index or comparison index mentioned.

**■ benchmark data**

the results of an investigation to determine how competitors and/or best-in-class companies achieve their level of performance.

**■ benchmarking**

the practice of reviewing the performance of an organisation, department, function or activity, by assessing it against the performance of - best in class - organisations, industry standards or internal departments.

### ■ benefit

a term used to indicate an advantage, profit or gain attained by an individual or organisation.

### ■ benefits management plan

a project statement of who is responsible for achieving the benefits the project is delivering and how they will be measured, managed and monitored.

### ■ benign report

a harmless document when it could have been detrimental to the firm.

### ■ best and final contract offer

final offer by the supplier to perform the work after incorporating negotiated and agreed changes in the procurement documents.

### ■ best and final offer

in negotiations, one or other of the parties declares that this is as far as they can go and it is up to the other to accept or reject and 'walk away'.

### ■ best efforts contract

a contract, usually a type of cost reimbursement contract, that obligates the contractor to do the best job possible under conditions of high risk and imposes no legal obligation to complete.

### ■ best of breed

technically proven investors in the private Equity and Hedge find range.

### ■ best practice

A process or methodology, which has been identified inside or outside the organisation and is recommended as a model. Also known by terms such as Better Practice in some organisations.

### ■ best practices

practical techniques, processes and methods gained from experience that have been shown to produce best results.

### ■ best value

the overall combination of quality, price and various elements of required services that in total are optimal relative to a public body's needs, as predetermined in a solicitation. Best value concepts may be applied when procuring goods and non-professional services, but not construction or professional services. The criteria, factors and basis for the consideration of best value and the process for the consideration of best value shall be as stated in the procurement solicitation.

### ■ beta

a risk measure, which indicates, how sensitive a plant, e.g. a fund, on market movements reacts, which are represented by the respective bench mark. Beta of 1, 2 means for example that one can expect a value movement of 12% with the fund, if one prognosticates a change of 10% for the market. The connection been based on historical observations and applies only approximately. It is the closer, the correlation between that bench mark and the investment trust is the higher.

■ **bid**

an offer to perform the work described in a set of proposal documents at a specified cost.

■ **bid bond**

a bond covering a bid.

■ **bid cost considerations**

consideration of suppliers' approach and reasonableness of cost, cost realism, forecast economic factors affecting cost and cost risks used in the cost proposal.

■ **bid documents**

a set of documents issued for purposes of soliciting bids in the course of the acquisition process.

■ **bid evaluation**

review and analysis of response to determine supplier's ability to perform the work as requested. This activity may include an evaluation of suppliers financial resources, ability to comply with technical criteria and delivery schedules, satisfactory record of performance and eligibility for award.

■ **bid list**

a list of suppliers invited to submit bids for goods or services as specified.

■ **bid package**

a subdivision of a project into separate workable components, usually consistent with the work breakdown structure, for purposes of inviting tenders from suitably qualified bidders. Often used by main contractors to parcel out work to specialist subcontractors on a large project.

■ **bid protests**

the process by which an unsuccessful supplier may seek remedy for unjust contract awards.

■ **bid qualifications**

a list of qualifiers that the supplier attaches to the submitted bid, which is contingent upon these requirements being met.

■ **bid response**

communications, positive or negative from prospective suppliers in response to the invitation to bid.

■ **bid technical consideration**

suppliers' technical competency, understanding of the technical requirements and capability to produce technically acceptable goods or services. Generally this evaluation ranks highest among all other evaluations.

■ **bid time consideration**

evaluation of suppliers' offer with regard to dates identified for completion of phases of the work and/or total work.

■ **bid/no bid decision**

The decision whether or not to submit a proposal in response to a request for proposal.

■ **bidder**

anyone who responds to a request for proposal (or quotation), i.e. one who submits a bid.

■ **bidders conference**

a meeting hosted by the buyer contracting organisation to assist prospective bidders in understanding the request for proposal.

■ **bidders source selection**

the pre- selection of qualified bidders from a given specialty. Tender invitations are then only distributed to those listed. If the list is large and there are multiple bid packages to be tendered bidders may be selected in rotation.

■ **bidding**

the process of soliciting or submitting bids.

■ **bidding strategy**

the manner in which bids are to be obtained. Options range from the stage of development of the project's definition or its inherent risk and hence the most suitable type of contract being offered, to the manner in which the work is divided, to the timing in the marketplace given the degree of competition available.

■ **bill**

an account for goods sold, services rendered or work done.

■ **Bill of Lading (BOL)**

Bill of Lading. A document used to acknowledge the receipt of products.

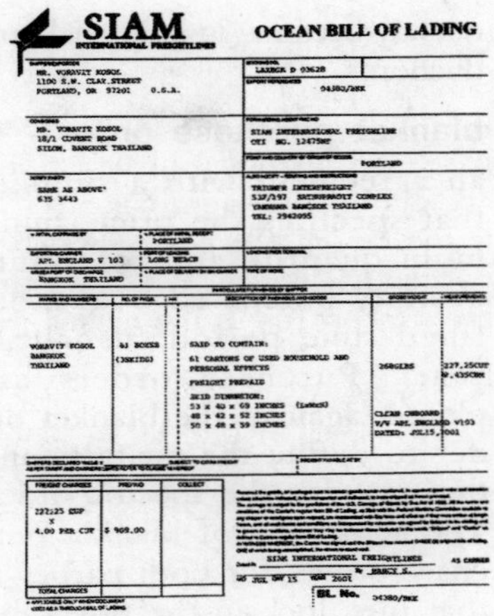
SIAM INTERNATIONAL FREIGHTLINES
OCEAN BILL OF LADING

MR. VORAVIT KOSOL
1100 S.W. CLAY STREET
PORTLAND, OR 97201 U.S.A.

LAXBGK D 93628
94380/BKK

MR. VORAVIT KOSOL
18/1 CONVENT ROAD
SILOM, BANGKOK THAILAND

SIAM INTERNATIONAL FREIGHTLINE
OTI NO. 12475NF

PORTLAND

SAME AS ABOVE'
635 3443

TRIUMPH INTERFREIGHT
537/197 SATHUPRADIT COMPLEX
YANNAWA BANGKOK THAILAND
TEL: 2942095

PORTLAND
APL ENGLAND V 103
LONG BEACH
BANGKOK THAILAND

VORAVIT KOSOL BANGKOK THAILAND
SAID TO CONTAIN:
61 CARTONS OF USED HOUSEHOLD AND PERSONAL EFFECTS
FREIGHT PREPAID
53 x 40 x 69 INCHES
48 x 42 x 52 INCHES
50 x 48 x 59 INCHES
CLEAN ONBOARD
V/V APL ENGLAND V103
DATED: JUL15,2001

FREIGHT CHARGES | PREPAID | COLLECT
4.00 PER CUF | $ 909.00

TOTAL CHARGES

SIAM INTERNATIONAL FREIGHTLINES AS CARRIER
JUL 15 2001
BL. No. 94380/BKK

■ **Bill of Material (BOM)**

a listing of components, parts and other items needed to manufacture a product, showing the quantity of each required for each intermediate item. The BOM is usually drawn as a 'tree structure' with the end items at the top. A bill of material is similar to a parts list except that it usually shows how the product is fabricated and assembled. The BOM is organised in 'levels' where each level is an 'inventoriable' item. Also called a product structure, formula, recipe or ingredients list.

■ **bimodal distribution**

a distribution with two identifiable curves within it, indicating a mixing of two populations such as different shifts, machines, workers, etc.

■ **biotechnology**

The employment of living, often genetically changed organisms (frequently bacteria) in industrial production.

### ■ blanket purchase order

an agreement with a supplier that specifies the price, minimum quantity and maximum quantity purchased over a defined time period (usually a year). Purchase orders are placed 'against' the blanket order to define the quantity and due date for the specific order. The advantage of blanket purchase orders for both parties is that they lock in the price and the parties only have to negotiate once every year or so. The supplier usually gives the customer a quantity discount for the blanket order. Another type of blanket P.O. does not specify the parts or the price. Purchasing issues a blanket P.O. for a 'not to exceed value'. Any company representative that knows the P.O. number can purchase items until the value of the P.O. is exceeded.

### ■ blind counts

describes method used in cycle counting and physical inventories where you provide your counters with item number and location but no quantity information.

### ■ blocking (a process, not football)

production is said to be 'blocked' when a process is not allowed to produce when the output storage area (container, kanban square) is full. Blocking is good for non-bottleneck processes.

### ■ blue chip

name for shares of prominent enterprises with first-class soil quality, high yield capacity and solid financial structure.

### ■ board

a committee with authority and ability to make decisions or strong recommendations.

### ■ boersenkapitalisierung

market value of an enterprise based on market prices of its shares multiplied by the amount of all pending titles. Also market capitalisation mentioned.

### ■ bond

a written instrument executed by a bidder or contractor (the principal) and a second party (the surety or sureties), to assure fulfilment of the principal's obligations to a third party (the obligee or agent identified in the bond. If the principal's obligations are not met, the bond assures payment, to the extent stipulated, of any loss sustained by the obligee.)

### ■ bonus

an added benefit. A sum paid to an employee over and above his/her regular pay.

### ■ bonus schemes

a scheme by which a contractor will receive extra pay or other rewards if certain targets or objectives are achieved. The targets are usually expressed as a certain quantity in a certain time, including completing a project by a fixed date.

**■ book profit**

the theoretical profit or loss on an investment due to their increase in value and/or its depreciation.

**■ bottleneck**

a bottleneck is any constraint in the system that holds the organisation back from greater achievement of its goals. In a system, a bottleneck is any resource that has capacity less than the demand placed on it. Note that sometimes the market is the bottleneck. When this is true the system can often become more flexible to the market's needs so that the firm can better achieve its goal of making more money.

**■ bottom up cost estimate**

an estimate derived by summing detailed cost estimates of individual work packages (labour and materials) and applying appropriate cost burdens.

**■ bounce an idea off someone**

to get someone's initial impression of an idea they have not heard before.

**■ boundary**

a limit line. Typically used to indicate some form of constraint.

**■ brainstorming**

a technique to develop alternative solutions through an unrestrained exchange of ideas.

**■ bread boarding**

the creation of an experimental device to determine the feasibility of an idea or a design and to develop it technically far enough to demonstrate the usefulness of the approach.

**■ breakdown**

identification of the smallest activities or task in a job according to a defined procedure.

**■ breakdown structure**

a hierarchical structure by which project elements are broken down or decomposed.

**■ break-even chart**

a graphic representation of the relation between total value earned and total costs for various levels of productivity.

**■ break-even point**

the productivity point at which value earned equals total cost.

**■ bring them along**

1. give a slow introduction over time.
2. incrementally spoon feed small amounts of possibly.
3. misleading information until the whole concept is accepted.
4. withhold distasteful information.

**■ browser**

**■ see web browser.**

**■ brush fire**

1. out of control.
2. growing wildly.

**■ bruttorendite**

with real estate fund the renting incomes in percent of the market value.

■ **budget**

when unqualified, refers to an estimate of funds planned to cover a project or specified period.

■ **Budget at Completion (BAC)**

the estimated total cost of the project when done.

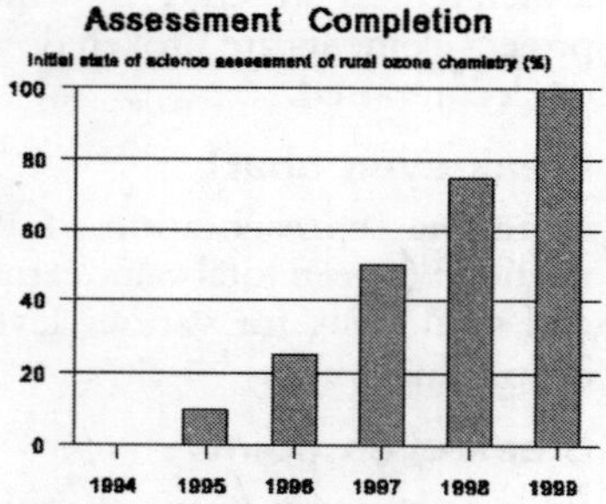


■ **budget cost**

the cost anticipated at the start of a project.

■ **budget decrement**

a reduction in the amount of money available for an activity.

■ **budget element**

the resources i.e. the people, materials or other entities needed to do the work of the programme. Budget elements are typically assigned to a work package, but can also be defined at the cost account level.

■ **budget period**

an interval of time into which a project period is divided for budgetary purposes, usually twelve months.

■ **budget presentation**

a formal representation of a project budget usually for purposes of obtaining approval to proceed.

■ **budget revision**

a formal document in which approval is sought or gained to change the contents of a budget.

■ **budget unit**

the base unit for calculation. Budget units are user defined and can be any appropriate unit of measure such as hours, dollars, linear feet or tons.

■ **budgeted**

an item for which expenditure has been provided, usually as a line item in the budget makeup.

■ **Budgeted Cost of Work Performed (BCWP)**

the sum of the approved cost estimates (including any overhead allocation) for activities (or portions of activities) completed during a given period (usually project-to-date).

■ **budgeting**

time phased financial requirements.

■ **buffer stock**

see **safety stock.**

■ **build**

1. a version of software that meets a specified subset of the requirements that the completed software will meet.
2. put parts together to form a unified whole, construct.

■ **bullish on**

1. in favour of.
2. to assert a belief that something will increase.

■ **burden**

overhead expenses distributed over appropriate direct labour and/or material base. For projects, the burden includes all costs not directly associated with tasks, such as project management costs.

■ **burn rate**

the rate at which funds or man-hours are being expended on a project.

■ **burst node**

in a network diagram, a node at which two or more activities commence after the completion of the preceding activity.

■ **business case**

a structured proposal for business improvement that functions as a decision package for organisational decision-makers. A business case includes an analysis of business process performance and associated needs or problems, proposed alternative solutions, assumptions, constraints and a risk-adjusted cost-benefit analysis.

■ **business data**

data about people, places, things, business rules and events used to operate a business. It is not metadata.

■ **business impact analysis**

identifies project constraints, alternatives and related assumptions as they apply to the initiation phase.

■ **business manager**

on a large project or programme this is the person responsible for managing the project's business functions such as contracting, sub-contracting, planning, budgeting, human resources, legal, etc.

■ **business objectives**

the business goals which the project's product is designed to satisfy.

■ **business plan**

model used by a manager for planning and scheduling project work.

■ **business problem**

a question, issue or situation, pertaining to the business, which needs to be answered or resolved.

■ **business process**

a collection of related, structured activities—a chain of events—that produces a specific service or product for a particular customer or customers.

■ **business process redesign**

an examination of key business processes in order to identify radical changes in order to achieve improved results.

■ **business process reengineering**

in government, a systematic disciplined improvement approach that critically examines, rethinks and redesigns mission-delivery processes and sub-processes within a process management approach. In a political environment, the approach achieves radical mission performance gains in meeting customer and stakeholder needs and expectations.

■ **business processes**

the systematic activities by which an enterprise conducts its affairs.

■ **Business Requirements Planning (BRP)**

BPR is a conceptual model showing how business planning, master planning, materials planning and capacity planning processes should work together.

■ **business transaction**

it is a unit of work acted upon by a data capture system to create, modify or delete business data. Each transaction represents a single valued fact describing a single business event.

■ **business unit**

any segment of an organisation or an entire business organisation, which is not divided into further segments.

■ **business vision**

a description of what senior management wants to achieve with the organisation in the future. A business vision usually addresses a medium to long-term period and is expressed in terms of a series of objectives.

■ **buy in**

1. agreement.
2. commitment.

■ **buy out**

assumptions of enterprises are named. The well-known forms are the management Buy Out (MBO), the company or range assumption by the management and the Leveraged Buy Out (LBO), with which new investors take over the firm majority using of outside capital. Buy Outs are used often also for successor-successfully in exempt private companies.

■ **CAI**

Computer Aided Inspection.

■ **calendar**

the calendar used in developing a project schedule. This calendar identifies project work days and can be altered so weekends, holidays, weather days, etc., are not included.

■ **calendar file**

a file containing calendar information for one or more individual calendars.

■ **calendar range**

the span of the calendar from the calendar start date through the last calendar unit performed. The calendar start date is unit number one.

■ **calendar start date**

the first calendar unit of the working calendar.

■ **calendar unit**

the smallest unit of the calendar produced. This unit is generally in hours, days or weeks. It can also be grouped in shifts.

■ **calm market**

a steady price.

## ■ cantilever rack

racking system in which the shelving supports are connected to vertical supports at the rear of the rack. There are no vertical supports on the face of the rack allowing for storage of very long pieces of material such as piping and lumber.

## ■ capability

the skills, competencies, resources and processes available to an organisation or individual to enable them to meet their objectives.

## ■ Capability Maturity Model (CMM)

a description of the stages through which software organisations evolve as they define, implement, measure, control and improve their software processes. The model is a guide for selecting the process improvement strategies by facilitating the determination of current process capabilities and identification of the issues most critical to software quality and process improvement.

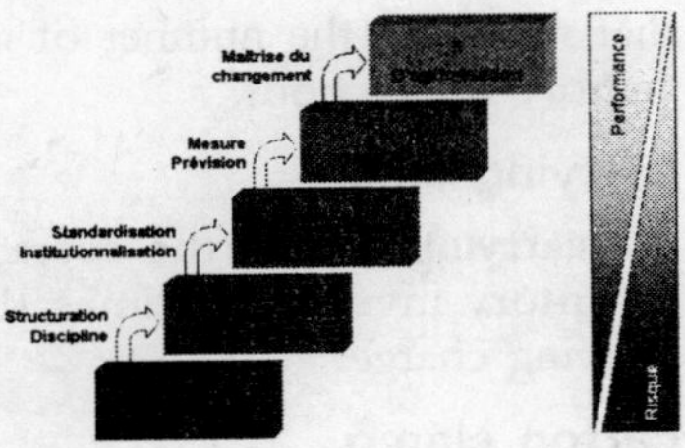


## ■ capability survey

a buyer survey of a seller's capability without specific regard to any project.

## ■ capacity

the maximum rate of output for a process, measured in units of output per unit of time. The unit of time may be of any length, a day, a shift or a minute. Note that it is redundant (and ignorant) to use the phrase 'maximum capacity' because a capacity is a maximum, just say 'capacity'. Some people make a distinction between nominal capacity, demonstrated capacity and theoretical capacity. Demonstrated capacity is the capacity that the process has actually been able to sustain over a long period. However, in the long run, the demonstrated capacity will never exceed the market demand. The theoretical capacity is the maximum production rate based on mathematical or engineering calculations, which sometimes do not consider all relevant variables, therefore, it is quite possible that the capacity can be greater than or less than the theoretical value. (It is not uncommon for factories to work at 110% of their theoretical capacity.) Do not confuse capacity with load. If an elevator has three people on it, what is its capacity? The answer is 'you don't know'. The capacity might be 2, 3, 20, etc. If it has three people on it, the elevator has a current load of three and probably has a capacity of at least three. The optimal capacity is that which minimises the total relevant cost, which is the sum of the capacity and waiting cost. All systems have a trade off between capacity utilisation and waiting time. These two variables have a non-linear relationship. As utilisation goes to 100%, the waiting time tends to go to infinity. Maximising utilisation is not the goal of the organisation. The goal in this case is to minimise the sum of two relevant—costs the cost of the capacity and the cost of waiting. For example, the optimal utilisation for a fire engine is not 100% it is closer to 1%.

**■ capacity building**

a term sometimes used in knowledge management to describe the process of enhancing an organisation's ability to implement knowledge management principles and practices.

**■ capital**

the assets of an enterprise including property, real estate and cash.

**■ capital appropriation**

a setting aside of funds for some approved expenditure, typically by an owner for all or part of a project.

**■ capital asset**

tangible property, including durable goods, equipment, buildings, installations and land.

**■ capital cost**

the total expenditure for acquiring an asset. The sum of all moneys spent on a project and transferred to the capital account of an organisation, usually upon completion.

**■ carousel**

type of automated material handling equipment generally used for high-volume small-parts order-picking operations. Horizontal carousels are a version of the same equipment used by dry cleaners to store and retrieve clothing. They have racks hanging from them that can be configured to accommodate various size storage bins. Vertical carousels consist of a series of horizontal trays on a vertical carousel. Vertical carousels are frequently used in laboratories and specialty manufacturing operations.

**■ carrying charge**

a rate parameter that is used in applying managerial economics for operations decision making with respect to inventory. The rate should be the sum of the weighted average cost of capital, a risk premium for obsolete inventory and a storage cost. Reasonable values are in the range of 15-40%. This rate should only reflect costs that vary with the size of the inventory and should not include costs that vary with the number of inventory transactions.

**■ carrying cost**

the carrying cost is the average inventory investment times the carrying charge.

**■ carton clamp**

lift truck attachment that operates like a paper roll clamp except the clamping surface is flat rather than circular.

### ■ case based reasoning

a branch of artificial intelligence that attempts to combine the power of narrative with the codification of knowledge on computers. Involves extraction of knowledge from a series of narratives or cases, about the problem.

### ■ cash burn rate

1. how quickly liquid assets are being spent.
2. the number of rupees of cash flow being lost each month or quarter.

### ■ cash flow

the inflow and outflow of funds. A time-based record of income and expenditures, often presented graphically.

### ■ cash flow management

the planning of project expenditures relative to income in such a way as to minimise the carrying cost of the financing for the project.

### ■ cash-flow

the cash-flow represents in one financial year obtained net proceeds before writings-off and resetting.

### ■ cash-flow net yield

net proceeds before writings-off and resetting in relation to current market prices, less accumulated yields contained in it.

### ■ CC

Critical Characteristic.

### ■ CCD, Charged Coupled Device

used to describe a type of barcode scanner that acts like a small digital camera taking a digital image of the barcode as opposed to the standard barcode scanner that uses a laser. CCD scanners are a low cost option for scanning barcodes at a short distance (usually within a few inches).

### ■ certificate of compliance

a document signed by an authorised party affirming that the supplier of a product or service has met the requirements of the relevant specifications, contract or regulation.

CERTIFICATE OF COMPLIANCE

This is to certify
that the Quality Management System of

UAB "SEIFUVA"

Pramonės g. 7, LT-4910 Lithuania (Lietuva)

has been assessed by LST Sert
and found to be in compliance
with the following quality standard

LST EN ISO 9001:1995

The Quality Management System is applicable to:

PRODUCTION OF SAFES AND OTHER ITEMS OF STORAGE

The compliance was assessed during the initial assessment
(Report number 2001-017-1)
Quality Management System has been certified since 2003-01-20
LST Sert will regularly undertake inspections
and grants recognition for the period

2003-01-20 - 2003-12-15

Certificate number 9000-025

### ■ certificate of conformance

a certificate signed by a contractor representative that the supplies or services required by the contract have been furnished in accordance with all applicable contract requirements.

■ **certification**

the procedure and action by a duly authorised body of determining, verifying and attesting in writing to the qualifications of personnel, processes, procedures or items in accordance with applicable requirements.

■ **CGI**

a set of rules that describe how a Web server communicates with another piece of software on the same computer and how the other piece of software (the 'CGI program') talks to the Web server. Any piece of software can be a CGI programme if it handles input and output according to the CGI standard.

■ **chain**

a series of elements joined together in sequence, such as a logical series of activities or occurrences.

■ **champion**

a person who proactively promotes something with the aim of persuading others of its benefits.

■ **change**

an increase or decrease in any of the project characteristics.

■ **change control**

the process of controlling, documenting and storing the changes to control items. This includes proposing the change, evaluating it, approving or rejecting it, scheduling it and tracking it.

■ **Change Control Board (CCB)**

a formally constituted group of stakeholders responsible for approving or rejecting changes to the project baselines.

■ **change documentation**

the official records of submitted project changes both accepted and rejected.

■ **change in scope**

a change in objectives, work plan or schedule that results in a material difference from the terms of previously granted approval to proceed.

■ **change management plan**

a defined process for making changes to a project plan.

■ **change management process**

a set of tasks or procedures established to ensure that project performance is measured to the baseline and changes are reviewed, approved or rejected and the baseline updated.

■ **change order**

a written order, signed by the organisation's contracting officer, directing a contractor to make a change that the changes clause authorises the contracting officer to order without the contractor's consent.

■ **change order/purchase order amendment**

written order directing the contractor to make changes according to the provisions of the contract.

## ■ changed conditions

a change in the contract environment. physical or otherwise, compared to that contemplated at the time of bid.

## ■ channel conflict

contention between players trying to sell to the same customers. Channel conflict is not a new phenomenon with the Internet but has become more obvious with the disruptions caused by the Internet.

## ■ channel partner

a firm that works with another firm to provide products and services to customers. Channel partners for a manufacturing firm generally include distributors, sales representatives, logistics firms, transportation firms and retailers.

## ■ characteristic

a physical, chemical, visual, functional or any other identifiable property of a product or material.

## ■ chart

a graphical display of quantitative or qualitative data.

## ■ chart of accounts

any numbering system used to monitor project costs by category (e.g., labour, supplies, materials). The project chart of accounts is usually based upon corporate chart of accounts of the primary performing organisation.

## ■ charter

a document prepared at the beginning of the project by the primary project participants that includes a mission statement, high level objectives, constraints and assumptions and any cost or schedule goals that are known. The charter is created during a chartering meeting where the project leads and the project sponsor agree on what will be accomplished by the project.

## ■ chase strategy

businesses that have seasonal demand can take two extreme approaches in meeting the demand. The chase approach keeps finished goods inventory quite low and matches the production rate to the seasonal demand. The level approach maintains a constant production rate and builds inventory in the off-season to meet the demand in the peak season. Many firms are able to economically implement a 'chase' strategy by offering counter-seasonal products such as snow skies and water skis to maintain a constant workforce but not build large inventories in the off-season.

## ■ checking

the process of verifying that an activity or object conforms to a given standard.

## ■ checklist

a list of items to help in the process of checking.

## ■ checkpoint

a scheduled technical and/or managerial control point.

■ **Chief Information Officer (CIO)**

a senior position with strategic responsibility for information management and information technology.

■ **Chief Knowledge Officer (CKO)**

a senior position with strategic responsibility for knowledge management.

■ **child**

a lower-level element in a hierarchical structure such as the requirements list or the work breakdown structure.

■ **CIM**

Computer Integrated Manufacturing.

■ **CIO**

abbreviation for Chief Information Officer.

■ **circular reasoning**

when a reason is the same as the object being explained. Thus, no explanation is offered. Example: We are giving small raises because we are not giving large raises.

■ **CKO**

an individual tasked with overall responsibility for managing the organisation's knowledge.

■ **CKO**

abbreviation for Chief Knowledge Officer.

■ **clamp down**

1. to reduce.
2. to slow to near zero.
3. to spend very little.

■ **clarification**

as a contractual term, refers to communication between a buyer and a seller to eliminate minor irregularities or apparent clerical errors in a document.

■ **clarification contact**

contact with an applicant by a grant team member before the department makes a funding decision in order to obtain more detailed information about programmatic and/or budgetary items in an application.

■ **classification**

the bringing together into classes of elements that are similar such as the grouping of costs, samples, tests, types of work, etc.

■ **classification of defects**

the enumeration of possible defects of the unit of product, classified according to their seriousness. Defects will normally be grouped into the classes of critical, major or minor, however, they may be grouped into other classes or into subclasses within these classes.

■ **click-and-mortar**

what dot-coms are attempting to become. A hybrid between a dot-com and a 'brick-and-mortar' operation.

■ **client**

the person or organisation for whom a project is implemented.

**client environment**

the conditions under which a client operates, such as the social factors found within the organisation.

**client quality services**

the process of creating a two-way feedback system to define expectations, opportunities and anticipated needs.

**closed fund**

investment trust in company form (normally as corporation) with fixed capital. A closed fund is not obligated to take spent portions back upon the requests of the portion owner. Opposite: open fund.

**close-out**

the completion of all work on a project. Can also refer to completion of a phase of the project.

**co-product**

The term co-product is used to describe multiple items that are produced simultaneously during a production run. Co-products are often used to increase yields in cutting operations, such as die cutting or sawing, when it is found that scrap can be reduced by combining multiple sized products in a single production run. Co-products are also used to reduce the frequency of machine set-ups required in these same types of operations. Co-products, also known as by-products, are also common in process manufacturing such as in chemical plants. Although the concept of co-products is fairly simple, the programming logic required to provide for planning and processing of co-products is very complicated and most off-the-shelf manufacturing software will have problems with co-product processing.

**coaching**

a one-to-one relationship that aims to bring about individual learning and performance improvement, usually focusing on achieving predefined objectives within a specific time period. The role of the coach is to create a supportive environment in which to challenge and develop the critical thinking skills, ideas and behaviour of the person being coached, so that they might reach their full potential. Related term: mentoring.

**coaching**

the process of assisting people to improve their performance.

**code and unit test**

the activities of writing software and performing the initial test.

**code of accounts**

any numbering system used to uniquely identify each element of the work breakdown structure.

**cognitive overload**

a psychological phenomenon characterised by an overload of information for a decision maker. The amount of information exceeds the person's cognitive capacity. DSS can positively or negatively impact the cognitive load for a decision maker.

## ■ COGS (Cost of Goods Sold)

accounting term used to describe the total value (cost) of products sold during a specific time period. Since inventory is an asset, it is not expensed when it is purchased or produced. It instead goes into an asset account (usually called inventory). When product is sold, the value of the product (the cost, not the sell price) is moved form the asset account to an expense account called cost of goods sold or COGS. COGS appears on the profit-and-loss statement and is also used for calculating inventory turns.

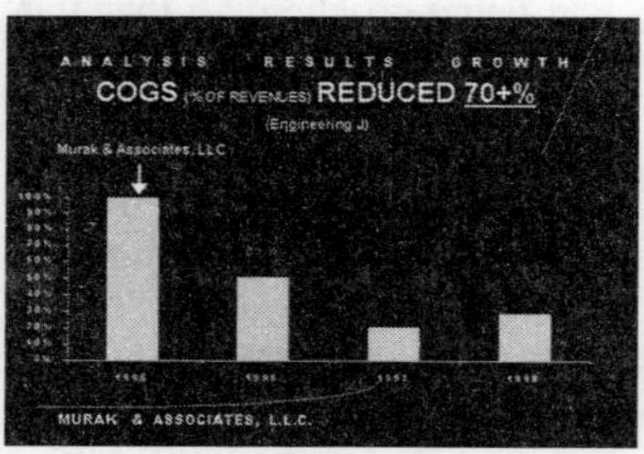


## ■ COI

abbreviation for Communities of Interest.

## ■ collaboration

working together, cooperation.

## ■ collaboration, collaborative working

a generic term that simply means teamwork or a group effort. It also has a more specific meaning in knowledge management, where it is often used to describe close working relationships involving the sharing of knowledge.

## ■ collaborative tools

tools such as groupware that enable both structured and free-flow sharing of knowledge and best practices.

## ■ commercial item description

specifications and other documentation that describe commercial products or services.

## ■ commissioning

activities performed for the purpose of substantiating the capability of the project to function as designed.

## ■ commissions

expenditure commission and cancelling commission. Fee, which during the design or cancelling is raised from fund portions.

## ■ commitment

the act of standing behind a policy whose value ends when the policy is concluded.

## ■ commitment package

a unit of work, typically part of a work breakdown structure, which is performed external to the organisation through a contract or purchase order.

## ■ committed costs

costs that will still be incurred even if the project is terminated.

## ■ commodity

in inventory management, the term commodity has a couple of definitions. Standard products commonly available from various sources are often called 'commodity items'. Specialised or custom products not widely available or proprietary products only available from a small number of sources would not be considered commodity items. The term commodity is also used to describe classifications of inventory. In this case, 'commodity codes' are used to distinguish groups of inventory items to be used for reporting and analysis. Note that commodity classifications can be used to describe any inventory item and are not limited to items that fall under the previous definition of commodity items.

### ■ commodity of find

investment trusts, which put on their fortune mainly in tradable raw goods. Also goods funds mentioned.

### ■ Commodity Traded Advisor (CTA)

CTAs exclusively invest in futures and other derivatives. The majority of the CTAs pursues 'following a trend' strategy. Reason is that there are temporary trends in the financial markets. They make profits both from falling and from rising markets. A further strategy is to recognise exactly these trend breaks and profit from it.

### ■ common cause

a source of variation that is always present as part of the random variation inherent in the process itself. Its origin can usually be traced to an element of the system which only management can correct.

### ■ communicating with groups

the means by which the project manager conducts meetings, presentations, negotiations and other activities necessary to convey the project's needs and concerns to the project team and other groups.

### ■ communicating with individuals

involves all activities by which the project manager transfers information or ideas to individuals working on the project.

### ■ communication

the effective transmission of information so that the recipient understands clearly what the receiver intends. Communications may occur in multiple forms: Oral, written, textural, numerical, graphic, body language, paper, electronic, physical, etc. For project communications, everything should be in writing as much as possible.

### ■ communication channels

the path along which the exchange of information takes place or is supposed to take place. Typically refers to the sequence of individuals in a chain of command.

### ■ communications management

the proper organisation and control of information transmitted by whatever means to satisfy the needs of the project. It includes the processes of transmitting, filtering, receiving and interpreting or understanding information using appropriate skills according to the application in the project environment. It is at once the master and the servant of a project in that it provides the means for interaction between the many disciplines, functions and activities, both internal and external to the project and which together result in the successful completion of that project.

■ **communications plan**

a statement of project stakeholders' communication and information needs and how they will be satisfied during the project.

■ **communications services**

service that includes telecommunications services, automated data processing services and management information systems that serve the needs of state agencies and institutions.

■ **communities of interest**

networks of people who share a common interest in a particular topic, either work-related or peripheral to work and who come together informally to share knowledge on that topic. Related term: communities of practice.

■ **communities of practice**

networks of people who work on similar processes or in similar disciplines and who come together to develop and share their knowledge in that field for the benefit of both themselves and their organisation(s). They may be created formally or informally and they can interact online or in person. Related term: communities of interest.

■ **company policy**

a written or verbal statement of a firm's stance on a topic.

■ **compelling case**

1. a winning argument.
2. overwhelmingly persuasive.

■ **compensation**

wages, salaries, honoraria, commissions, professional fees and any other form of remuneration provided directly or indirectly for services rendered. Also, something given on account of goods provided, services, some form of loss or misuse. Usually financial, to offset an adverse situation such as a claim.

■ **compensation and evaluation**

the measurement of an individual's performance and the financial payment provided to employees as a reward for their performance and as a motivator for future performance.

■ **competence**

the ability to handle a situation through knowledge, skills, relationships, values, will and commitment.

■ **competency (in project management )**

the measurement of both a person's knowledge and their demonstrated capability in project management.

■ **competitive advantage**

a widely-used term in the private sector to describe something that differentiates a company from its competitors in the same industry and makes it more likely to gain profits than the others.

### ■ competitive analysis

an investigation to find out if others are already doing the same thing.

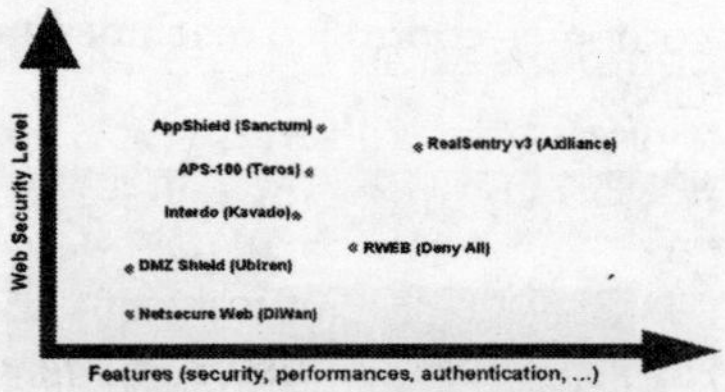


### ■ compile

to collect or put together.

### ■ completed activity

an activity with an actual finish date and no remaining duration.

### ■ completed units

the number of units completed to date.

### ■ completion

the process of finishing.

### ■ completion date

the date calculated by which the project could finish following careful estimating, planning and risk analysis taking into account resource limitations and contingency.

### ■ complexity

unnecessary work. Any activity that makes a work process more complicated without adding value to the resulting product or service.

### ■ compliance

an affirmative indication or judgment that the supplier of a product or service has met the requirements of the relevant specifications, contract or regulation also the state of meeting the requirements.

### ■ compliance labels

standardised label formats used by trading partners. Compliance labels are used as shipping labels, container/pallet labels, carton labels or piece labels and usually contain bar codes. Many bar-code labelling software products now have the more common compliance label standards set up as templates.

### ■ component

any raw material, substance, piece, part, software, firmware, labelling or assembly which is intended to be included as part of the finished, packaged and labelled device.

### ■ component integration and test

assembling units into the next higher assembly and testing the integrated unit.

### ■ components/equipment

reparable assemblies which currently require repair parts support or will require it when introduced into an inventory.

### ■ compound risk

a risk made up of a number of inter-related risks.

### ■ comprehensive plan

regional, state or local documents that describe community visions for future growth. Comprehensive plans describe general plans and policies for how communities will grow and the tools that are used to guide land use decisions and give general, long range recommendations for community growth. Typical elements include, land use, housing, transportation, environment, economic development and community facilities.

**■ compromise**

both sides agree such that each wins or loses a few points.

**■ compromising, in negotiating**

a search for middle ground that involves some degree of sacrifice by both sides.

**■ Computer Aided Inspection (CAI)**

a system for performing inspection through the use of computer hardware and software technologies.

**■ computer database**

a structured collection of data or records residing in a computer.

**■ computer hardware**

devices capable of accepting and storing computer data, executing a systematic sequence of operations on computer data or producing control outputs. Such devices can perform substantial interpretation, computation, communication, control or other logical functions.

**■ Computer Numerical Control (CNC)**

Computer Numeric Controls is a type of controller that is typically found on machining centres and other machine tools. These controls process part programmes in the form of M and G codes that describe tool paths required to machine production parts. Robots that are not machine tools are not considered CNC. Note that not all computer-controlled machines are CNC.

**■ computer program**

a combination of computer instructions and data definitions that enable computer hardware to perform computational or control functions.

**■ Computer Software Component (CSC)**

a functionally or logically distinct part of a computer software configuration item. Computer software components may be top-level or low-level.

**■ Computer Software Configuration Item (CSCI)**

a software item, which is identified for configuration management. An aggregation of software that satisfies an end use function and designated for separate configuration management.

■ **concept**

an imaginative arrangement of a set of ideas.

■ **concept of execution**

represents the dynamic relationships of the components. It can include such descriptions as flow of execution control, data flow, dynamically controlled sequencing, state transition diagrams, timing diagrams, priorities among units, handling of interrupts, etc.

■ **concept phase**

the first of four sequential phases in the generic project life cycle. Also known as idea, economics, feasibility or pre- feasibility phase.

■ **concept study**

consideration of an idea that includes a review of its practicality, suitability, cost-effectiveness, etc. usually followed by a recommendation whether or not to proceed with a/the project.

■ **conceptual project planning**

the process of developing broad-scope project documentation from which the technical requirements, estimates, schedules, control procedures and effective project management will all flow.

■ **concession**

permission to use or release a product that does not conform to specified requirements.

■ **concurrency**

a requirement that development and the extension of infrastructure occurs at the same time. Used to prevent sprawling development in areas that do not have infrastructure in place and to ease the financial burden on the localities that build it.

■ **concurrent**

happening at the same time such as activities carried out in parallel.

■ **concurrent delays**

two or more delays that take place or overlap during the same period, either of which occurring alone would have affected the ultimate completion date.

■ **concurrent engineering**

an approach to project staffing that, in its most general form, calls for implementers to be involved in the design phase. Sometimes confused with fast tracking.

■ **concurrent tasks**

tasks in a project that can be worked on at the same time.

■ **condition**

the key circumstances, situations, etc., that are causing concern, doubt, anxiety or uncertainty. In a risk statement, the condition phrase is the phrase at the beginning of the statement.

■ **conditional risk**

risk that occurs under certain conditions or is accepted provided that certain conditions are met.

■ **conditions**

the existence of or setting of, certain requirements before agreement can be reached or work can begin, etc.

**conducting**

the carrying out of such things as audits, inquiries, reviews, etc.

**confidence in the future**

1. assurance that a plan of action will work out
2. to imply prior knowledge of future events.

**confidence level**

a level of confidence, stated as a percentage, for a budget or schedule estimate. The higher the confidence level, the lower the risk.

**configuration**

the functional and/or physical characteristics of hardware/software as set forth in technical documentation and achieved in a product.

**configuration breakdown**

the separation of configuration items into logical groupings.

**configuration control**

the systematic evaluation, co-ordination, approval or disapproval and dissemination of proposed changes and implementation of all approved changes in the configuration of any item after formal establishment of its configuration baseline.

**configuration control board**

a board composed of technical and administrative representatives who approve or disapprove proposed engineering changes to an approved baseline.

**configuration documentation**

configuration documentation is the sum of all the documents that define the physical and functional characteristics of a system, subsystem, CSCI, HWCI or designated equipment, for example, specifications, design documents, engineering drawings, source code listings.

**configuration elements**

specifications, drawings, source code, etc., that define the configuration of a CSCI.

**configuration identification**

the current approved or conditionally approved technical documentation for a configuration item as set forth in specifications, drawings and associated lists and documents referenced therein.

**configuration item**

a component of a configuration that has a defined function and is designated for configuration management.

**Configuration Item (CI)**

a configuration item is an aggregation of hardware or software that satisfies an end use function and is designated by the acquirer for separate configuration management.

**configuration item acceptance review**

the acceptance of a CI by the system integrator that authorises the CI to be integrated into the system for further verification testing and system acceptance.

**configuration item verification**

proving compliance with the CI 'Design-to' specification using test, demonstration, analysis and inspection.

**■ Configuration Management (CM)**

Configuration Management is a formal discipline that provides project team members and customers with the methods and tools that are used to identify the product developed, establish baselines, control changes to these baselines, record and track status and audit the product.

**■ configuration management board**

the authoritative committee of qualified senior representatives responsible for configuration control.

**■ configuration management plan**

the configuration management plan defines the implementation (including policies and methods) of configuration management on a particular program/project.

**■ configuration relationships**

a description of the technical interfaces between configuration items.

**■ Configure-to-Order (CTO)**

in a configure-to-order system, a firm sells standard products that require that certain parameters, adjustments or modules be added in response to a customer order. Examples include setting the height of a seat for a riding mower, selecting the language option for a software package.

**■ conflict management**

the process by which the project manager uses appropriate managerial techniques to deal with the inevitable disagreements, both technical and personal in nature, that develop among those working toward project accomplishment.

**■ conflict resolution**

to seek a solution to a problem, five methods in particular have been proven through confrontation, compromise, smoothing, forcing and withdrawal.

**■ conformance**

an affirmative indication or judgment that a product or service has met the requirements of the relevant specifications, contract or regulation, also the state of meeting the requirements.

**■ conformance quality**

the degree to which the product or service design specifications (standards) are met. Conformance quality is generally measured by the yield rate (the percentage of units started that are not defective) or the scrap rate (the percentage of units started that have to discarded because they are defective).

**■ conformance to requirements**

when a product meets all aspects of its specification, it is said to be in conformance to requirements.

**■ conformity**

the fulfilling by an item or service of specification requirements.

■ **consensus**

in project team decision-making, full agreement within the group of a course of action including all its details. This approach requires negotiation within the group of all the precise details.

■ **consensus decision process**

group decisions resulting from members engaging in full and open discussion and then reaching consensus to live with and openly support the resulting decision.

■ **consent**

in project team decision-making, acquiescence or agreement to a course of action commonly characterised by comfort with the general direction though not necessarily with all the specific details. In project decision-making, consent is considered a more practical approach than consensus.

■ **consequence**

the possible negative outcomes of the current conditions that are creating uncertainty. In a risk statement, the consequence phrase is the phrase at the end of the statement.

■ **conservation easements**

conservation easements are voluntary, legally binding agreements for landowners that limit parcels of land or pieces of property to certain uses. Land under conservation easements remains privately owned and most easements are permanent.

■ **consignment inventory**

inventory that is in the possession of the customer, but is still owned by the supplier. Consignment inventory is used as a marketing tool to make it easier for a customer to stock a specific supplier's inventory. The customer pays for the inventory only after it is resold or consumed.

■ **consignment stock**

an inventory held by a customer that is owned by the supplier. Payment is made only when stock is sold or used by the customer.

■ **consolidation**

the firing of employees and/or the reduction of plant and equipment.

■ **constituents**

anyone who is impacted by a project, often as members of the public, but not directly involved as participants.

■ **constraint**

applicable restriction, which will affect the scope. Any factor, which affects when an activity can be scheduled.

■ **construction**

all the work involved in assembling resources and putting together the materials required to form a new or changed facility.

■ **construction contractor**

a corporation or individual who has entered into a contract with the organisation to perform construction work.

■ **Construction Management (CM)**

the process by which a potential owner of a capital facility engages a professional agent, referred to as a construction manager, to coordinate, communicate and direct the entire process of construction from the project planning stage through design, procurement, construction and start-up, in terms of scope, quality, time and cost.

■ **construction manager**

the title of a position on the project team. This person is responsible to the project manager for directing the construction of a project within authority and responsibility limits, usually established by the contract. On smaller projects, a construction contractor may assign this role to a superintendent.

■ **construction stage**

that part of a project life cycle during which the construction work is carried out.

■ **construction work**

the construction, rehabilitation, alteration, conversion, extension, demolition or repair of buildings, highways or other changes or improvements to real property, including facilities providing utility services. The term also includes the supervision, inspection and other on- site functions incidental to the actual construction.

■ **consultant**

one who provides some specialised service based on their special qualifications, education or experience.

■ **consumable**

a type of item or products that is used up (consumed) in the process (e.g. paper, oil, grease, etc.). Many firms make more money selling consumable products than they do in selling capital goods or other products.

■ **consumable resource**

a type of resource that remains available until consumed (for example, a material).

■ **consumer goods**

products sold to non-business end users. Clothing, food, Music CDs, are examples of consumer goods.

**Trade in Automotive Products, Growth in 2000 over 1999, by Categories**

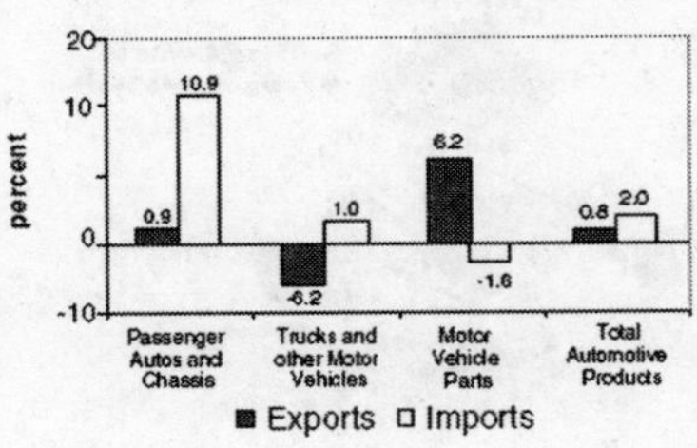


■ **consumer's risk**

the risk of receiving a shipment of poor quality product and believing that it is good quality.

### ■ contemplated change notice

a form issued to a construction contractor requesting its quotation for a proposed change in the scope of work that would be included in its contract.

### ■ content

the intrinsic information and data contained in a variety of formats, including bibliographic data-sets, statistical and qualitative data, moving and still images, sound, textual resources and manuscripts.

### ■ content management

the management of the electronic content line with the business objectives of the organisation or business unit, including demand and supply management.

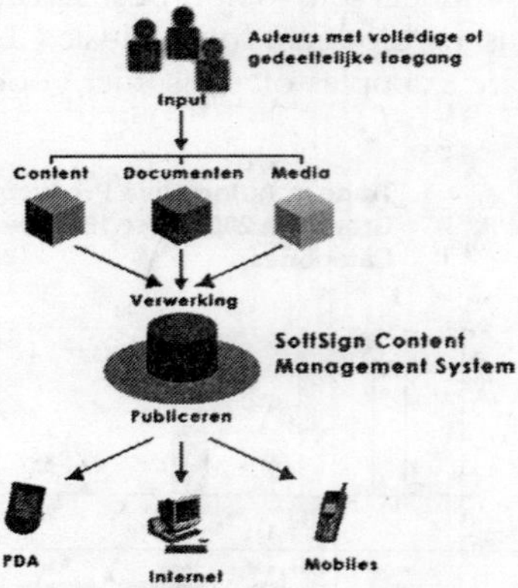


### ■ content mapping

identifying and organising a high-level description of the meaning contained in a collection of electronic document.

### ■ content type

the subdivision of contents into separate groupings or types.

### ■ context

the background within which something is reviewed, determined, decided or otherwise happens.

### ■ contingencies

specific provision for unforeseeable elements of cost within the defined project scope particularly important where previous experience relating estimates and actual costs has shown that unforeseeable events which will increase costs are likely to occur. If an allowance for escalation is included in the contingency it should be a separate item, determined to fit expected escalation conditions for the project.

### ■ contingency plan

a plan that identifies key assumptions beyond the project manager's control and their probability of occurrence. The plan identifies alternative strategies for achieving project success.

### ■ contingency planning

the development of a management plan that identifies alternative strategies to be used to ensure project success if specified risk events occur.

### ■ contingency reserve

a separately planned quantity used to allow for future situations. Some reserves may be planned for only in part (sometimes called 'known unknowns').

■ **continual improvement**

recurring activity to increase the ability to fulfil requirements.

■ **continuous improvement process**

the ongoing enhancement of work processes for the benefit of the customer and the organisation. Activities devoted to maintaining and improving work process performance through small and gradual improvements as well as radical innovations.

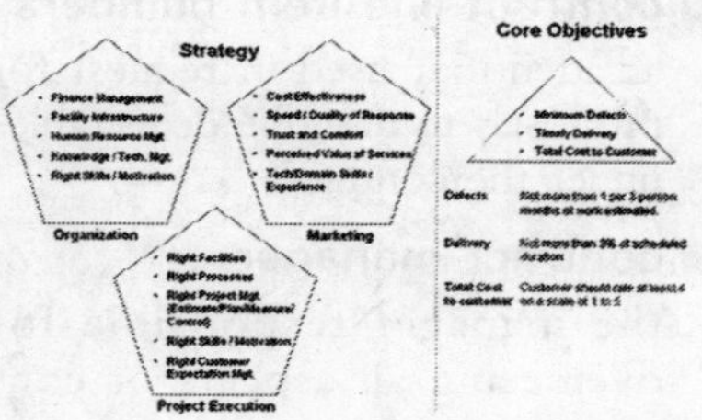


■ **continuous reporting**

reports available on- line from data that is entered in real time.

■ **contract**

a mutually binding legal relationship obligating the seller to furnish the supplies or services (including construction) and the buyer to pay for them. It includes all types of commitments that obligate the acquirer to an expenditure of appropriate funds and that, except otherwise authorised, are in writing. In addition to bilateral agreements, contracts include, but are not limited to, awards and notices of awards, job orders or task letter issued under purchase orders, under which the contract becomes effective by written acceptance or performance and bilateral modifications.

■ **contract**

a binding agreement to acquire goods and/or services in support of a project.

■ **contract administration**

managing the relationship with the seller.

■ **contract award**

the final outcome of the acquisition process in which generally the contract is awarded to one prospective supplier, through acceptance of a final offer generally either by issuing a purchase order or the signing of a legally binding contract formalising the terms under which the goods/ services are to be supplied.

■ **contract breakdown**

the breakdown of a contract into measurable packages, measurable activities such as units of work performed or milestones verifiable by corresponding checklists.

■ **contract change**

an authorised modification to some terms of the contract. This may involved any of the following: a change in the volume or conditions of the work involved, the number of units to be produced, the quality of the work or units, the time for delivery and/or the consequent cost involved.

■ **contract closeout**

completion and settlement of the contract, including resolution of all outstanding items.

■ **contract data requirements list**

that portion of a contract that identifies deliverable data products.

■ **contract dates**

the dates specified in the contract that impact the project plan.

■ **contract dispute**

disagreement between the parties. This may occur during contract execution or at completion and may include misinterpretation of technical requirements and any terms and conditions or due to changes not anticipated at the time of contract award.

■ **contract document system**

the system in place to store, retrieve, reference and update contract documentation.

■ **contract documents**

the set of documents, which form the contract.

■ **contract elements**

to be legally enforceable, a contract must include the following: an offer, an acceptance, consideration, execution by competent parties, legality of purpose and clear terms and conditions.

■ **contract financial control**

exercise of control over contract costs.

■ **contract form**

the formal legal cover sheet that is signed by the parties that gives effect to the contract.

■ **contract funds status report**

a report normally required on cost or incentive type contracts to inform the buyer of funds used and status of remaining funds.

■ **contract guarantee**

a legally enforceable assurance of performance of a contract by a contractor.

■ **contract line item numbers**

an identifier used in request for proposals to describe deliverables under the contract.

■ **contract manager**

the manager responsible for overseeing all aspects of contract preparation and administration.

■ **contract negotiation**

method of procurement where a contract results from a bid, which may be changed through bargaining.

■ **contract order modifications**

changes in a contract during its execution to incorporate new requirements or to handle contingencies that develop after contract placement. Changes may include price adjustments or changes in scope.

## ■ contract performance control

control of work during contract execution.

## ■ contract plan

the conditions, methods, schedule, etc. for carrying out the work of the contract as agreed between the parties at the time of signing the contract.

## ■ contract pre-award meetings

meetings with prospective suppliers before final award determination to aid ranking and/or finalise terms of agreement between parties.

## ■ contract quality requirements

the technical requirements in the contract relating to the quality of the product or service and those contract clauses prescribing inspection and other quality controls incumbent on the contractor, to assure that the product or service conforms to the contractual requirements.

## ■ contract requirements

in addition to specified performance requirements, contract requirements include those defined in the statement of work, specifications, standards and related documents. The contract requirements list, management systems and contract terms and conditions.

## ■ contract risk

the potential and consideration of risk in procurement actions. Generally the forces of supply and demand determine who should have the maximum risk of contract performance but the objective is to place on the supplier the maximum performance risk while maintaining an incentive for efficient performance. In a fixed price contract, the supplier accepts a higher risk than in a cost type contract in which supplier's risk is lowest.

## ■ contract risk analysis

analysis of the consequences and probabilities that certain undesirable events will occur and their impact on attaining the contract/procurement objectives.

## ■ contract warehouse

a contract warehouse is a business that handles shipping, receiving and storage of products on a contract basis. Contract warehouses will generally require a client to commit to a specific period of time (generally in years) for the services. Contracts may or may not require clients to purchase or subsidise storage and material-handling equipment. Fees for contract warehouses may be transaction and storage based, fixed, cost plus or any combination.

**■ Contract Work Breakdown Structure (CWBS)**

a customer-prepared breakout or subdivision of a project, which subdivides the project into all its major hardware, software and service elements, integrates the customer and contractor effort, provides a framework for the planning, control and reporting.

**■ contract, cost-plus-a-fixed-fee**

a cost-reimbursement type contract that provides for the payment of a fixed fee to the contractor. The fixed fee, once negotiated, does not vary with the actual cost but may be adjusted as a result of any subsequent changes in the scope of work or services to be performed under the contract.

**■ contract, cost-plus-a-percentage-of-cost**

a form of contract which provides for a fee or profit at a specified percentage of the contractor's actual cost of accomplishing the work. Except in case of emergency affecting the public health, safety or welfare and for some insurance contracts, no public contract shall be awarded on the basis of cost plus a percentage of cost.

**■ contract, fixed price**

a contract that provides for a firm unit or total price to be established at the time of order placement or contract award. The contractor bears the full risk for profit or loss.

**■ contract/procurement management**

the function through which resources (including people, plant, equipment and materials) are acquired for the project (usually through some form of formal contract) in order to produce the end product. It includes the processes of establishing strategy, instituting information systems, identifying sources, selection, conducting proposal or tender invitation and award and administering the resulting contract.

**■ contracting**

the business of entering into and/or undertaking contracts.

**■ contractor**

an individual, partnership, company, corporation, association or other service, having a contract with an acquirer for the design, development, manufacture, maintenance, modification or supply of items under the terms of a contract.

**■ contractor claims release**

certificate to release and hold harmless from future claims by the contractor.

**■ contractor evaluation**

the collection of background, experience, past performance and current capabilities of potential contractors for purposes of soliciting bids from qualified contractors.

**■ contractor furnished equipment**

contractor equipment that is committed to be used to satisfy a contract as opposed to equipment furnished by the client or by the government.

■ **contractor project office**

the contractor's project manager and associated immediate staff.

■ **contractor short listing**

a process whereby a short list of contractors is assembled and designated for receipt of an invitation to bid. This process has the effect of avoiding dealing with proposals by contractors who do not qualify for some reason.

■ **control**

the process of comparing actual performance with planned performance, analysing variances, evaluating possible alternatives and taking appropriate corrective action as needed.

■ **Control Account Point (CAP)**

the management control unit in which earned value performance measurement takes place. The old name was cost account point.

■ **control chart**

1. a graphic representation of a characteristic of a process, showing plotted values of some statistic gathered from that characteristic and one or two control limits.

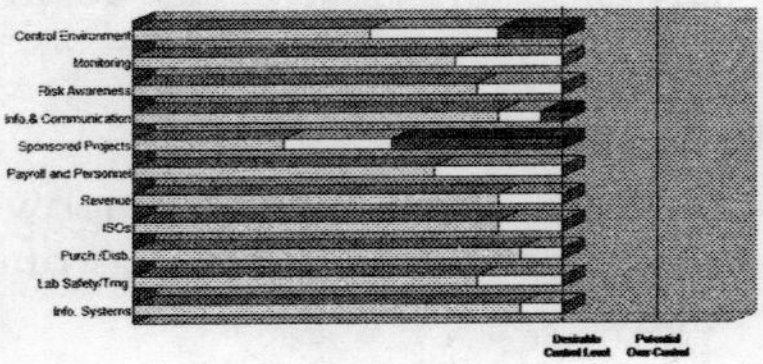


2. A line graph that identifies the variation occurring in a work process over time, helps distinguish between common-cause variation and special-cause variation.

■ **control cycle**

a cycle that usually includes: planning, measuring, monitoring and taking corrective action based on the results of the monitoring.

■ **control item**

a project element that is considered a unit for the purpose of change and configuration management. This includes such items as software modules, versions of software systems, the project design document, the project plans and so forth.

■ **control limit**

a line (or lines) on a control chart used as a basis for judging the significance of the variation from subgroup to subgroup. Variation beyond a control limit is evidence that special causes are affecting the process. Control limits are calculated from process data and are not to be confused with engineering specifications.

■ **control plans**

written descriptions of the systems for controlling parts and processes.

■ **control requirements**

the specified conditions under which control is to be exercised.

■ **control system**

a mechanism that reacts to the current project status in order to ensure accomplishment of project objectives.

**controllable risks**

those risks to the project which, if they occur, can be mitigated by the project team by adopting a 'work-around' or by changing the method by which something risky is done.

**controllable variables**

decision variables that can be changed and manipulated by a decision maker, such as quantity to produce, amount of resources to allocate, etc.

**coordinated matrix organisation**

an organisational structure where the project leader reports to the functional manager and doesn't have authority over team members from other departments.

**coordination**

bringing together the separate work elements of a project to form a workable whole.

**COP**

abbreviation for Communities of Practice.

**core capabilities**

constitute a competitive advantage for a firm. They have built up over time and cannot be easily imitated. They are distinct from both supplemental and enabling capabilities, neither of which is sufficiently superior to those of competitors to offer a sustainable advantage.

**core competence**

1. skills that differentiate a firm from its competitors.
2. a set of organisational skills and systems that is perceived by customers as providing exceptional value in the marketplace. A true core competence is unique, hard to copy and can lead the firm into new products and markets.

**core portfolio**

the core portfolio is the part of the portfolio (dynamic) of a security fund, with which the capital protection is to be guaranteed. The plants take place usually in geldmarktanlagen respectively. Obligations in the reference currency of the fund.

**core processes**

processes that have clear dependencies and that require the same order on most projects.

**core rigidities**

refers to the idea that a firm's strengths are also – simultaneously – its weaknesses. The dimensions that distinguish a company competitively have grown up over time as an accumulation of activities and decisions that focus on one kind of knowledge at the expense of others. Companies, like people, cannot be skilful at everything. Therefore, core capabilities both advantage and disadvantage a company.

**corporate**

a group of individuals empowered to transact business as one body.

■ **corporate amnesia**

the loss of collective experience and embedded tacit knowledge.

■ **corporate constraints**

limitations to the activities of a corporation. These may be as a result of the corporation's charter, its philosophy or mission or due to market conditions.

■ **corporate culture**

acceptable behaviour at a company.

■ **corporate governance**

in accordance with a study of the OECD as structure of relations and mutual responsibility between the management and the shareholders one defines.

■ **corporate memory**

1. the collective tacit or explicit understanding of the people, process or products within an organisation. Corporate memory is strategically important, but it can also be a serious liability if it inhibits an organisation from adjusting quickly to the changing environment.
2. a term used to describe an organisation's historic records and experience, essential for reliable estimating and forecasting. Can be either in documentation or in the collective experience of the employees and management. When employees leave, so does this experience. Every effort should be made to capture past experience in a form usable by others to avoid the loss of this type of asset.

■ **corporate philosophy**

the underlying assumptions that result in a corporation behaving in a particular way.

■ **corporate planning system**

usually a model-driven decision support system based upon a financial model that assists in planning decisions that cut across organisational units and involve all of an organisation's functions (i.e., operations, finance, marketing, personnel, etc.).

■ **corporate project strategy**

the overall direction set by the corporation of which the project is a part and the relationship of specific procurement actions to these corporate directions.

■ **corporate quality standards**

the overall quality standards espoused at the corporate level.

■ **corporate resources**

the resources available to the corporation, usually from internal sources.

■ **corporate responsibility matrix**

a responsibility matrix depicted at the corporate level and from the corporate perspective.

■ **corporate standards**

the overall standards espoused at the corporate level.

■ **corporation**

a group of individuals legally empowered to transact business as one body. Ownership in the corporation is issued as shares of stock. In a publicly-owned corporation the stock is traded on the open markets. In a privately-held corporation the stock is owned by a few individuals and not bought or sold on the open market.

**■ correction**

action to eliminate a detected non-conformity.

**■ corrective action**

changes made to bring expected future performance of the project into line with the plan.

**■ corrective action plan**

a plan for correcting a process or part quality issue.

**■ correlation**

the relationship between two or more variables.

**■ cost**

the cash value of project activity.

**■ Cost Account Manager (CAM)**

a member of a functional organisation responsible for cost account performance and for the management of resources to accomplish such tasks.

**■ Cost Account Plan (CAP)**

the management control unit in which earned value performance measurement takes place.

**■ cost accumulation methods**

the various ways in which the entries in a set of cost accounts may be aggregated to provide different perspectives on the information.

**■ cost analysis**

the analysis of the cost elements of a proposal or on-going work. It includes verification of cost data, evaluation of all elements of costs and projection of these data to determine the effect on price.

**■ cost applications**

the processes of applying cost data to other techniques that have not been described in the other processes.

**■ cost avoidance**

an action taken in the present designed to decrease costs in the future.

**■ cost benefit**

the comparison of the cost versus the benefit expected (of a project) usually for purposes of evaluating alternative forms of investment.

**■ Cost Benefit Analysis (CBA)**

a technique used to compare the various costs associated with an investment with the benefits that it proposes to return. Both tangible and intangible factors should be addressed and accounted for.

| Cost Factor | Annual Recurring Cost | 5 Year Net Present Value Total |
|---|---|---|
| **Personnel Salaries and Fringe Benefits** | | |
| Computer Operations (Enterprise) | $500,693 | $2,212,114 |
| Telecommunications (Monies) | $71,528 | $316,016 |
| Applications Maintenance (Integration) | $643,748 | $2,844,147 |
| Office of Mailing Services | $143,055 | $632,033 |
| **Hardware (Lease and Maintenance)** | | |
| Mainframe Processor Costs | $0 | $0 |
| RAID | $0 | $0 |
| DASD | $0 | $0 |
| STK Tape Silos | $0 | $0 |
| FileNet Optical Disk Storage Unit | $0 | $0 |
| Printers | $148,700 | $609,699 |
| Printer Usage | $14,760 | $60,519 |
| New Hardware (Maintenance) | $24,209 | $76,635 |
| **Software (License and Maintenance)** | | |
| Mainframe Operating system | $0 | $0 |
| Utility software | $0 | $0 |
| COTS Applications | $77,235 | $246,383 |
| **External Vendor Services** | | |
| Inter-Agency Timesharing (Legis. Branch) | $230,000 | $943,045 |
| Disaster Recovery/Back-Up | $20,000 | $82,004 |
| NCOA Services (Gov't or Comm. Vendor) | $0 | $0 |
| **Total Recurring Costs** | **$1,873,928** | **$8,022,596** |

■ **Cost Breakdown Structure (CBS)**

a hierarchical structure that rolls budgeted resources into elements of costs, typically labour, materials and other direct costs.

■ **cost budgeting**

allocating the cost estimates to individual project components.

■ **cost containment**

the firing of employees and/or the reduction of plant and equipment.

■ **cost control**

controlling changes to the project budget.

■ **cost control point**

the point within a programme at which costs are entered and controlled. Frequently, the cost control point for programme is either the cost account or the work package.

■ **cost control system**

any system of keeping costs within the bounds of budgets or standards based upon work actually performed. Cost control is typically a level in the budget element breakdown structure.

■ **cost curve**

a graph plotted against a horizontal time scale and cumulative cost vertical scale.

■ **cost distribution**

usually refers to the distribution of overhead (indirect) costs on some logical basis, e.g. the time or cost of all associated direct cost activities.

■ **cost effective**

better value for money or the best performance for the least cost.

■ **cost element**

a unit of costs to perform a task or to acquire an item. The cost estimated may be a single value or a range of values.

■ **cost engineering**

technique for planning and controlling costs.

■ **cost envelope**

the area bounded by a cost curve based on early start dates of activities and a cost curve based on late start dates of activities.

■ **cost estimating**

estimating the cost of the resources needed to complete project activities.

■ **cost estimating relationship**

a technique used to estimate a particular cost or price by using an established relationship with an independent variable.

■ **cost forecasting**

the activity of predicting future trends and costs within the project duration. These activities are normally marketing oriented. However, such items as sales volume, price and operating cost can affect the projected profitability analysis. Items that affect the cost management functions are: predicted time/cost, salvage value, etc.

■ **cost growth**

the net change of an estimated or actual amount over a base figure previously established.

**■ cost incurred**

costs identified through the use of the accrued method of accounting or costs actually paid. Costs include direct labour, direct materials and all allowable indirect costs.

**■ cost management**

the firing of employees and/or the reduction of plant and equipment.

**■ cost model**

s tabulated presentation of logical element cost estimates summed to a total estimate for the whole.

**■ cost of quality**

the costs incurred to ensure quality. The cost of quality includes quality planning, quality control, quality assurance and rework.

**■ cost overrun**

the amount by which actual costs exceed the baseline or approved costs.

**■ cost performance measurement baseline**

the formulation of budget costs, measurable goals, (particularly time and quantities). for the purposes of comparisons, analysis and forecasting future costs.

**■ cost plan**

sub divides the total project budget into meaningful cost classes each with its own related outline specification or scope. It provides the first principal frame of reference required for a valid cost control system.

**■ cost plus contract**

a form of contract in which the contractor is reimbursed for the costs it incurs in performing the work plus a lump sum or percentage fee hence, cost-plus. This type of contract is favoured where the scope of the work is indeterminate or highly uncertain and the kinds of labour, material and equipment needed are also uncertain.

**■ Cost Plus Fixed Fee Contract (CPFF)**

provides reimbursement of allowable cost plus a fixed fee, which is paid proportionately as the contract progresses.

**■ Cost Plus Incentive Fee Contract (CPIF)**

provides the supplier for cost of delivered performance, plus a predetermined fee as a bonus for superior performance.

**■ Cost Plus Percentage Of Cost Contract (CPPC)**

provides reimbursement of allowable cost of services performed plus an agreed upon percentage of the estimated cost as profit.

**■ cost reimbursable contract**

a contract that provides for payment of allowable incurred costs, to the extent prescribed in the contract. These contracts establish an estimate of total cost for the purpose of obligating funds and establishing a ceiling that the contractor may not exceed (except at its own risk) without the approval of the contracting officer.

**■ cost reimbursement**

payment of direct costs and directly associated overhead costs, but without any allowance for profit.

**■ cost reimbursement type contracts**

a category of contracts based on payments to a contractor for allowable estimated costs, normally requiring only a 'best efforts' performance standard from the contractor. Risk for all growth over the estimated value rests with the project owner.

**■ cost reviews**

planned, systematic and rigorous reassessments of the estimated cost at completion of the scope of work in a cost class. Every design review should be accompanied by a reforecast of cost.

**■ cost savings**

an action that will result in a smaller than projected level of costs to achieve a specified objective.

**■ cost sharing contract**

a contract that provides payment for only a share of allowable costs. Cost sharing contracts are often awarded to motivate development of new technologies.

**■ cost to complete**

the projected cost to complete the project from its present state.

**■ Cost Variance (CV)**

any difference between the estimated cost of an activity and the actual cost of that activity.

**■ Cost/Schedule Impact Analysis (CSIA)**

the process followed to determine the cost and/or schedule impact of a specific change with a project.

**■ cost-effectiveness**

a systematic quantitative method for comparing the costs of alternative means of achieving the same stream of benefits or a given objective.

**■ costing**

the process of determining actual costs from actual expenditures. There is often a large difference between the way that costs are estimated initially and the way the money is actually spent as the project progresses.

**■ costing systems**

systems established to determine current costs and their trends up or down so that appropriate management action can be taken.

**■ counselling**

the process of advising or assisting an individual concerning career plans, work requirements or the quality of work performed.

**■ coupon**

the one security added interest or dividend coupon. It confirms the owner's claim to yield.

**■ course**

price for portions of investment trusts, which are listed at the stock exchange or are off-board acted (real estate funds). The course forms by offer and demand on the market, while the expenditure and withdrawal price of the portions are specified due to the net asset value by the fund line.

**■ CPG, Consumer Packaged Goods**

describes inventory that is in a form ready for sale to consumers (end-users).

**■ CQA**

Certified Quality Auditor.

**■ CQE**

Certified Quality Engineer.

**■ CQMGR**

Certified Quality Manager.

**■ crash costs**

the cost of reducing an activity to its crash duration.

**■ crashing**

taking action to decrease the total project duration by analysing a number of alternatives to determine how to get the maximum duration compression for the least cost. Sometimes defined as: action to decrease the duration of an activity or project by increasing the expenditure of resources.

**■ CRE**

Certified Reliability Engineer.

**■ create value**

1. make a better product or service.
2. to increase a customer's perception of something's usefulness.

**■ crisis**

an adverse situation in which urgent decisions are required to prevent the situation from deteriorating further.

**■ crisis management**

1. to control and limit the impact of major unforeseen problems.
2. a management style that only acts after a crisis has occurred.

**■ criteria**

a statement that provides objectives, guidelines. procedures and standards that are to be used to execute the development, design and/or implementation portions of a project.

**■ critical**

an activity or event that, if delayed, will delay some other important event, commonly the completion of a project or a major milestone in a project.

**■ critical activity**

any activity on a critical path. Most commonly determined by using the critical path method. Although some activities are 'critical' in the dictionary sense without being on the critical path, this meaning is seldom used in the project context.

**■ critical chain**

The set of tasks that determines the overall duration of a project, talking into account both precedence and resource dependencies.

**■ critical event**

a happening that may serve to change the course of a project.

**■ critical factors**

favourable or adverse conditions that may exist or be expected that may significantly influence the course of a project.

## ■ critical incidents technique

a method for identifying the underlying dimensions of customer satisfaction. The method involves collecting a large number of customer complaints and complements and analysing each one to identify the underlying quality dimension (timeliness, friendliness, etc.). We can use this method to identify the key dimensions of service quality for use on a customer satisfaction survey. The technique is used in a variety of contexts other than quality improvement.

## ■ critical path

the critical path is the longest path through a project-planning network. Note that it is possible to have two or more critical paths. Management should focus its attention only on critical path activities and not allow non-critical activities to become critical. The only way to speed up a project is to reduce the task time for activities along the critical path. This is sometimes called 'crashing'. Crashing non-critical activities will not improve the project completion date.

## ■ Critical Path Method (CPM)

a network analysis technique used to predict project duration by analysing which sequence of activities (which path) has the least amount of scheduling flexibility (the least amount of float). Early dates are calculated by means of a forward pass using a specified start date. Late dates are calculated by means of a backward pass starting from a specified completion date.

**Critical Path Method**

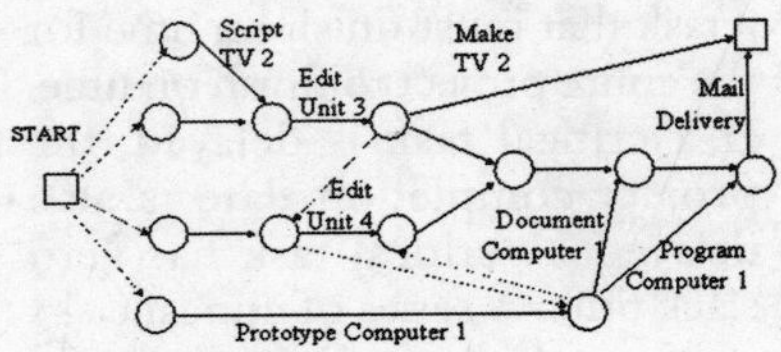


## ■ Critical Path Network (CPN)

a plan for the execution of a project, which consists of activities and their logical relationships to one another.

## ■ critical ratio

a ratio that measures an important characteristic. This ratio is often plotted or tracked in some way to determine priorities among items or events.

## ■ critical sequence

a sequence of activities having zero float after resource limits are taken into account in calculating float.

## ■ critical sequence analysis

a process of calculating a critical sequence of activities while taking into account resource limits that reflect an activity's flexibility.

## ■ critical success factors

defines how progress and outcomes will be measured on a project—sometimes called objectives. Some typical critical success factors include technology (specifications, performance, quality), time (due dates, milestones) and cost (total investment, required cash flow, profits.)

**■ critical task**

a task that must finish on time for the entire project to finish on time. If a critical task is delayed, the project completion date is also delayed. A critical task has zero slack time. A series of critical tasks make up the project's critical path.

**■ criticality index**

a measure of how often an activity appears on the critical path during a Monte Carlo simulation.

**■ CRM**

abbreviation for Customer Relationship Management.

**■ cross functional**

involving the cooperation of two or more departments within the organisation (e.g., Marketing and Product Development).

**■ cross-docking**

in its purest form cross-docking is the action of unloading materials from an incoming trailer or rail car and immediately loading these materials in outbound trailers or rail cars, thus eliminating the need for warehousing (storage). In reality, pure cross-docking is rare outside of transportation hubs and hub-and-spoke type distribution networks. Many 'cross-docking' operations require large staging areas where inbound materials are sorted, consolidated and stored until the outbound shipment is complete and ready to ship. This staging may take hours, days or even weeks in which case the 'staging area' is essentially a 'warehouse'.

**■ CRP, Capacity Requirements Planning**

process for determining amount of machine and labour resources required to meet production.

**■ cube utilisation**

term used in Warehouse Management Systems. Cube logic is often incorporated but seldom used in WMS systems because of its tendency to treat your product as liquid (fitting a round peg in a square hole).

**■ current budget**

the budget at the current point in time, specified at the last date where accurate budget information is available.

**■ current finish date**

the current estimate of the point in time when an activity will be completed.

**■ current start date**

the current estimate of the point in time when an activity will begin.

**■ current status**

the current degree of completion of the project or of tasks in comparison to the base lined schedule.

**■ customer**

the ultimate users of a product or service.

**■ customer acceptance criteria**

the criteria that the customer will use to determine if he/she is satisfied with the final deliverables.

**■ customer capital**

the value of the organisation's relationship with its customers.

**■ customer expectations**

the 'needs' and 'wants' of a customer that define 'quality' in a specified product or service.

**■ customer relationship management**

a business strategy based on selecting and proactively managing the most valuable customer relationships. It requires a customer-focused philosophy to support effective marketing, sales and customer service processes.

**■ customer satisfaction**

customer's perception of the degree to which the customer's requirements have been fulfilled.

**■ customer/client personnel**

those individuals working for the organisation that will assume responsibility for the product produced by the project when the project is complete.

**■ customisation flexibility**

the ability to provide a wider range of 'respond to order' products and still be profitable. This is sometimes called mass customisation.

**■ cut-off date**

the ending date in a reporting period. Also refers to a 'no-later-than' date for a deliverable.

**■ cutover**

the event or action that takes place when the product, service or project element contracted for by the client is placed in operation or turned over to the client. Also called the implementation date.

**■ cycle count**

refers to process of regularly scheduled inventory counts (usually daily) that 'cycles' through your inventory. User determines how often certain items/locations are counted.

**■ cycle time**

historically, cycle time was defined as the time between completions of a process step. For example, you could look at the end of manufacturing process and time how look it took from the completion time of one part to the completion time of the next part. However, it is now common to talk about the 'cycle time' for a factory as the cumulative time required for a product from start to end, which can be measured as the completion time minus the start time. In other words, it is now common to use the terms manufacturing throughput time and cycle time synonymously.

**■ dangle**

an activity in a network, which has neither predecessors nor successors.

**data**

1. facts, observations and data points.
2. a set of facts, concepts or statistics that can be analysed.
3. to produce information.

**data application**

the development of a data base of risk factors both for the current project and as a matter of historic record.

**data collection**

the gathering and recording of facts, changes and forecasts for reporting and future planning.

**data date**

the point in time that separates actual (historical) data from future (scheduled) data. Also called as-of-date.

**data dictionary**

a database about data and database structures. A catalogue of all data elements, containing their names, structures and information about their usage. A central location for metadata.

**data element**

the most elementary unit of data that can be identified and described in a dictionary or repository, which cannot be subdivided.

**data item description**

a completed document that defines the data required of a supplier (contractor). The document specifically defines the data content, format and intended use.

**data mining**

a technique for analysing data in very large databases and making new connections between the data in order to reveal trends and patterns.

**data quality**

high quality data is accurate, timely, meaningful and complete.

**data recorded information**

regardless of medium or characteristics, of any nature, including administrative, managerial, financial and technical.

**data refinements**

rework or redefinition of logic or data that may have previously been developed in the planning subfunction as required to properly input milestones, restraints, priorities and resources.

**data structure organisation**

the logical and systematic arrangement of information elements.

**data type**

the characteristic indicating whether a data item represents a number, date, character string, etc.

**data warehouse**

a database designed to support decision making in organisations. It is batch updated and structured for rapid online queries and managerial summaries. Data warehouses contain large amounts of data. A data warehouse is a subject-oriented, integrated, time-variant, non-volatile collection of data in support of management's decision making process.

■ **database**

a collection of related data stored in one or more computerised files in a manner that can be accessed by users or computer programmes via a database management system.

■ **database management system**

an integrated set of computer programmes that provide the capabilities needed to establish, modify, make available and maintain the integrity of a database.

■ **data-driven DSS**

this type of DSS emphasises access to and manipulation of a time-series of internal company data and sometimes external data. Simple file systems accessed by query and retrieval tools provide the most elementary level of functionality. Data warehouse systems that allow the manipulation of data by computerised tools tailored to a specific task and setting or by more general tools and operators provide additional functionality.

■ **date of acceptance**

the date on which the client agrees to the final acceptance of the project. Commitments against the capital authorisation cease at this time. This is an event.

■ **day work account**

a method of payment for work not included in the scope of the contract that the construction contractor is obliged to perform at the request or direction of the owner or its agent. Generally, such day-work-account is paid for on unit-price or Cost-Plus terms.

■ **DC**

a distribution centre. This is a location that is used to warehouse and ship products.

■ **deactivation plan**

the document that describes the approach and critical processes required to convert the project to the safe, deactivated or disposed state. It includes methods of shutdown, disposition of records and hardware, security issues and transition to new or follow-on systems. The plan may include lessons learned, disposition of items of historical interest, environmentally sensitive and hazardous materials issues, etc.

■ **deactivation procedures**

step-by-step instructions to safely deactivate and dispose of a system.

■ **deadline date**

the date by which an applicant must mail a discretionary grant or cooperative agreement application for it to be considered for funding by the Department. Under some competitions, the Department requires that the application be received by the deadline date.

■ **deal with**

1. handle and/or dispose of something in such a way that.
2. it may not solve and/or answer anything directly.
3. a postponement and/or avoidance.

■ **debriefing**

in the procurement process, informing bidders about the strengths and weaknesses of their proposal.

■ **decision**

the choice of one from among a number of alternatives. A statement indicating a commitment to a specific course of action.

■ **decision documentation**

the recording of the terms and results of a decision and the assumptions and reasoning behind the decision.

■ **decision making**

the process for arriving at a decision.

■ **decision making process**

the sequence of decisions made as a part of the project life cycle.

■ **decision room**

a physical arrangement for a group DSS in which workstations are available to participants. The objective for using a decision room is to enhance and improve the group's decision-making process.

■ **decision support system**

a sophisticated computer programme to assist managers in making decisions. It may include simulation programs, mathematical programming routines and decision rules.

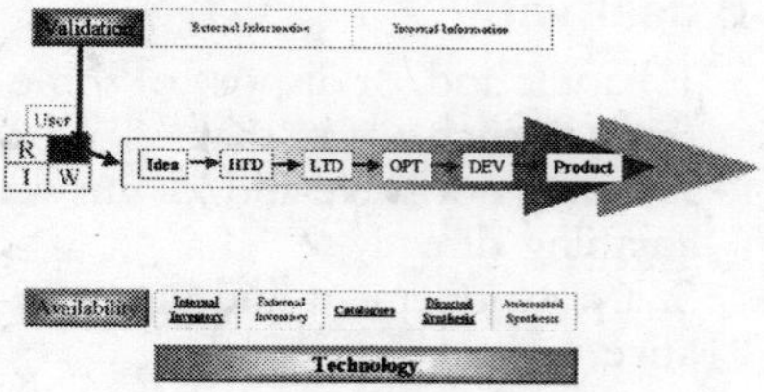


■ **decision systems**

are computer based programmes and technologies intended to automate and make routine decisions, monitor and control processes and aid or assist decision makers in structured and routine decision situations.

■ **decision theory**

a technique for helping to reach decisions under uncertainty and risk. All decisions are based to some extent on uncertain forecasts. Given the criteria selected by the decision maker, Decision Theory points to the best possible course whether or not the forecasts are accurate. For example, used to determine the best product capacity level for a project.

■ **decision tree**

a graphical representation of the decision process. Sequential decisions are drawn in the form of the branches of a tree, stemming from an initial decision point and extending all the way to the final outcomes. Each path through the branches of the tree represents a separate series of decisions and probabilistic events.

■ **decision variables**

in a model-driven DSS, a decision variable is a changing factor in a model that is determined by a decision maker. The possible range of values for decision variables constrain the choices of a decision maker.

■ **decisive action**

1. a change by the firm which will affect its future performance.
2. a deterministic stance.

■ **decomposing (decomposition)**

the process of breaking down activities and the work package to a manageable level.

■ **default**

failure to fulfil the terms of a contract.

■ **defect**

the non-fulfilment of intended usage requirements.

■ **defective**

a unit of product, which contains one or more defects.

■ **defects-per-hundred-units**

the number of defects-per-hundred units of any given quality of product is the number of defects contained therein divided by the total number of units of product, the quotient multiplied by one hundred (one or more defects being possible in any unit of product).

■ **deficiency**

all or part of an item that does not comply with its governing requirements or specification.

■ **deficiency list**

a listing of deficiencies.

■ **defined**

the software process for both management and engineering activities is documented, standardised and integrated into a standard software process for the organisation. All projects use an approved, tailored version of the organisation's standard software process for developing and maintaining software.

■ **definition**

phase of project.

■ **definition phase**

the second of four sequential periods in the generic project life cycle. Also known as planning phase or development phase.

■ **definitive**

precisely described or defined.

■ **definitive estimate**

a definitive estimate is prepared from well defined data, specifications, drawings, etc. This category covers all estimate ranges from a minimum to maximum definitive type. These estimates are used for bid proposals, bid evaluations, contract changes, extra work, legal claims, permit and government approvals. Other terms associated with a definitive estimate include check, lump sum, tender, post contract changes. etc.

■ **deflection**

the act of transferring all or part of a risk to another party, usually by some form of contract.

■ **degradation**

a lowering of quality, performance or status.

■ **dehire**

the firing of employees.

■ **delay**

an interruption or hindrance to planned progress.

■ **delaying resource**

in resource scheduling, inadequate availability of one or more resources may require that the completion of an activity be delayed beyond the date on which it could otherwise be completed. The delaying resource is the first resource on an activity that causes the activity to be delayed.

■ **delegating**

the process by which authority is distributed from the project manager to an individual working on the project.

■ **deliverable**

any measurable, tangible, verifiable outcome, result or item that must be produced to complete a project or part of a project. Often used more narrowly in reference to an external deliverable, this deliverable is subject to approval by the project sponsor or customer.

■ **deliverable deadline**

the delivery date of a deliverable to its customer.

■ **deliverables management**

the planning organising and control of end items.

■ **delivery**

the transfer or handover of a product from one party to another.

■ **delphi technique**

a process where a consensus view is reached by consultation with experts. Often used as an estimating technique.

■ **demand**

the need for a specific item in a specific quantity.

■ **demand chain management**

supply chain management that focuses on using signals from the customer to trigger production.

■ **demand filter**

a control tool for time series forecasting. When the forecast error is very large or small, an exception report is generated to warn the user. The simplest rule is to test if the forecast error is larger than plus or minus three standard deviations of the forecast error.

■ **demand flow**

another word for JIT manufacturing.

■ **demand management**

the practice of affecting demand to better meet the capacity. This can be done through pricing, advertising, promotions, replacing unscheduled arrivals with scheduled arrivals (e.g., appointments) and with customer communications.

■ **deming cycle**

a model that describes the cyclical interaction of research, sales, design and production as a continuous work flow, so that all functions are involved constantly in the effort to provide products and services that satisfy customers and contribute to improved quality.

**■ demonstrate**

to show clearly the merits or workings of an element or issue.

**■ demonstration**

verification by witnessing operation.

**■ department improvement team**

made up of all members of a department and usually chaired by the manager or supervisor, department improvement teams function as a vehicle for all employees to continuously participate in ongoing quality improvement activities.

**■ dependability**

the state of being counted on or trusted.

**■ dependencies**

relationships between products or tasks. For example, one product may be made up of several other 'dependent' products or a task may not begin until a 'dependent' task is complete.

**■ dependency diagram**

another name for a network or precedence diagram that shows the dependencies (precedence) between tasks.

**■ dependency links**

different types of links connecting activities in a precedence network.

**■ dependency management**

management of the relationships or dependencies between activities or elements of a project.

**■ dependent demand**

demand generated from scheduled production of other items.

**■ dependent demand inventory**

this term has two meanings: demand from internal customers, rather than external customers and demand that should be planned rather than forecasted. In other words, the demand for a dependent demand item can be calculated from the production plan of a higher-level item under the firm's control. Demand for a component that goes into an end-item is considered dependent demand, because this demand is planned based on the production plan for the end-item. This dependent demand should not be forecasted. Dependent demand has to do with boundaries of the firm. Demand for items under the firm's control is dependent, whereas, demand for items outside of the firm's control is considered independent demand. Given that many firms can now get detailed long-range demand information from their customers, this term may now be less meaningful now than it used to be.

**■ deployment plan**

the document that defines that approach to transition the system from the factory environment to the staging site or operational mode.

**deployment procedures**
the document that defines the step by step instructions for carrying out the deployment plan. Typically includes details of marking, packaging, shipping, transportation, precautions, transportation environment, unpacking, assembly and special risk management actions.

**deployment readiness review**
a control gate to approve readiness for deployment into the staging or operational environment.

**depot bank**
bank, which is responsible for the fortune of a fund kept and for the expenditure and cancelling of the fund portions. It supervises the adherence to the regulations of the investment trust law and the fund folder by the fund line.

**depot guidance price**
annually raised price for the verwahrung and administration of securities.

**depreciation**
a charge to current operations, which distributes the cost of a tangible capital asset, less estimated residual value, over the estimated useful life of the asset in a systematic and logical manner. It does not involve a process of valuation.

**derivatives**
financial instruments, e.g. options and futures, which are derived from to reason lying base values, frequently shares or foreign exchange.

**design**
those characteristics of a system or CSCI that are selected by the developer in response to the requirements, such as definitions of all error messages. Others will be implementation related, such as decisions about what software units and logic to use to satisfy the requirements.

**design alternatives**
during the feasibility and the design/development phases, the product designer will identify several technical solutions that all satisfy the functional requirements and the standards that constrain the choices. The alternate designs are compared in terms of cost effectiveness, often using an analysis of trade-offs to arrive at an optimum solution.

**design and development**
set of processes that transforms requirements into specified characteristics or into the specification of a product, process or system.

**design appraisal**
an appraisal of the complete design for a project or a component deliverable.

**design authority**
an organisation responsible for the detailed design of materiel to approved specifications and authorised to sign certificates of design or certified sealed drawings in accordance with procedures identified in the programme 'Configuration Management Plan'.

**design baseline**

the design, which forms the basis of the project control estimate.

**design bid build**

the traditional delivery method where design and construction are sequential and contracted for separately with two contracts and two contractors.

**design build contract**

combining design and construction in a single contract with one contractor.

**design completeness**

the design shall be complete from a total system element viewpoint (hardware, facilities, personnel, computer software, procedural data).

**design concept**

an early stage in the design development process, in which the design for a project is presented in some imaginative form such as a broad description, sketches, models, etc.

**design contract**

a contract for design work.

**design control**

a system for monitoring project scope, schedule and cost during the project's design stage.

**design development**

the process of identifying and verifying technical solutions to meet the requirements of the conceptual design. It brings a conceptual design to the next level of detail, but not as detailed as the detailed design stage. Depending on the size and nature of the project, it may be a separate stage in the project life cycle.

**design documents**

technical documents that lay out in detail the anticipated design of the project deliverable.

**Design Failure Mode and Effects Analysis (DFMEA)**

an analytical technique used by a design responsible engineer/team as a means to assure, to the extent possible, that potential failure modes and their associated causes/mechanisms have been considered and addressed.

**Design for Assembly (DFA)**

a set of methodologies and principles that can be used to guide the design process so that product assembly will have low cost, low assembly time, high labour productivity, low manufacturing cycle time and high conformance quality.

**Design for Disassembly (DFD)**

DFD is a set of principles used to guide designers in designing products that are easy to disassemble for re-manufacturing and/or repair operations. DFD enables a product and its parts to be easily reused, re-manufactured, refurbished or recycled at end of life. In the long run, DFD could make it possible to eliminate the need for landfills and incineration of mixed waste. Products would be designed so as never to become waste, but instead inputs into new products at the end of their useful lives. DFD is a key strategy within the larger area of Sustainable Product Design, which is concerned with a more proactive approach to environmentally responsible design. This approach has been most widely and successfully adopted by the product design industry.

### ■ design for manufacturability and assembly

a simultaneous engineering process designed to optimise the relationship between design function, manufacturability and ease of assembly.

### ■ design input

the physical and performance requirements of a device that are used as a basis for device design.

### ■ design management

management of the complete design process specific to the technology involved.

### ■ design management plan

a deliverable developed by the project manager stating how the design phase will be managed, including known design constraints, trade-offs, approval processes, roles and responsibilities, etc.

### ■ design of experiment

the planning of an experiment to minimise the cost of data obtained and maximise the validity range of the results. Requirements for a good experiment include clear treatment comparisons, controlled fixed and experimental variables and maximum freedom from systematic error. The experiments should adhere to the scientific principles of statistical design and analysis. Each experiment should include three parts: the experimental statement, the design and the analysis.

### ■ design records

design records refers to all technical documentation necessary to define the design, manufacture, packaging, testing, installation and maintenance of the system and its comprising elements.

### ■ design review

a proactive process to prevent problems and misunderstandings.

### ■ design simplicity

the concept of design simplicity and standardisation shall be evident.

### ■ design to cost

a concept that establishes cost elements as management goals to achieve the best balance between life-cycle cost, acceptable performance and schedule. Under this concept, cost is a design constraint during the design and development phases and a management discipline throughout the acquisition and operation of the system or equipment.

### ■ design validation

testing to ensure that product conforms to defined user needs and/or requirements. Design validation follows successful design verification and is normally performed on the final product under defined operating conditions. Multiple validations may be performed if there are different intended uses.

■ **design verification**

testing to ensure that all design outputs meet design input requirements. Design verification may include activities such as: design review, performing alternate calculations,
understanding tests and demonstrations and review of design stage documents before release.

■ **design-to specifications**

documents that specify the 'Design-to' requirements and may include functionality, performance, interfaces, constraints, effectiveness and verification.

■ **detail documentation**

a written description at an exacting level, rather than a high level overview, of any part of the project or product.

■ **detail schedule**

a schedule used to communicate the day-to-day activities to working levels on the project.

■ **detailed**

1. provide another level to a description.
2. very little extra substance when the starting level is high enough.

■ **detailed design**

the conversion of design-to specifications into designs and associated build-to and code-to documentation. Includes behaviour analysis, requirements flow down, concept trades, risk management, concept testing, producability analysis, models, etc.

■ **detailed design phase**

that part of a project life-cycle during which working drawings, standards, specifications and tender documents are prepared.

■ **detailed planning**

the lowest level of planning adopted in a project.

■ **detailed resource plan**

a plan implemented when it is necessary to plan and control a certain major activity within a stage. The plan sets costs and resource usage that correspond to the detailed technical plan.

■ **detailed schedule**

a plan of activities for all work. The detailed schedule would typically cover activities up to at least the next major milestone. The detailed schedule supports and is consistent with the master schedule.

■ **detailed technical plan**

a plan providing a detailed breakdown of selected major activities, e.g. system testing and produced as and when required. A detailed technical plan should be established on all but the very smallest projects.

■ **detection or inspection**

a past-oriented strategy that attempts to identify unacceptable output after it has been produced and separate it from the good output.

**■ deterministic**

an approach that presumes the presence of fixed constraints.

**■ deterministic network**

a project schedule network with no ability to accommodate probabilistic dependencies. Precedence networks are said to be deterministic.

**■ developer**

An organisation that develops products ('develops' may include new development, modification, reuse, reengineering, maintenance or any other activity that results in products) for itself or another organisation.

**■ development**

the actual work performed to accomplish, effect or bring about the Project.

**■ development phase**

the second of four sequential phases in the generic project life cycle. Also known as definition phase and sometimes as a feasibility phase.

**■ development plan**

a plan for moving a project concept to a viable project.

**■ deviation**

any variation from planned performance. The deviation can be in terms of schedule, cost, performance or scope of work. Deviation analysis is the heart of exercising project control.

**■ deviation permit**

written authorisation, prior to production or provision of a service, to depart from specified requirements for a specified quantity or for a specified time.

**■ deviations**

a specific written authorisation, granted prior to the manufacture of a configuration item, to depart from a particular performance or design requirement of a specification, drawing or other document for a specific number of units or a specific period of time. A deviation differs from an engineering change in that an approved change requires a corresponding revision of the documentation defining, the affected item, whereas a deviation does not contemplate revision of the applicable specification or drawing.

**■ DFA**

Design for Assembly.

**■ DFM**

Design for Manufacturing.

**■ DFMEA**

Design Failure Mode and Effects Analysis.

**■ Dialog Generation and Management System (DGMS)**

a software management package in a DSS whose functions in the dialog subsystem is similar to that of a DBMS in a database .

■ **direct cost**

any cost that is specifically identified with a particular activity.

■ **direct costs**

those costs (labour, material and other direct costs) that can be consistently related to work performed on a particular project. Direct costs are best contrasted with indirect costs that cannot be identified to a specific project.

■ **direct labour**

labour, i.e. man-hours, that is specifically identified with a particular activity.

■ **direct net yield**

payment per portion in per cent of the stock exchange course.

■ **direct project costs**

the costs directly attributable to a project, including all personnel, goods and/or services together with all their associated costs, but not including indirect project costs, such as any overhead and office costs incurred in support of the project.

■ **discipline**

a broad general body of knowledge, skills and competence (expertise) that logically belong together and which are required by a company in order to provide its products or service or to provide other functions necessary for its continued existence.

■ **discontinuous activity**

an activity in which the interval between the start and finish dates is allowed to exceed its duration in order to satisfy start-to-start and finish-to-finish relationships with other activities.

■ **discontinuous processing**

this option assigns the discontinuous attribute to all activities for a time analysis session, except where overridden by a specific activity type.

■ **Discounted Cash Flow (DCF)**

a calculation of present value of a projected cash flow based on some assumed rate of inflation or interest.

■ **discounting**

the process of reducing a future amount of money to a present value.

■ **discrete activity**

a task that has a deliverable, is measurable and has a definite start and finish. An item on the Work Breakdown Structure would be an example of a discrete activity.

■ **discrete effort**

tasks that have a specific measurable end product or end result. Discrete tasks are ideal for earned value measurement.

■ **discrete manufacturing**

describes manufacturing of distinct items (items you can easily count, touch, see) such as a pencil, a light bulb, a telephone, a bicycle, a fuel pump, etc. Discrete as apposed to process manufacturing.

**■ discrete milestone**

a milestone that has a definite scheduled occurrence in time.

**■ discrete task**

a measurable activity with an output.

**■ discrimination**

the requirements imposed on the organisation and the procedures implemented by the organisation to assure fairness in hiring and promotion practices.

**■ discussion**

dialogue explaining implications and impacts on objectives. The elaboration and description of facts, findings and alternatives.

**■ diseconomies of scale**

an economics term that suggests that as the volume produced increases, the cost per unit also increases. For example, it is said that the optimal hospital size is about 400 beds and that larger hospitals tend to become less personal and less efficient due to complexity of the operation and the distance that people have to travel. This is also said to be true of high schools. The optimal student body size is probably between 400-600 students. The point at which a plant becomes too large and, as volume continues to increase, the average cost per unit of output increases rather than drops. Increase in long-run average costs, which may set in as the scale of production increases. Although the unit cost of production may fall as plant size increases, there are several reasons why this process is eventually reversed: (a) the different processes within a plant will probably not have the same optimum scale. For example, a car-body press might be at its most efficient at 150,000 units a year, while an engine transfer machining line may be optimal at 100,000 units a year. When 150,000 cars are produced, it will be necessary either to have a sub optimal engine line with a capacity of 50,000 in addition or to run a second line at 50 per cent capacity. (b) As firm size increases, problems of administration and coordination increase and there is a growth of bureaucracy. (c) If output for a national or international market is concentrated at one large plant in a single location, transport costs of raw materials and finished goods to and from distant markets may offset scale economies of production at the large plant. These are internal diseconomies. External diseconomies are said to arise as a geographic region sees larger-scale production - these might include traffic congestion or pollution, for example.

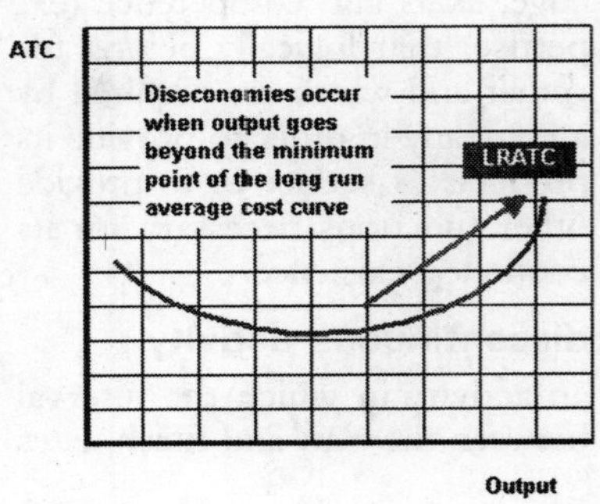

■ **disintermediation**

displacing a distributor in the channel. For example, a manufacturing firm replaces its distributors with a web site to sell directly to its customers has 'disintermediated' its distributors. A wholesale distributor is an intermediary between manufacturers and customers. If you remove an intermediary, you have disintermediation.

■ **dispatching**

the process of determining the next job (order) to be processed in a factory (or job shop). Typical rules include earliest due date, shortest processing time, short slack time and critical ratio.

■ **display**

a pictorial, verbal, written, tabulated or graphical means of transmitting findings, results and conclusions.

■ **dispute**

disagreements not settled by mutual consent, which could be decided by litigation or arbitration.

■ **dissemination**

the distribution of information to as many people as possible.

■ **distinguishing constraint**

a dummy which distinguishes two activities which may have the same start and finish dates.

■ **distributed**

the results of allocation, division or otherwise spreading around of components such as allocable project overhead costs to their respective activities or other information such as memos and directives to the parties concerned.

■ **distribution**

The population (universe) from which observations are drawn, categorised into cells and form identifiable patterns. It is based on the concept of variation that states that anything measured repeatedly will arrive at different results. These results will fall into statistically predictable patterns. A bell-shaped curve (normal distribution) is an example of a distribution in which the greatest number of observations occur in the centre with fewer and fewer observations falling evenly on either side of the average.

■ **distribution**

describes the process of storing, shipping and transporting goods. Also describes the facilities (distribution operations, distribution centres) that conduct these activities. In statistical analysis, describes the measurement of a group of events or occurrences.

■ **distribution list**

a list of people receiving information for a particular purpose.

■ **distribution of information**

the dissemination of information for the purpose of communication, approval or decision-making.

■ **distribution of minutes**

the circulation to attendees of meeting of a record of their discussion, conclusions and action items.

## distribution statement

a statement used in marking a technical document to denote the extent of its availability for distribution release and disclosure without the need for additional approvals and authorisations from the controlling agency.

## document

a record of an event or knowledge, taken so that the information will not be lost. Documents are usually written, but they can also be made up of images or sound. Documents can also be put into electronic or digital form and stored in a computer.

## document control

a system for controlling and executing project documentation in a uniform and orderly fashion.

## document management

1. systems and processes for managing documents including the creation, editing, production, storage, indexing and disposal of documents. This usually refers to electronic documents and uses specific document management software. 2. a process for managing the life cycle of a document, from inception, version creation, publication, storage, retention and disposal. This usually refers to electronic documents and uses specific document management software.

## documentation

written material defining the process to be followed (e.g. test procedure, quality manual, operation sheets).

## documentation change notice

a notification of change to holders of controlled documentation.

## documentation matrix

a communication project control tool used to identify all project document names, their revision data and number, who is responsible for keeping the document updated, what format the document is presented in and how often a safety back is performed.

## documented procedure

a written description of a course of action to be taken to perform a given task.

## DOE

Design of Experiments.

## dog and pony show

a project briefing which uses a number of viewgraphs, slides, flip charts or similar aids, usually with a view to persuading the audience to a particular point of view.

## domain

the part of the external world, including users and inmates of the system that affects and is affected by the system.

## double declining balance

book value is multiplied by a fixed rate, often double the straight-line rate. Initially, the asset's cost is the book value. For subsequent periods, the book value at the end of one period becomes the next period's beginning book value. Once the book value is reduced to the expected salvage value, no more depreciation may be recognised. Similar to Sum-of-the-Years'-Digits, larger amounts of depreciation are taken in the early years of the asset's life.

## ■ double-loop learning

in contrast to single-loop learning which involves using knowledge to solve specific problems based on existing assumptions and often based on what has worked in the past, double-loop learning goes a step further and questions existing assumptions in order to create new insights. For example, take the problem 'how do we prevent earthquakes from killing people?' The single-loop answer would be to learn how earthquakes happen and try to predict them in order to be prepared. The double-loop answer would question our notion of 'earthquake' and might conclude that earthquakes do not kill people, falling buildings do.

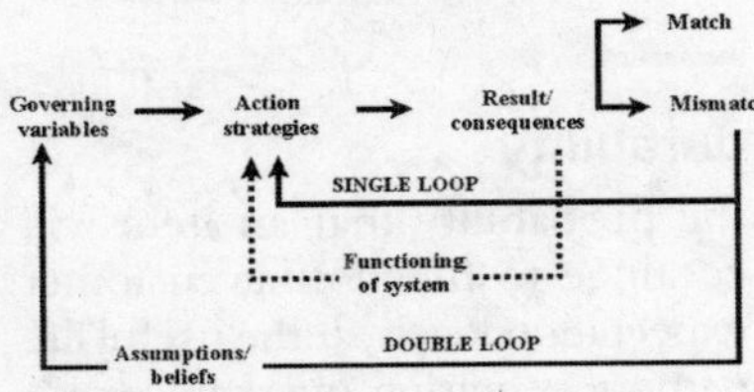


## ■ downsize

to fire some employees and/or reduce plant and equipment.

## ■ downzoning

a change in zoning classification to less intensive use and/or development.

## ■ drawings

a drawing is the means of conveying information and in this context includes all item lists, drawing lists, etc., in connection with a drawing or group of drawings.

## ■ drill down

to increase the amount of detail about a topic, the amount of additional detail is relative to the starting level.

## ■ drill down/up

an analytical technique that lets a DSS user navigate among levels of data ranging from the most summarised (up) to the most detailed (down).

## ■ drive home a point

1. to emphasise.
2. repetition used instead of additional information.

## ■ drop ship

when a distributor (or retailer) has a supplier send an order directly to a customer, it is said to be 'drop-shipped' to the customer. This reduces the customer's lead-time, but usually increases the distribution cost for the system.

## ■ DRP, Distribution Requirements Planning

process for determining inventory requirements in a multiple plant/warehouse environment. DRP may be used for both distribution and manufacturing. In manufacturing, DRP will work directly with MRP. DRP may also be defined as Distribution Resource Planning, which also includes determining labour, equipment and warehouse space requirements.

■ **drum-handling attachments**

describes the various designs of lift-truck attachment used to handle 55 gallon drums. Some are smaller versions of a paper roll clamp while others may engage the upper rim of the drum or the lower rings. Some drum attachments are capable of picking up multiple drums at the same time.

■ **DSS development tools**

software components (such as editors, code libraries, specific objects, visual interfaces) that facilitate the development of a specific DSS.

■ **DSS generator**

computer software package that provides tools and capabilities that help a developer quickly and easily build a specific decision support system. Excel is an example of a DSS Generator.

■ **dual responsibility**

the acceptance of functional responsibility from one person and project responsibility from another.

■ **dummy**

an activity denoting a dependency, but not an action.

■ **dummy activity**

an activity of zero duration used to show a logical relationship in the arrow diagramming method. Dummy activities are used when logical relationships cannot be completely or correctly described with regular activity arrows. Dummies are shown graphically as a dashed line headed by an arrow.

■ **dupont analysis**

an economic analysis that can be used to show the return on investment as a function of many other variables. Operations managers sometimes use this analysis to show that a small reduction in inventory can reduce cost, increase sales and reduce investment and if you increase the numerator and decrease denominator of ratio at the same time, the ratio gets much larger.

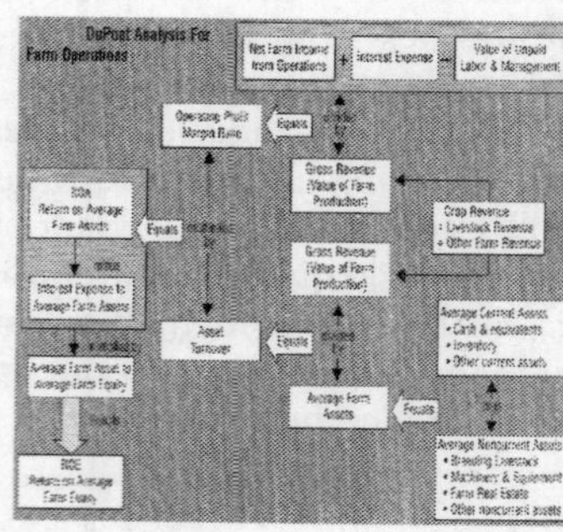


■ **durability**

the probability that an item will continue to function at customer expectation levels, at the useful life without requiring overhaul or rebuild due to wear out.

■ **duration**

the number of work periods (not including holidays or other nonworking periods) required to complete an activity or other project element. Usually expressed as workdays or workweeks. Sometimes incorrectly equated with elapsed time.

■ **duration**

the number of work units (not including holidays or other nonworking periods) required to complete an activity or other project element. Usually expressed as work days or work weeks.

■ **duration compression**

shortening the project schedule without reducing the project scope. Duration compression is not always possible and often requires an increase in project cost.

■ **duty and tax administration**

action taken to legally minimise duties and taxes applicable to the goods/services supplied.

■ **earliest feasible date**

the earliest date on which the activity could be scheduled to start based on the scheduled dates of all its predecessors, but in the absence of any resource constraints on the activity itself. This date is calculated by resource scheduling.

■ **earliest finish**

the earliest day that the work item can finish if it starts on its earliest start and is completed in its expected time.

■ **earliest start**

the earliest day that the work item can start provided every preceding work item starts at its earliest start day and is completed in its expected time.

■ **early dates**

calculated in the forward pass of time analysis, early dates are the earliest dates on which an activity can start and finish.

■ **early finish**

in the critical path method, the earliest possible date on which the uncompleted portions of an activity (or the project) can finish based on the network logic and any schedule constraints. Early finish dates can change as the project progresses and changes are made to the project plan.

■ **Early Finish Date (EF)**

In the critical path method, the earliest possible point in time on which the uncompleted portions of an activity (or the project) can finish based on the network logic and any schedule constraints. Early finish dates can change as the project progresses and changes are made to the Project Plan.

■ **early start date**

in the critical path method, the earliest possible point in time on which the uncompleted portions of an activity (or the project) can start, based on the network logic and any schedule constraints. Early start dates can change as the project progresses and changes are made to the Project Plan.

■ **early warning system**

a monitoring system that provides advance notification or indication of potential problems in a project. Many computerised project management systems incorporate early warning functions.

**■ earned hours**

the time in standard hours credited as a result of the completion of a given task or a group of tasks.

**■ Earned Value (EV)**

1. a method for measuring project performance. It compares the amount of work that was planned with what was actually accomplished to determine if cost and schedule performance is as planned.
2. the budgeted cost of work performed for an activity or group of activities.

**■ earned value analysis**

analysis of project progress where the actual money budgeted and spent is compared to the value of the work achieved.

**■ earned value cost control**

the quantification of the overall progress of a project in rupee terms so as to provide a realistic yardstick against which to compare the actual cost to date.

**■ earned value management**

a management technique that relates resource planning to schedules and to technical cost and schedule requirements. All work is planned, budgeted and scheduled in time-phased increments constituting a cost and schedule measurement baseline.

**■ e-business**

the use of electronic information systems (especially internet technologies) in business processes.

**■ e-commerce**

the use of electronic information systems (especially internet technologies) to perform transactions i.e. buy and sell things.

**■ economic analysis**

a systematic approach to one or more options designed to assist the programme or project manager in making a choice.

**■ economic evaluation**

the process of establishing the value of a project in relation to other corporate standards/bench marks, project profitability, financing, interest rates and acceptance.

**■ economic life**

the period of time over which the benefits to be gained from a project may reasonably be expected to accrue.

**■ Economic Order Quantity (EOQ)**

the optimal order quantity (batch size) that minimises the sum of the carrying and ordering cost. The equation for the total incremental cost is $TIC=(D/Q)S+(Q/2)ic$, where D is the annual demand, Q is the order quantity, S is the order cost, i is the carrying charge and c is the unit cost. Taking the first derivative of this function and setting it to zero, we find that the optimal order quantity (the EOQ) is given by . The EOQ model is considered to be of little practical value for three reasons. First, it is very difficult to estimate the parameters of the model. Second, even with perfect estimates of the parameters, the total incremental cost function is very flat near the optimal solution, which means that the total incremental cost is not sensitive to errors in the EOQ. Third, managerial intuition is usually good at finding the EOQ without the equation. It is obvious to most managers that costly items should be ordered more often and in smaller quantities. In other words, the EOQ really does not matter very much — except on the exams in all major business schools. On the positive side: the EOQ model does help people get a better understanding of lotsizing issues, in some cases the tradeoffs do have a significant economic impact and the EOQ model is the foundation for other models such as the quantity discount model.

Determining the optimum inventory level

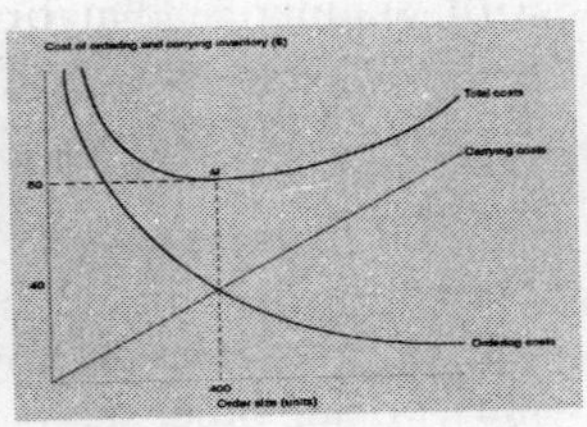


## ■ economic success

the success of a project in terms of achieving its economic value.

## ■ economic value

the value of a project in terms of its expected financial returns from the perspective of the enterprise's overall commercial strategic objectives.

## ■ economy of scale

a concept from economics where a reduction in cost per unit results from increased production, realised through operational efficiencies. Economies of scale can be accomplished because as production increases, the cost of producing each additional unit falls. See **diseconomies of scale, economy of scope.**

## ■ economy of scope

a concept from economics that states that the cost per unit will decline as the variety of products increases. In other words, economies of scope arise from synergies in the production of similar goods. A firm with economics of scope can reduce its cost per unit by having a wide variety of products that share resources.

## ■ effectiveness

extent to which planned activities are realised and planned results achieved.

## ■ effects fund

investment trust with plants in securities and value rights, which at a stock exchange or at another regulated, which public openly standing market are acted. Real estate funds and remaining funds compare.

## ■ efficiency

1. ratio of average processing time to some standard processing time. For example, if a process has a standard time of 100 minutes per unit and the operator can do the process in 90 minutes per unit, the operator is said to have an efficiency of 100/90 = 111%. An efficient process is one that can

perform at a very low cost compared to some standard.
2. relationship between the result achieved and the resources used.

■ **efficiency factor**

a measure of overall performance used in a work measurement system. It is calculated by dividing the standard time to perform the work by the actual time.

■ **Efficient Consumer Response (ECR)**

a consumer goods (primarily grocery) initiative aimed at reducing inefficient practices and waste in the supply chain.

■ **effort**

the number of labour units required to complete an activity or other project element. Usually expressed as staff hours, staff days or staff weeks. Should not be confused with duration.

■ **effort**

the number of labour units required to complete an activity or other project element. Usually expressed as staff hours, staff days or staff weeks.

■ **effort remaining**

the estimate of effort remaining to complete an activity.

■ **effort-driven activity**

an effort-drive activity provides the option to determine activity duration through resource usage. The resource requiring the greatest time to complete the specified amount of work on the activity will determine its duration.

■ **elapsed duration**

the amount of time needed to complete a task.

■ **elapsed time**

the total number of calendar days (excluding non-work days such as weekends or holidays) that is needed to complete an activity. It gives a 'real world view' of how long an activity is scheduled to take for completion.

■ **electronic collaboration**

a process through which project partners can contribute jointly to works in progress via email, groupware, public networks, etc.

■ **Electronic Data Interchange (EDI)**

Electronic Data Interchange (EDI) is a system (and a related set of standards) that firms can use to communicate routine business transactions between computers without human intervention. EDI transactions can include information for inquiries, planning, purchasing, acknowledgments, pricing order status, scheduling, test results, shipping and receiving, invoices, payments and financial reporting. The simplest

form of EDI is to send purchase orders to suppliers. More advanced forms of EDI include sending invoices, electronic payments and planned orders (requirements).

■ **element**

a basic component e.g. of the work breakdown structure.

■ **element definition dictionary**

a listing of terms and their meanings representing the contents or elements of a work breakdown structure.

■ **e-mail**

short for electronic mail. Uses internet technologies to send messages and documents to and from computers around the world in a matter of seconds. Sending or receiving e-mail requires internet access and an e-mail address.

■ **e-meetings**

a term for a meeting supported by full-motion video, audio and Web meeting tools. One or more participants in the meeting is participating remotely in the meeting. It is possible that all participants are in different physical locations.

■ **emerging economies bond**

obligations from Latin America, Eastern Europe and Asia, which promise high net yields, due to which political or economic uncertainty in these countries however are afflicted with a larger risk.

■ **emerging market fund**

investment trusts, which invest in developing countries, e.g. in Asia or Latin America. See **also emerging markets.**

■ **emerging markets**

emerging markets or threshold markets are countries - particularly in Asia, Eastern Europe and Latin America -, which develop rapidly, whose national economies and boersenplaetze did not achieve however yet western standard.

■ **eminent domain**

the legal right of government to take private property for public use, provided the owner is offered just compensation for the taking of property.

■ **emission**

expenditure of new securities.

■ **emitter**

legal entity or public body, who spends securities for the procurement of outside capital.

■ **employee relations**

those formal activities and procedures used by an organisation to administer and develop its workforce.

■ **empowerment**

to give responsibility and some authority to one or more employees. The amount of authority may not be sufficient to fulfil the responsibility.

■ **empty statements**

descriptions which add little to understanding.

**■ enablers of knowledge management**

systems and infrastructures, which ensure knowledge is created, captured, shared and leveraged. These include culture, technology, infrastructure and measurement.

**■ enabling capabilities**

necessary [to enter a market] but not sufficient in themselves to competitively distinguish a company.

**■ end activity**

an activity with no logical successors.

**■ end stage assessment**

a mandatory management control at the end of each stage. Work may not proceed on the next stage until the project board has approved current status and future resource plans and technical plans at this assessment.

**■ end-item**

a deliverable item, which is formally accepted by the acquirer in accordance with requirements of a detail specification.

**■ endorsement**

written approval. Endorsement signifies personal understanding and acceptance of the thing endorsed and recommends further endorsement by higher levels of authority if necessary. Endorsement of commitment by a person invested with appropriate authority signifies authorisation.

**■ engineering change notice**

the formal release of an engineering change.

**■ Engineering Change Order (ECO)**

a change made in the product design (or process). The timing for an ECO can be dependent on the current inventory. This is a major opportunity for improvement for many firms, given that ECOs tend to be error-prone and the timing is complicated by current inventories, documentation, training, etc.

**■ engineering change request**

a request to consider a technical change to the technical baseline submitted to a change control board.

**■ engineering cost estimate**

cost estimate derived by summing detailed cost analysis of the individual work packages and adding appropriate burdens. Usually determined by a contractor's performing organisations, price analysts and cost accountants.

**■ engineering decision trace ability**

significant engineering decisions shall be traceable to the system engineering process activities on which they were based.

**■ engineering management**

the management of the engineering and technical effort to transform a conceptual requirement into an operational system. It includes the system performance parameters and preferred system configuration to satisfy the requirement, the planning and control of technical programme tasks, integration of the engineering specialties and the management of a totally integrated effort of design engineering, computer software engineering, test engineering, safety engineering, security engineering, logistics engineering, production engineering and specialty engineering (EMC, environmental, etc.,) to meet cost, technical performance and schedule objectives.

■ **engineering process**

the set of activities relating to a construction output.

■ **engineering specialty integration**

the timely and appropriate intermeshing of engineering efforts and disciplines such as reliability, maintainability, logistics engineering, human factors, safety, value engineering, computer software, standardisation, transportability, etc., to insure their influence on system design.

■ **enterprise portal**

a means of presenting a business professional with clear, consistent and ordered access to multiple information sources and / or applications via a corporate intranet.

■ **Enterprise Programme Management (EPM)**

an Information Technology Investment Management-based methodology to manage programmes and projects of enterprise significance. EPM focuses on the management of multiple related programmes and projects that individually support the same mission or ongoing activity.

■ **enterprise project management**

the application of the project management discipline throughout an enterprise.

■ **Enterprise Resources Planning (ERP)**

integrated applications software that manufacturing corporations can run to run their business. ERP systems typically include accounts payable, accounts receivable, general ledger, payroll, MRP (Manufacturing Resources Planning) and many other interrelated systems.

■ **enterprise technology programme**

a group of related IT projects aggregated for management purposes, that support a defined enterprise.

■ **enterprise-wide DSS**

a DSS that supports a large group of managers in a networked client-server environment with a specialised data warehouse as part of the DSS architecture.

■ **environment characteristic**

a particular property of the environment.

■ **environment, project**

the combined internal and external forces, both individual and collective, which assist or restrict the attainment of the project objectives. These could be business or project related or may be due to political, economic, technological or regulatory conditions.

■ **environmental requirements**

regulatory conditions that pertain to the natural environment that must be met in the planning and execution of a project.

■ **EOQ (Economic Order Quantity)**

result of a calculation that determines the most cost effective quantity to order (purchased items) or produce (manufactured items). The formula basically finds the point at which the combination of order cost and carrying cost is the least. The standard formula is EOQ = Square Root [2 (Annual Usage) (Order Cost) / (Annual Carrying Cost/unit)]. The difficult part of implementing the formula is getting accurate values for order cost and carrying cost.

■ **e-procurement**

a web-based information system that improves corporate purchasing operations by handling the specification, authorisation, competitive bidding and acquisition of products and services through catalogues, auctions, request for proposals and request for quotes.

■ **equipment procurement**

the acquisition of equipment/material to be incorporated into the project.

■ **equitable adjustment**

the price or target cost adjustment to which a contractor is entitled upon the occurrence of some special event, such as the issuance of a contract change.

■ **ergonomics**

the science of designing work to be consistent with the capabilities (and limitations) of the human body. This science is usually taught in an industrial engineering department. It is concerned with minimising the cumulative trauma disorders related to motions and forces applied to the body in the workplace.

■ **ERP (Enterprise Resource Planning)**

describes software systems designed to manage most or all aspects of a manufacturing or distribution enterprise (an expanded version of MRP systems). ERP systems are usually broken down into modules such as Financials, Sales, Purchasing, Inventory Management, Manufacturing, MRP, DRP. The modules are designed to work seamlessly with the rest of the system and should provide a consistent user interface between them. These systems usually have extensive set-up options that allow you to customise their functionality to your specific business needs. Unfortunately, in the real world, ERP systems rarely are sufficient to meet all business needs and a myriad of other software packages such as Customer Relationship Management (CRM), Manufacturing Execution Systems

(MES), Advanced Planning and Scheduling (APS), Warehouse Management Systems (WMS) and Transportation Management Systems (TMS) are being sold to make up for these deficiencies.

■ **error**

a discrepancy between a computed, observed or measured value or condition and the true, specified or theoretically correct value or condition.

■ **error probability**

the likelihood of a mistake.

■ **escalated base price**

the base price estimate adjusted for inflation up to the time of tender.

■ **escalation**

an anticipated rise in uncommitted costs of resources (labour, material, equipment) over time, due to reduced purchasing power of money. A component of a cost type. The allowance for escalation is a component within the anticipated award cost of a cost class.

■ **ESFR (Early Suppression Fast Response)**

sprinkler system technology that executes faster and with a substantially greater volume of water. ESFR sprinklers may eliminate the need for in-rack sprinkler systems in many warehouses, thus reducing the cost of installation and, more importantly, the risk of water damage caused by damage to in-rack sprinklers. Retrofitting ESFR into older warehouses is not always feasible due to limited water pressure in old systems.

■ **essential characteristics**

the minimum operational, functional, maintenance, performance, reliability and safety requirements, which must be fulfilled to meet the needs of the user(s).

■ **establish**

define, document (in writing or electronically) and implement.

■ **estimate**

an assessment of the likely quantitative result. Usually applied to project costs and durations and should always include some indication of accuracy (e.g., +/- x percent). Usually used with a modifier (e.g., preliminary, conceptual, feasibility). Some application areas have specific modifiers that imply particular accuracy ranges (e.g. order-of-magnitude estimate, budget estimate and definitive estimate in engineering and construction projects).

■ **Estimate at Completion (EAC)**

the expected total cost of an activity, a group of activities or of the project when the defined scope of work has been completed. Most techniques for forecasting EAC include some adjustment of the original cost estimate based on project performance to date.

■ **estimate class a**

a detailed projection of time and costs for next planning horizon, having an expected precision variance of 10% or less, team involved in this estimate and willing to commit to it.

**■ estimate class b**

an estimate based on at least two levels of a documented work breakdown structure, having an expected precision variance of 25% or less, project manager and/or subject matter experts developed this estimate.

**■ estimate class c**

ballpark estimate used only in preliminary discussion of feasibility having a precision variance of 50% or more, not to be used for making commitments.

**■ estimate class d**

an estimate based on a comprehensive statement of requirements in mission terms and an outline solution. Such an estimate is strictly an indication of the final cost and completion date.

**■ estimate conversion**

the re-assembly of the components of an estimate into a fiscal or project budget, typically for approval and control purposes.

**■ estimated completion date**

the predicted date at which all requirements for a defined task will be completed.

**■ Estimated Cost to Complete (ECC)**

the remaining costs to be incurred to satisfy the complete scope of a project at a specific data date. The difference between the cost to date and the forecast final cost.

**■ estimating**

calculating approximately the probable cost or value.

**■ estimating costs**

the process of forecasting a future result in terms of cost, based upon information available at the time.

**■ estimating factor**

a multiple used to estimate cost or price based on a linear relationship with a product characteristic or an element of cost.

**■ eternal loans**

obligations without day of maturity. Eternal or infinite loans carry regularly interest payments out, however never erase the nominal amount, in order to get its capital back, an investor must sell such obligations at the stock exchange.

**■ evaluation**

the process of determining whether an item or activity meets specified criteria.

**■ evaluation factors**

those elements (technical, cost, management, etc.) the buyer considers most important and is the basis for proposal evaluation.

**■ evaluation of IT investments**

a structured process to provide a systematic method to minimise risks and maximise return on IT investments.

**■ evaluation of progress**

a careful assessment of the work completed to date as compared to the baseline plan.

**■ even loading**

an even distribution of budget over an activity or project's duration.

**■ event**

an event is an identifiable single point in time on a project.

**■ event driven**

with event driven strategies information about announced events fast and above all profit is used bringing. With this strategy one assumes the markets evaluate information too optimistically or too pessimistically. Pro find knowledge and experience during the evaluation of securities and the entrance to current information are with event driven strategies the success factor number unity.

**■ event management**

term used to describe software functionality that triggers specific actions based upon the occurrence of a specific event or combination of events. This is another one of those terms used primarily by software vendors and consultants to push 'new' technology. In reality, business software has been providing event-management functionality for years. If inventory dropping below a predetermined level (reorder point) triggers a message to a planner (or even a listing on a reorder report), this is essentially event management.

**■ event oriented**

a planning approach focusing on events rather than activities.

**■ event oriented schedule**

systems, which present information in terms of events (i.e. points in time).

**■ evidence-based medicine, evidence-based practice**

evidence-based medicine involves integrating individual clinical experience with the best available external clinical evidence from systematic research when making decisions about patient care. Evidence-based practice is a term strongly associated with healthcare and so is often taken to mean the same, although it is now also being used in other fields so can have a broader meaning.

**■ evolutionary (iterative) design process**

a systematic process for system development that is recommended for use in creating DSS. A portion of the DSS system is quickly constructed, then tested, improved and enlarged in systematic steps. This methodology is similar to prototyping.

**■ evolutionary development**

a development approach where successive increments build on previous versions. The product 'evolves' to its final state rather than being developed that way in a single development effort.

**■ evolutionary prototype**

the progressive maturing of a software or hardware product by building a model and developing it into the final product by the progressive introduction of required performance.

**■ examination**

an element of inspection consisting of investigation, without the use of special laboratory appliances or procedures, of supplies and services to determine conformance to those specified requirements which can be determined by such investigations. Examination is generally non-destructive and includes, but is not limited to visual, auditory, olfactory, tactile, gustatory and other investigations. Simple physical manipulation, gauging and measurement is needed.

**■ exception**

an exclusion or deviation from a specified or accepted reference set.

**■ exception reporting**

the process of documenting those situations where there are significant deviations from the specifications of a project. The assumption is made that the project will be developed within established boundaries. When the process falls outside of those boundaries, a report is made on why this deviation occurred.

**■ excusable compensable delays**

delays that are caused by the owner's actions or inactions. Also, the contractor is entitled to a time extension and damage compensation for extra costs associated with the delay. See also excusable delays, excusable non-compensable delays, non-excusable delays.

**■ excusable delays**

delays that are not attributable to the contractor's action or inactions. Excusable delays when founded, entitle the contractor to a time extension if the completion date is affected. See also excusable compensable delays, excusable non-compensable delays, non-excusable delays.

**■ excusable non-compensable delays**

delays that are neither the contractor's nor the owner's fault. The contractor is entitled to a time extension but not to damage compensation. Non-excusable Delays are delays that are caused by the contractor's or its subcontractor's actions or inactions. Consequently, the contractor is not entitled to a time extension or delay damages. On the other hand the owner may be entitled to liquidated or other damages. See also excusable delays, excusable compensable delays, non-excusable delays.

**■ execution period**

see execution phase.

**■ execution phase**

the period within the project life cycle during which the actual work of creating the project's deliverables is carried out.

**■ executive authority**

the individual or collective body representing the source of project management's authority. This authority may be channelled through a project sponsor or project director.

## ■ executive control gate

a control gate identified, defined and included in the project schedule by executive management.

## ■ executive control point

a point between project stages when top management has the opportunity to review the project status, the plan for the ensuing stage, verify its consistency with their latest business objectives and give or withhold, approval to proceed.

## ■ Executive Information Systems (EIS)

a computerised system intended to provide current and appropriate information to support executive decision making for managers using a networked workstation. The emphasis is on graphical displays and an easy to use interface that present information from the corporate database. They are tools to provide canned reports or briefing books to top-level executives. They offer strong reporting and drill-down capabilities. An early term for a sophisticated data-driven DSS targeted to senior executives.

## ■ executive steering committee (or executive improvement team)

includes top executives and is chaired by the CEO, encourages and participates in a quality initiative by reviewing, approving and implementing improvement activities.

## ■ exit interview

a survey that is conducted with an employee when he or she leaves an organisation. The information from each exit interview is used to provide feedback on why employees are leaving, what they liked about their employment and what areas of the organisation need improvement. Exit interviews can also be used as part of knowledge harvesting to extract knowledge from the departing employee so that it is kept in-house.

## ■ expanding

in an outline, making visible the collapsed tasks that are immediately subordinate to summary tasks.

## ■ expectations

looking forward to events that are about to happen.

## ■ expected monetary value

the product of an event's probability of occurrence and the gain or loss that will result.

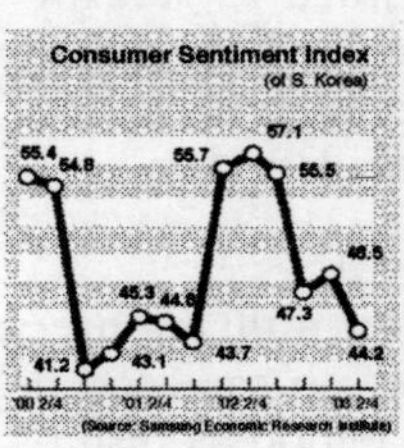


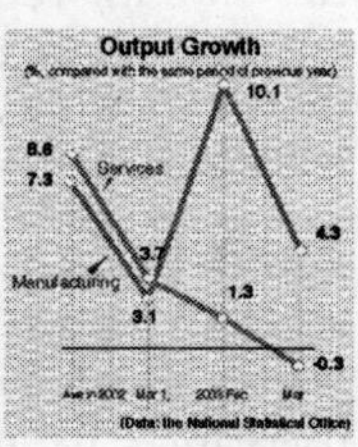


## ■ expected value

a way for comparing the values/costs of different scenarios. It is calculated by multiplying the probability of an outcome times the estimated cost of that outcome.

■ **expected working period**

a proposed period of work or the normal working day, week, month, year, that is expected of an employee.

■ **expediting**

facilitating and accelerating progress by the removal of obstacles.

■ **expenditure authority**

the senior management responsible for giving permission for or the actual approval of, disbursement of funds.

■ **expenditure commission**

commission, that is loaded by the spending fund company with the design of portions the buyer.

■ **expenditure to budget**

a comparison of or the difference between, the amount expended and the corresponding budget allocation.

■ **expenditure to date**

the amount recorded as actually disbursed and accrued on an activity or whole project up to the current cut-off or data date.

■ **expense**

cost of operation and maintenance of activities on the accrual basis for a fiscal period as distinguished from cost of acquisition of property.

■ **expense management**

1. to limit wasteful spending.

2. to keep a record of what is spent.

■ **experience**

refers to what we have done and what has happened to us in the past.

■ **experiment**

an effort to discover or confirm some principle or effect usually in some scaled down form such as a mock-up or surrogate form such as a computer model.

■ **expert**

one who is skilled in a particular area by virtue of learning and experience.

■ **expert system**

branch of artificial intelligence that develops computer applications to simulate human decisions.

■ **expertise**

a specialised, in-depth body of knowledge, skills and competence that is a major, identifiable component of the relevant discipline.

■ **expertise directory, experts directory (or skills directory)**

a staff directory in the form of a database that includes details of people's skills, knowledge, experience and expertise so that users can search for people with specific know-how.

■ **explicit knowledge**

explicit knowledge is formal and systematic and can be easily captured, codified and conveyed to others.

**explosion-proof lift trucks**

lift trucks designed to work in hazardous environments where highly combustible materials are present. Vehicles are designed to avoid sparks and components reaching combustible temperatures. Special electrical systems and materials are used to achieve this.

**extended price**

1. a high price.
2. a price that may be reduced in the future.

**external**

literally: outside. Usually refers to someone or some influence, that is not part of or from the organisation or the project team.

**external constraint**

a constraint from outside the project network.

**external costs**

costs, which are not contained in the market prices, since they are not carried by the actual causer, as external costs designated. To it for example the costs of the forest dying, health damage, building and material damages, climatic change etc. belong.

**external procurement sources**

extra-firm sources including industry contacts, market data, competitive intelligence and regulatory information which could aid procurement decision-making.

**external structure**

refers to customer and supplier relationships and the organisation's image. That's assets such as image, relationships with customers, vendors and also competitors and other associations. In short, external structure refers to assets that depend on relationships outside your organisation As an accounting term it refers to assets in a balance sheet that are not 'tangible', such as copyrights, acquired goodwill, patents, brands.

**externalisation**

the process of making tacit knowledge explicit.

**extinction**

the end of all activity on a project, usually before meeting its stated objectives. The end results of a project terminated by extinction are neither terminated by inclusion or integration.

**extra works**

requirements that require additional effort that were not contemplated in the original contract or agreement.

**extranet**

a website that links an organisation with other specific organisations or people. Extranets are only accessible to those specified organisations or people and are protected via passwords.

**facilitating processes**

interactions among processes that are more dependent on the nature of the project.

**facilitator**

a person(s) who manages the use of a group decision support system from initial planning through actual operation.

## fair trade

fair trade means fair trade with rural cooperatives and plantagen. That means among other things: cost-hitting a corner prices, guaranteed minimum wages for female workers and workers as well as long-term trade relations. But the enterprises cultivate their products in accordance with strict guidelines and ensure thereby a high quality.

## fast tracking

compressing the project schedule by overlapping activities that would normally be done in sequence, such as design and construction. Sometimes confused with concurrent engineering.

## faxban

a modification of a kanban system that faxes forms to signal demand. It is identical to any other kanban system except that it uses faxes rather than kanban cards or squares.

## feasibility study

a formal document that analyses and discusses a possible solution to a technical or business issue and determines if the solution is practical, reasonable and doable.

## feel good about

1. optimistic.
2. can accept.

## FIFO

First-in-first-out. In warehousing describes the method of rotating inventory to used oldest product first. Actually an accounting term used to describe an inventory costing method.

## fill rate (unit, line order)

the unit fill rate is the percent of the units filled immediately from stock. The line fill rate is the percent of lines on purchase orders that filled immediately from stock. An order fill rate is the percent of orders filled immediately from stock. The order fill rate is generally a lower number than the others and therefore is a more difficult fill rate to satisfy. The terms 'fill rate' and 'service level' are often used synonymously in many make-to-stock firms.

## Final Assembly Schedule (FAS)

the final assembly schedule is a schedule for the assemble-to-order portion of a manufacturing process. The firm will use MRP to plan the production of all major components and then use the FAS to schedule the final assembly for specific customer orders after those orders arrive.

## financial audit

a thorough examination of a project by an evaluation team that includes a detailed overview of the project's financial procedures, budgets, records, etc. It may deal with a project as a whole or the separate individual parts of a project.

## financial closure

the process of completing and terminating the financial and budgetary aspects of the project being performed. It includes both (external) contract closure and (internal) project account closure.

■ **financial drag**

expenses that are higher than desired.

■ **find of find**

investment trusts, which limit their plants to portions of other investment trusts.

■ **finite scheduling**

creating a sequence of activities with associated times so that no resource (person, machine, tool, etc.) is assigned to work more than the time available. A 'due-date feasible' finite schedule will satisfy all due date requirements for all tasks (orders). A start-date feasible schedule will start after the current time — as opposed to the situation where you should have started 2 weeks in order to get done on time. The opposite of finite scheduling is infinite planning that ignores capacity constraints when a schedule is created. (The words finite loading and infinite loading are sometimes used.) While many ERP systems and project management tools have finite scheduling capabilities, nearly firms use infinite planning for both ERP and project management and then resolve resource contention after the plan (schedule) has been created.

■ **firewall**

software that protects an organisation's computer systems from problems such as viruses that can be carried by internet technologies or hackers seeking to gain unauthorised access.

■ **firmware**

the combination of hardware device and computer instructions and/or computer data that resides as read-only software on the hardware device.

■ **first pick ratio**

during order picking, the percentage of orders or lines for which 100% completion was achieved from the primary location or picking face.

■ **fiscal impact analysis**

the analysis of the estimated taxes that a development project would generate in comparison to the cost of providing municipal services demanded by that project.

■ **fit**

the ability of an item to physically interface or interconnect with or become an integral part of another item.

■ **five s (the 5s's)**

5S is a methodology for simplifying organising, cleaning, developing and sustaining a productive work environment. The methodology originated in Japan and is based on the simple idea that the foundation of a good production system is a clean and safe work environment. Translated from Japanese words that begin with an 'S', the closest English equivalents are: sort — get rid of clutter. Set in order — organise the work area. Shine — clean the work area.

Standardise — use standard methods to keep sort, set in order and shine at a high level. Sustain — maintain through empowerment, commitment and discipline. If we combine the above list we have the following 5S's: Sort, separate and scrap Get rid of clutter. Set in order, straighten and store Organise the work area (red/yellow campaign, shadow boards). Shine and scrub Clean the work area. Standardise and sustain Use standard methods to maintain the above at a high level. Systematise and sustain Spread through the entire organisation through empowerment, commitment and discipline. Benefits of an 5S programme include: improved safety, reduced waste, improved morale, ownership of workspace, improved productivity, improved quality, improved maintenance and a better impression on customers. Not only will employees feel better about where they work, the effect on continuous improvement can lead to less waste, better quality and shorter lead times. Any of which will make your organisation more profitable and competitive in the market place. Indications that a firm needs a 5S programme: (1) space crowded with parts and tools, (2) unneeded items are stacked between workers, (3) excess inventory, (4) excess items and machines make it difficult to improve process flow, (5) equipment is dirty and a collection point for miscellaneous materials and (6) needed equipment such as tools are difficult to find.

■ **flex conveyor**

portable conveyor that can be expanded, contracted and flexed around curves.

■ **flexibility**

the ability to change. From a strategic point of view, only four kinds of flexibility exist.

■ **Flexible Manufacturing System (FMS)**

an FMS is an integrated set of machines that have automated materials handling between them and an integrated information system. Often oversold by vendors in this author's opinion.

■ **float**

the amount of time that an activity may be delayed from its early start without delaying the project finish date. Float is a mathematical calculation and can change as the project progresses and changes are made to the Project Plan. Also called slack, total float and path float.

■ **floater**

a direct labour employee used to fill in on a production line when the regular worker is absent.

■ **floating rate notes**

variable interest-bearing notes.

■ **floor**

value lower bound, under which the invested capital at a certain deadline is not to sink.

■ **flow rack**

racking system that incorporates sections of conveyor to allow the cartons or pallets to flow to the face of the rack. Stocking is performed from the rear of the rack.

### ■ FMCG (Fast Moving Consumer Goods)

description of common high volume products such as food, hygiene product or cleaning supplies. These would be products that the average consumer would frequently purchase such as soda, toothpaste or dish soap.

### ■ FMEA Method (FMECA)

Failure Mode and Effect (and Criticality) Analysis, a powerful method of risk assessment and failure analysis for use in risk management and product liability control.

### ■ focused factory

a focused factory is a process that is 'aligned with its market' and therefore requires a limited range of operations objectives. A factory focused on making high volumes of standard products at low cost will likely have minimum wage workers, fairly automated processes, MRP systems and JIT delivery of supplies. A focused factory reduces the 'variability' of the requirements in the process and therefore can help the process achieve its stated operations objectives. 'You can't be everything to everyone' is an old phrase, which suggests that you cannot do everything well at least not in one process. A focused factory is a means of implementing a strategic direction in your operations. A firm might have many 'focused factories' in any one factory.

### ■ focused on

1. give a great deal of attention to.
2. the attention given by some to one of many things.

### ■ follow up on

1. to check on progress at a later date.
2. to not promise to take any corrective action in the future.

### ■ forecast

a forecast is an estimation of future demand. Most forecasts use historical demand to calculate future demand. Adjustments for seasonality and trend are often necessary.

### ■ forecast bias

the average forecast error over time. Forecast bias can be defined mathematically as , where Et is the forecast error in period t and T periods of data have been collected so far. A simple recursive approach for handling this is to define Rt =Rt-1 + Et . The ideal forecast has a zero forecast bias. An exception report called a tracking signal is used to signal that the forecast bias is large and requires an intervention.

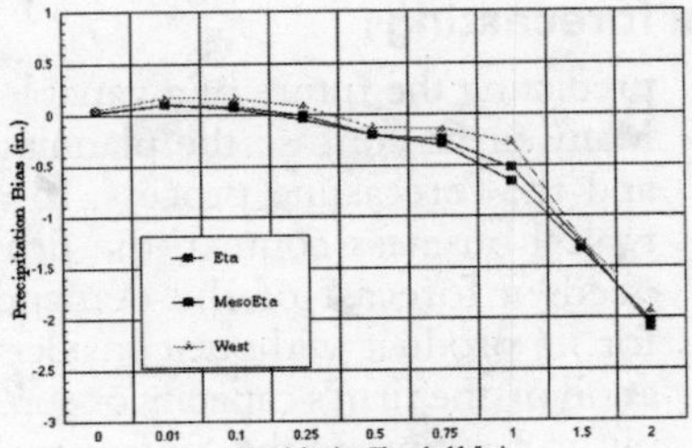

**■ forecast consumption**

forecast consumption describes the method(s) your inventory management software uses to reduce forecasted demand by the actual demand that occurs during the forecast period. Incorrectly set up forecast consumption parameters or lack of functionality related to forecast consumption can often create serious problems with planning systems.

**■ forecast error**

the demand minus the forecast in a period. Using standard mathematical notation, Et=Dt-Ft, where Et is the forecast error in period t, Dt is the demand in period t and Ft is the forecast made for period t. See **forecast bias.**

**■ forecast horizon**

the number of time periods ahead that a firm forecasts. For example, if a firm has a 6-month manufacturing lead time, it should clearly forecast at least six months into the future. The forecast error increases quickly with the forecast horizon. It is often more practical to reduce the manufacturing lead time (and the corresponding forecast horizon) than it is to improve the forecast error.

**■ forecasting**

predicting the future of a variable. Many firms confuse the planning and the forecasting process. In a typical business context, the firm needs a forecast of the demand for its product without consideration of the firm's capacity or supply. In response to this 'unfettered' (unconstrained) demand forecast, the firm makes production and inventory plans. In some periods, the firm might plan to have inventory greater than the demand. In other periods, the firm might plan to have inventory well short of the demand. In many firms, they use the term 'forecast' for what is essentially their production plan and therefore lose important stock-out (opportunity cost) information from the rest of the firm.

**■ foreign loans**

obligations, which a debtor spends outside of his homeland in the currency of the issue market.

**■ fork positioner**

fork positioners are lift truck attachments that allow the operator to adjust the distance between the forks without getting off of the truck. Used primarily in high volume operations where there is a great variety of pallet and crate sizes handled.

**■ form**

the defined configuration of an item including the geometrically measured configuration, density and weight or other visual parameters which uniquely characterise an item, component or assembly. For software, form denotes the language, language level and media.

**■ formal testing**

the process of conducting testing activities and reporting results in accordance with an approved test plan making provision for customer involvement.

## ■ format

documents shall be prepared on A4 (210 x 297 mm) 80 gsm copier paper (hard copy) and/or the form of electronic media specified in the requirements. Each page of a document shall be numbered in Arabic numerals consecutively from Section 1 to the appendices. Documents may be printed on one or both sides of each page (single sided or double sided). On single sided documents, the document control number shall be on the top right hand side. For double sided, all even pages shall have document control numbers on the top left hand side and on odd pages on the top right hand side. Each page prior to section 1 shall be numbered in lower-case roman numerals.

## ■ forward buy

the practice of purchasing raw materials, components, etc. ahead of the need, usually in anticipation of a price increase.

## ■ forward loading (forward scheduling)

a finite scheduling method that begins with the start date (which could be the current time) and plans forward in time, never violating the capacity constraints. The complete date is an output of the process.

## ■ forward pass

the calculation of the early start and early finish dates for the uncompleted portions of all network activities.

## ■ four-year investment cost

the planned project and ongoing support costs for the current and following budget biennium in which the project is authorised.

## ■ fraction

see parliamentary group.

## ■ free float (ff)

the amount of time an activity can be delayed without delaying the early start of any immediately following activities.

## ■ free seminar

sales presentation.

## ■ frequency distribution

a statistical table that presents a large volume of data in such a way that the central tendency and distribution are clearly displayed.

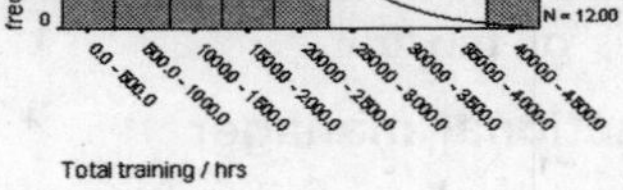


## ■ FTA

Fault Tree Analysis.

## ■ fulfilment

describes the activity of processing customer shipments. Though most manufacturing and warehouse operations will process customer shipments, this term usually refers to operations that ship many small orders (usually parcels) to end users as opposed to operations that process larger shipments to other manufacturers, wholesalers or resellers. Examples of fulfilment operations would include operations that process shipments for mail-order catalogues, internet stores or repair parts.

■ **fully paid moving expenses**

1. pay for some part of each major expense incurred for employee relocation.
2. pay only the minimum fees for services such as moving insurance.

■ **function**

the action or actions, which an item is designed to perform.

■ **function point**

unit of measure to quantify the overall size and complexity of a computer application.

■ **functional area**

a distinct group of system performance requirements which, together with all other such groupings forms the next lower-level breakdown of the system on the basis of function.

■ **functional manager**

a manager responsible for activities in a specialised department or function (e.g., engineering, manufacturing, marketing.)

■ **functional organisation**

an organisation structure in which staff are grouped hierarchically by specialty (e.g., production, marketing, engineering and accounting at the top level with engineering, further divided into mechanical, electrical and others).

■ **functional requirements**

what the systems/products are, do or provide from the customer's point of view.

■ **functional verification**

testing to ensure the part conforms to all customer and supplier engineering performance and material requirements.

■ **function-specific DSS**

a decision support system that has knowledge relevant for assisting in decisions about a specific function an organisation performs (e.g., a marketing function, a production function).

■ **fund assets**

the term 'fund assets' (also 'net fund assets' mentioned) is named the fund assets computed to market values less possible commitments. With real estate funds are to be taken off except the mortgage acre and other debts also still the taxes presumably resulting with the liquidation.

■ **fund domicile**

the fund has its domicile in the country, in which it established and/or which was announced there supervisory authority for registration.

■ **fund line**

the fund line administers the investment trust to be paid by of the investors. It decides in particular on the plants and makes valid all the investment trust for rights belonging to. It can delegate the plant decisions and further subtasks, is responsible however for actions from it assigned as for own acting.

■ **funding offer**

an instance when the Department proposes to a successful applicant, either orally or in writing, a level of funding less than the applicant request. Occurs when the Department either does not accept certain items of cost in the applicant's original budget or does not have a sufficient level of programmes appropriations to fund all recommended projects at the requested level.

■ **futures**

futures obligate the contracting parties to take over (buyers) or supply a standardised quantity of a base value at an agreed upon price on a certain time (salesmen).

■ **fuzzy front end**

it is the process for determining customer needs or market opportunities, generating ideas for new products, conducting necessary research on the needs, developing product concepts and evaluating product concepts up to the point that a decision is made to proceed with development. This process is described as the fuzzy front end because it is the least defined and most unstructured part of product development.

■ **Gantt chart**

a graphical project planning tool that shows horizontal bars that depict the beginning and ending time for each task. While a Gantt chart is powerful tool for communicating a project plan, it does not clearly show the precedence relationships and therefore is not a particularly helpful tool for project planning.

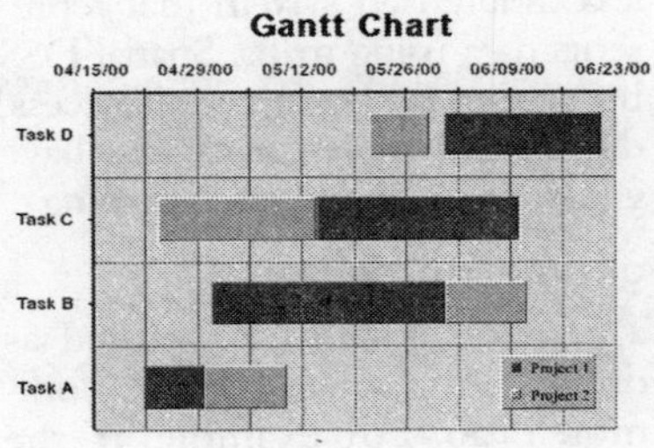


■ **gas cell technology**

a gas cell produces river and warmth during an electro-chemical process by the combination of hydrogen and oxygen. As by-product only water develops and no exhaust gases as with a combustion engine.

■ **geld market funds**

investment trusts, which invest in short term, papers at fixed interest (running time under one year) in certain currencies.

**generally implied**

custom or common practice for the organisation, its customers and other interested parties, that the need or expectation under consideration is implied.

**Geographic Information Systems (GIS)**

a computerised system that represents data using maps. Spatial DSS built using GIS help people access, display and analyse data that have geographic content and meaning.

**geometric decay**

a geometric series is defined as dt+1 = rdt, where r is the common ratio. For example, if the demand in period 1 is 100 and r=.8, then the demand in period 2 is .8( 100)=80. The demand in period T is dt+T = rTdt. The geometric time series model can be used to forecast demand for either a finite or an infinite number of periods into the future.

**get a handle on**

investigate and learn about something when very little is known before hand.

**give a comment**

to provide words on a topic that may have little or no meaning.

**give a talk**

to provide words on a topic that may have little or no meaning.

**given a mandate**

told to do something with few employees or resources assigned to the task.

**GMP**

Good Manufacturing Practice.

**go a long way toward**

get a good start on.

**goal-seeking**

the capability of asking the computer software what values certain variables must have in order to attain desired goals. It is a tool that uses iterative calculations to find the value required in one cell (variable) in order to achieve a desired value in another cell. A common use of the goal-seeking feature in a spreadsheet is calculating a break-even quantity.

**going forward**

in the future.

**good meeting**

1. a discussion with nothing unexpected happening.
2. a uneventful meeting.

**goods**

material, equipment, supplies, printing and automated data processing hardware and software.

**GR&R**

Gage Repeatability and Reproducibility.

**grade**

a category or rank used to distinguish items that have the same functional use (e.g., 'hammer') but do not share the same requirements for quality (e.g., different hammers may need to withstand different amounts of force.)

**■ granularity**

detail.

**■ Graphical Evaluation and Review Technique (GERT)**

a network analysis technique that allows for conditional and probabilistic treatment of logical relationships (i.e., some activities may not be performed.)

**■ Graphical User Interface (GUI)**

a programme interface that uses a computer's graphics capabilities to make the programme easier to use. Graphical interfaces use a pointing device to select objects, including icons, menus, text boxes, etc. A GUI includes standard formats for representing text and graphics.

**■ gravity conveyor**

types of conveyor that use gravity to move materials. Skate-wheel conveyer and roller conveyor are the most common types of gravity conveyor used, however, even a simple steel chute is essentially a gravity conveyor.

**■ gravity model**

the gravity model for retail store location can a retailer locate one or more new retail stores given that they know some basic information about your competitors in the area — which might include some of your own stores. The basic concept of the model is that large stores that are close to a set of customers have a high 'gravitational pull' on the customers — and that stores that are smaller or farther away have less 'gravitational pull' on the customers. This is really an application of Newton's Law, which states that the gravitational pull between two heavenly bodies is directly proportional to the mass of the bodies and inversely proportional to the square of the distance between them.

**■ great confidence in**

to have a belief that something is likely when little proof may exist

**■ green manufacturing**

manufacturing that is environmentally conscious.

**■ Group Decision Support Systems (GDSS)**

an interactive, computer-based system that facilitates solution of unstructured and semi-structured problems by a set of decision-makers working together as a group. A GDSS aids groups in analysing problem situations and in performing group decision making tasks. Any of the five generic types of DSS can be built as a group DSS.

**groupware**
networked system applications that facilitate information/knowledge sharing and exchange.

**growing**
an increase in sales or an increase in the number of employees.

**growth management**
government programmes that control timing, location and character of land use and development.

**GSI**
abbreviation for Government Secure Intranet.

**guidance systems**
guidance systems are used to guide automated guided vehicles through plants, guide lift trucks in very-narrow-aisle storage areas. Wire-guided and rail-guided tend to be the most common guidance systems, but others including laser and optical systems are also available.

**guidelines**
are directives and specifications, similar to standards, but advisory in nature. In essence, guidelines constitute recommendations, which are not binding on agencies and institutions of higher education.

**half-life curve**
a mathematical model that relates a performance metric such as defects, costs, percent tardy or cycle time to time. The half-life concept suggests that the performance metric will be cut in half every so many periods. For example, if the half-life is 6 months and the defect rate is 10% at time zero, at month six, the defect rate should be 5% and at month twelve the defect rate should be 2.5%. The basic equation for the half-life curve is , where exp(x) is the function that takes e to the x power and e 2.718281. y(t) is the value (cost, labour time per unit, etc.) at time t. The constants are and $t_{1/2}$, where the half-life (in periods) is . The value for b can be estimated with regression using historical data.

**half-yearly report**
See annual report.

**hammock**
an aggregate or summary activity (a group of related activities is shown as one and reported at a summary level). A hammock may or may not have an internal sequence.

**hanger**
an unintended break in a network path. Missing activities or missing logical relationships usually causes hangers.

**hardware**
tangible, discrete product with distinctive form.

**Hardware Configuration Item (HWCI)**
an aggregation of hardware that satisfies an end use function and is designated for separate configuration management by the acquirer.

**■ health care delivery system**
the medical services (doctors, nurses, hospitals, clinics, equipment and medicines) available to an employee and the method used to pay for them.

**■ health informatics**
the understanding, skills and tools that enable the sharing and use of information to deliver healthcare and promote health.

**■ hedge of find**
against their name (English tons hedge = secure) security business is not by any means the principal purpose of such funds. With the goal of gaining absolute yields rather plants are transacted, the conventional funds are not permitted. Thus hedge of find can obtain positive net yields independently of the market situation.

**■ hedging**
securing plants against losses.

**■ heritage**
a firm's traditional lines of business which are rarely abandoned.

**■ heuristics**
the informal, judgmental knowledge of an application area that constitutes the 'rules of good judgment' in the field. Heuristics also encompass the knowledge of how to solve problems efficiently and effectively, how to plan steps in solving a complex problem, how to improve performance and so forth.

**■ high watermark**
is used in connection with success-dependent fees (performance fees). The fund manager computes his profit-sharing on the basis of the increase in value beyond the last highest level of the net asset value. This has the consequence that the performance fee results only after possible losses were again completely caught up.

**■ high yield of find**
obligation funds, which invest in papers of debtors of smaller soil quality. Such titles offer higher interest, in addition, at the same time the loss risk - the danger that a debtor does not pay the interest or the repayment precipitates - is larger.

**■ high-density storage**
describes storage methods where unitised loads are stored more than one unit deep and/or high. Stacked bulk floor storage, drive-in/drive-thru rack, push-back rack, flow rack and, to a lesser extent, double-deep rack, are examples of high-density storage.

**■ high-piled combustible storage**
term used in fire codes to refer to codes relating to floor or racked storage exceeding 12 feet in height or high-hazard commodity storage exceeding 6 feet in height.

**■ hired gun**
a consultant with an expertise who may or may not have better knowledge than almost any employee.

■ **historic area**

an area or building in which historic events occurred or one which has special value due to architectural or cultural features relating to the heritage of the community. Elements in historic areas have significance that necessitates preservation or conservation.

■ **historic pricing**

account method in the fund business. The investor knows the net asset value of the fund at the time of the design/return. Opposite: forward pricing.

■ **hockey-stick phenomenon**

a pattern of sales or shipments that increase dramatically at the end of the week, month or quarter. This pattern looks a like a hockey stick because it is low at the beginning of the period and high at the end. The hockey stick phenomenon is nearly always a logical result of reward systems based on sales or shipments. The large changes causes 'variance' in the system, which often results in increased inventories, stock-outs, overtime, idle capacity, frustrated workers and other significant problems. Clearly, the solution is the change reward systems to motivate workers to produce and sell at the market demand rate.

■ **honeycombing**

honeycombing refers to the unused pallet positions in high-density storage that result when the number of unit-loads for an item does not completely fill the storage lane.

■ **human capital**

1. the competence and capabilities of an organisation's employees.
2. the knowledge, skills and competencies of the people in an organisation. Human capital is one component of intellectual capital.

■ **I think**

to state that the following is one's own opinion. The speaker protects the firm by stating something as his own opinion. Also, the opinion is accurately stated even if the opinion is poor. No promise or commitment has been made. The statement must be assumed to be an honest opinion. Few would disagree that it is an opinion. Example: I think raises will be good this year.

■ **ICE**

ICE (Information Content and Exchange) is a protocol aiming to develop a consistent vocabulary for describing and managing the exchange of content and electronic assets.

■ **ICT**

abbreviation for Information Communication Technology.

■ **ICT - Information Communication Technology**

merging of computing and high-speed communications links carrying data, sound and video.

■ **IEC**

International Electro-technical Commission.

**■ IEEE**

Institute of Electrical and Electronic Engineers.

**■ impact**

the loss or effect on the project, programme or enterprise if the risk occurs. Impact is one of the three attributes of a risk.

**■ impact fees**

costs imposed on new development to fund public facility improvements required by new development and ease fiscal burdens on localities.

**■ impact statement**

a cause and effect report generated at the manager level to show the impact that new projects will have on current schedules and resources as they enter the work stream.

**■ implementation**

occurs when products that have completed testing are moved into production or into their working environment. Normally used as a term on Information Technology projects.

**■ improved data quality**

sending information via electronic means can improve quality because it eliminates almost all the human data entry from the process. With the rapid growth of e-commerce, many expect that the phrase 'EDI' will soon die. E-commerce will, of course, serve the same purposes as EDI and will have to include all of the same functionality.

**■ improved forecast accuracy**

forward visibility of your customer's requirements can dramatically improve forecast accuracy. For many firms, this is the most important benefit.

**■ improving steering council (also known as quality steering committee)**

a group of people with representation from all functions in the organisation, usually drawn from management levels, chartered to develop and monitor a quality improvement process in their own functions. This group is often responsible for deciding which improvement projects or work processes will be addressed and in what priority.

**■ in depth**

to some degree of detail.

**■ in some sense**

1. partially.
2. related in some way.

**■ in sourced**

use resources owned by the firm to produce a good or provide a service.

**■ independent demand**

demand generated from forecasts, customer orders or service parts.

**■ independent demand inventory**

this term that has two meanings. Demand from external customers, rather than a higher-level assembly or warehouse and demand that must be forecasted rather than planned. This concept is no longer very helpful given that many firms can now get detailed long-range demand information from their customers. Typical examples of independent demand include retail inventory demand, demand for an item sold from a distributor's warehouse and demand for an end-item for a manufacturing firm. Demand for a component that goes into an end-item would be considered dependent demand, because this demand is planned based on the plan for the end-item.

Inventory Systems for Independent Demand

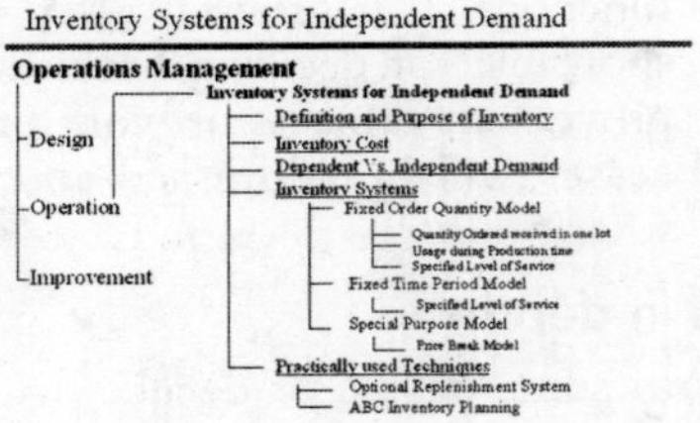


## ■ independent project oversight

a process that employs a variety of quality control, inspection, test measurement and other observation processes to ensure that project objectives are achieved in accordance with an approved plan. Project oversight is usually done by an independent entity (separate from the project team) trained or experienced in a variety of management and technical review methods. Project oversight includes both technical and management oversight.

## ■ independent variables

variables in a model-driven DSS that are controlled by the environment and that influence the results of a decision (also called input variables, parameters, givens).

## ■ Independent Verification and Validation (IV&V)

IV&V is performed by an organisation that is technically, managerially and financially independent of the development organisation. Verification and validation (V&V) is a system engineering process for evaluating the correctness and quality of a product throughout its life cycle.

## ■ index

characteristic number of the development of the courses to one or more markets. The most well-known and at the same time oldest share index is the Dow Jones. Indices permit it, the performance of a fund, which is invested on a certain market to compare with the development of this market. Comparisons also bench mark.

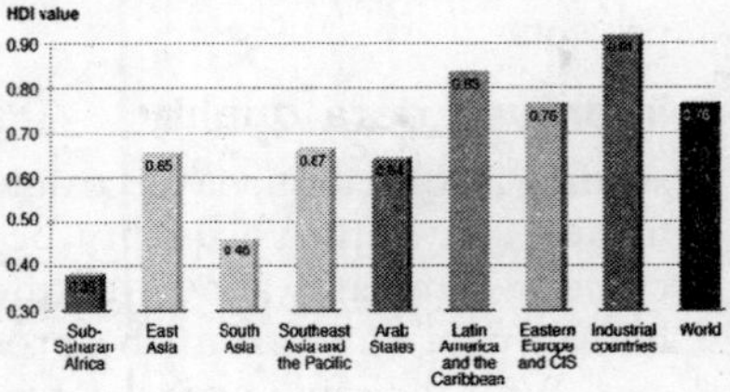


## ■ index fund

investment trusts, which copy one as exactly as possible in their title lesson and weighting in advance the selected stock price averages.

■ **indirect costs**

costs of an organisation incurred for common or joint objectives, which cannot be readily and specifically identified with a particular grant project or other institutional activity.

■ **individual competence**

refers to the capacity of employees to act in a wide variety of situations. It's their education, skills, experience, energy and their attitudes that will make or break the relationships with the customers and the products or services that are provided.

■ **industry fund**

investment trusts, which put on their fortune exclusively in securities of a certain sector of the economy.

■ **infill development**

infill projects use vacant or underutilised land in previously developed areas for buildings, parking and other uses.

■ **information**

a collection of data that has been organised within a context and translated into a structure that conveys meaning.

■ **information assets**

collections of information, which can be exploited by the organisation for business value.

■ **information audit**

a process which reviews and maps organisational information need, creation, use, flow and storage. Identifies gaps, duplication, costs and value and uncovers the barriers to effective information flow.

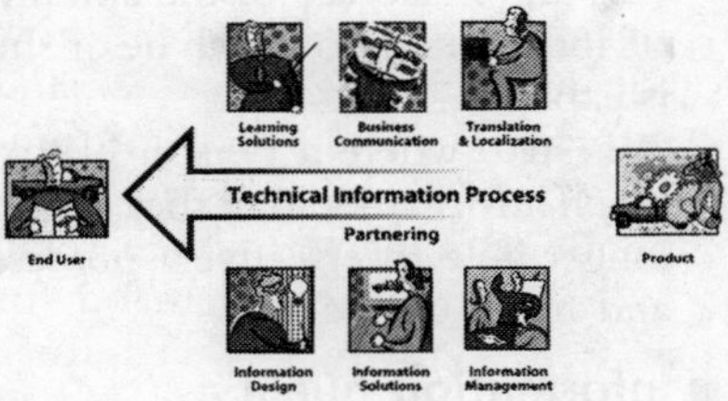


■ **Information Communication Technology (ICT)**

technology that combines computing with high-speed communications links carrying data, sound and video.

■ **information management**

1. an umbrella term for the various activities that contribute to the effective production, co-ordination, storage, retrieval and dissemination of information, in whatever format and from internal or external sources, leading to the more efficient functioning of the organisation.

2. the management of an organisation's information resources in order to improve the performance of the organisation. Information management underpins knowledge management, as people derive knowledge from information.

■ **information mining**

tools and techniques for finding and analysing electronic textual information stores designed to identify trends and patterns within the data/information.

**information overload**

1. a state where the individual is no longer able effectively to process and make use of the amount of information to which he or she is exposed.
2. a state where a person has so much information that they are no longer able to effectively process and make use of it.

**information quality**

measures of the reliability, accuracy, currency and usability of information.

**information system**

the organised collection, processing, transmission and dissemination of information in accordance with defined procedures, whether automated or manual. Information systems include non-financial, financial and mixed systems.

**information systems architecture**

a formal definition of the business processes and rules, systems structure, technical framework and product technologies for business information systems.

**Information Technology Investment Management (ITIM)**

an integrated approach to managing IT investments that provides for the continuous identification, selection, control, life cycle management and evaluation of IT investments. ITIM uses structured processes to minimise risks and maximise return on IT investments. ITIM is the basis for the Commonwealth's approach to technology management.

**infostructure**

the information, technology and communication architectures that enable the effective creation of information and dissemination of information for re-use.

**infrastructure (of an organisation)**

system of facilities, equipment and services needed for the operation of an organisation.

**initial**

the software process is characterised as ad hoc and occasionally even chaotic. Few processes are defined and success depends on individual effort and heroics.

**initial risk identification**

the process during the initial concept phase of identifying risks that might impact a project. The risk identification process is recommended for agencies to evaluate a project.

**initiation**

committing the organisation to begin a project phase.

**inland loans**

obligations of native debtors in the own currency on the home market.

**innovation**

the creation of something new or different. The conversion of knowledge and ideas into a new benefit, such as new or improved processes or services.

## ■ innovation capital

renewal strength in a company, expressed as protected commercial rights, intellectual property and other intangible assets.

## ■ innovator

innovators are by the majority smaller and recent enterprises, whose products and services offer a provable environmental use and a high resources efficiency.

## ■ inspection

1. the process of checking parts that have already been completed to make sure that they were done correctly. Inspection can be done for either an accept/reject decision for a batch of parts (batch control) or to check to see if a process is still in control (process control). Inspection can be done by the operator (self-check, source inspection), the next person in the process (successive check), the last step (final inspection) or some combination of the above. Ideally, inspection is done at the source (quality at the source) so that the process has immediate feedback and has a sense of ownership of quality. Most firms conduct final inspection before a product is delivered to a customer. Inspection should be done just before a bottleneck so that valuable bottleneck time is not wasted on a bad part. (Attention to parts that have gone through the bottleneck because valuable bottleneck capacity has been invested in these parts.) Many firms are eliminating incoming inspection by having the supplier certify that the parts meet certain quality standards. This saves money and time for both parties. An ideal process has no inspection the product and process are carefully designed so that inspection, which is fundamentally a non-value adding activity, is not needed.

**2.** activities, such as measuring, examining, testing or more characteristics of a product or service and comparing these with specified requirements to determine conformity.

## ■ intangible asset

1. the non-financial assets of an organisation which contribute to its success.

**2.** the non-physical resources of an organisation. An example might be the reputation linked to a brand name or the loyalty of customers to a company. These assets are not generally accounted for in an organisation's financial statements, but they are of great value to the organisation.

## ■ Integrated Product Development (IPD)

Integrated Product Development (IPD) is a philosophy that systematically employs a teaming of functional disciplines to integrate and concurrently apply all necessary processes to produce an effective and efficient product that satisfies the customer's needs. There is no checklist for implementing IPD because there is no one solution...each application will be unique.

**■ intellectual assets management**

the management of an organisation's intellectual assets in order to improve the performance of the organisation. In theory, synonymous with knowledge management but in practice, intellectual assets management tends to focus on issues relating to intellectual property such as organising and exploiting patents, copyrights, trademarks and other intellectual property rights.

**■ intellectual capital**

1. the sum of human capital and structural capital.
2. knowledge that is of value to an organisation - made up of human capital, structural capital and customer capital.

**■ intellectual property**

1. intellectual assets that qualify for legal or commercial protections e.g. patents, trademarks, copyrights and trade secrets.
2. explicit intellectual assets (or knowledge assets) that are protected by law. Includes things like patents, trademarks, copyrights, licences etc.

**■ intellectual property rights**

the legal rights associated with intellectual property.

**■ interact with**

1. to be in physical proximity to or connected to over.
2. some communication medium.
3. some amount of talking with.

**■ interdependent decisions**

a series of decisions that are interrelated. A sequential set of decisions are usually interdependent.

**■ interested party**

person or group having an interest in the performance or success of an organisation.

**■ interface**

the functional and physical characteristics required to exist at a common boundary. In development, a relationship among two or more entities in which the entities share, provide or exchange data. An interface is not a CSCI, HWCI, software unit or other system component. It is a relationship among them.

**■ interface control**

interface control comprises the delineation of the procedures and documentation, both administrative and technical, contractually necessary for identification of functional and physical characteristics between two or more configuration items which are provided by different contractors/ acquiring agencies and the resolution of the problems thereto.

**■ intermodal**

transportation term describing the use of multiple modes of transportation for a shipment. Ocean containers that are picked up by a truck, delivered to port, transported by ship and then picked up by another truck are a common example of intermodal transportation. In the trucking industry, intermodal usually refers to the combination of trucking and rail transportation.

### ■ internal customer

anyone in the organisation who relies on you for a product or service.

### ■ internal efficiencies

reductions in the cost of production whose cost savings may come from a firing of employees and/or the reduction of plant and equipment.

### ■ internal structure

...that's your organisation... and includes assets like patents and brand names, manuals, systems processes...everything that constitutes what we normally call 'organisation', including very fuzzy areas called culture. Managers are also part of internal structure because it's their task to maintain and keep it viable over the long run, thereby ensuring the viability of the organisation.

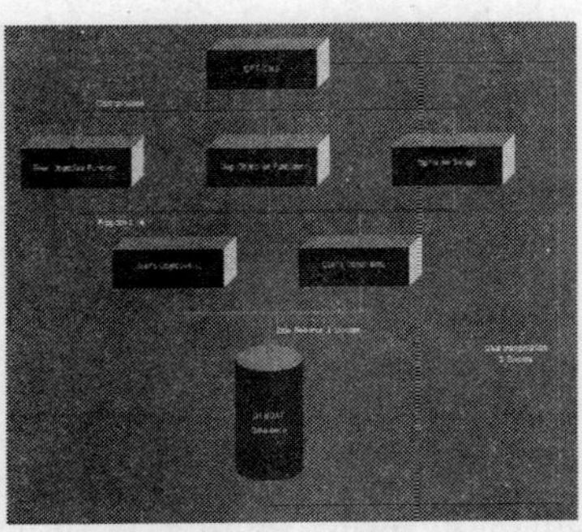

### ■ internal supplier

anyone in the organisation you rely on for a product or service.

### ■ internalisation

the process of absorbing explicit knowledge and making it tacit.

### ■ intranet

a private application of the same internetworking technology, software and applications within a private network, for use within an enterprise. It may be entirely disconnected from the public internet, but is usually linked to it and protected from unauthorised access by security firewall systems. More loosely, the term may include extranets, as well. Web based technology that is typically used within an organisation's internal network to centralise applications or data. An intranet is usually segmented into data or applications that all employees have access to and data or applications that are restricted to only authorised users. The term intranet refers to a private network as opposed to internet that is the public network.

### ■ inventory position

the on-hand plus on-order minus allocated inventory quantities. Allocated inventory is that which has been promised to customers or other orders.

### ■ inventory turn

number of times inventory turns during a one year period. Generally calculated by dividing the average inventory level (or current inventory level) into the annual inventory usage (annual cost of goods sold).

■ **inventory turnover**

this is the cost of goods sold divided by the average inventory investment. The inverse of the inventory turnover ratio is an estimate of the cycle time. It can be proven mathematically that inventory turnover should increase as the demand increases. If sales double, the turnover ratio should increase by roughly or 41%. Therefore, caution should be used in benchmarking inventory turnover ratios between firms (or divisions) that have differing demand rates — or within a firm if the demand rate is changing drastically over time. Technically, sales divided by the average inventory investment is 'coverage' but many managers mistakenly call this 'turnover'. See **cycle time.**

■ **inventory value**

actual assets of a fund divided by the number itself of portions in the circulation.

■ **investment policy**

the investment policy describes the procedure, like the investment objective to be reached is (title selection, purchase and sales times, portion of liquid means etc.).

■ **Investment Review Board (IRB)**

a decision-making body, made up of senior programme, financial and information managers, that is responsible for making decisions about IT projects and systems, based on comparisons and tradeoffs between competing projects and an emphasis on meeting mission needs and improving organisational performance.

■ **investment strategy fund**

investment trusts, which copy the investment strategies of the respective offers for the different risk classes. Investment strategy funds invest world-wide in different plant instruments, depending upon risk class shares and/or obligations are over-weighted. Investment strategy fund also ate allocation of find, strategy of find, portfolio fonds, investment objective fund, administration of an estate fund or mixed funds called.

■ **investment trust**

an investment trust is a fortune, which due to public advertisement by a multiplicity from each other independent investor is applied to the joint investment and administered by a fund line after the principle of the diversification to be paid by of the investors.

■ **investments in ERP systems**

the developers and sellers of software usually believe they know more than you do about your business and most managers are too quick to concede that the experts are right. Most companies simply do not know what they want to achieve even with the software and are hoping for.

■ **investor**

investor, owner of fund portions. With the purchase of portions the investor acquires the right to his portion corresponding a participation in the fortune and in the yield of the fund.

**■ invisible assets**

sometimes used as a synonym to intangible assets.

**■ invisible equity**

is the difference between the market value of a company and the visible equity.

**■ is hot**

1. current and up to date.
2. topical in the media.
3. a growing field.

**■ ishikawa diagram (fishbone diagram)**

a graph tool often used as a brainstorming approach for identifying the root causes of a problem. Also called a Cause-and-Effect or Fishbone Diagram. The diagram illustrates the relationships among the wide variety of possible contributors to the effect. Note that this tool is referred to by several different names: Ishikawa diagram, Cause-and-Effect diagram, Fishbone diagram and Root Cause Analysis. The first name is after the inventor of the tool, Kaoru Ishikawa (1969) who first used the technique in the 1960s. The basic concept in the Cause-and-Effect diagram is that the name of a basic problem of interest is entered at the right of the diagram at the end of the main 'bone'. The main possible causes of the problem (the effect) are drawn as bones off the main backbone. The 'Four-M' categories are typically used as a starting point: 'Materials', 'Machines', 'Manpower' and 'Methods'. Different names can be chosen to suit the problem at hand or these general categories can be revised. The key is to have three to six main categories that encompass all possible influences. Brainstorming is typically done to add possible causes to the main 'bones' and more specific causes to the 'bones' on the main 'bones'. This subdivision into ever increasing specificity continues as long as the problem areas can be further subdivided. The practical maximum depth of this tree is usually about four or five levels. When the fishbone is complete, one has a rather complete picture of all the possibilities about what could be the root cause for the designated problem.

**■ ISIN number**

Internationally Securities Identification Number. Internationally security index recognised.

**■ ISO**

International Organisation for Standards.

**■ ISO14001**

certification standards created by the International Organisation for Standardisations related to environmental impact. The standard specifies requirements for an environmental management system to enable an organisation to formulate a policy and objectives taking into account legislative requirements and information about significant environmental impacts. It applies to those environmental aspects that the organisation can control and over which it can be expected to have an influence.

## ■ ISO9000

Certification Standards created by the International Organisation for Standardisations in 1987 that now play a major role in setting process documentation standards for global manufacturers. These standards are recognised in over 100 countries. Some people summarise ISO as an external motivation to 'document what you do and do what you document'. Some criticises ISO as a non-value added activity. Others argue that ISO was created by Europeans as a barrier to entry and that its primary value for North American firms is to help them sell their products in Europe. ISO9000 provides general requirements for various aspects of a firm's operations including purchasing, design controls, contracts, inspection, calibration, etc. For example, ISO9001 requires that statistical process controls (SPC) be applied to a firm's operations. This is more than simply documenting activities. The most recent standard is ISO9001:2000 which is a bit different than the older ISO9001:1994 standard in its emphasis on SPC and process flow diagrams.

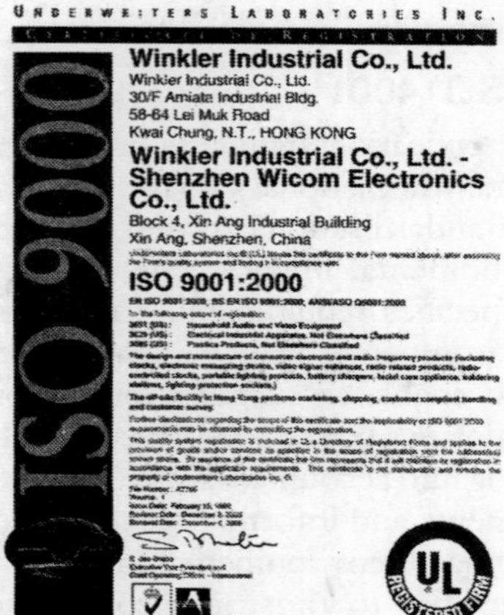
UNDERWRITERS LABORATORIES INC.

ISO 9000

Winkler Industrial Co., Ltd.

Winkler Industrial Co., Ltd.
30/F Amiata Industrial Bldg.
58-64 Lei Muk Road
Kwai Chung, N.T., HONG KONG

Winkler Industrial Co., Ltd. - Shenzhen Wicom Electronics Co., Ltd.

Block 4, Xin Ang Industrial Building
Xin Ang, Shenzhen, China

ISO 9001:2000



## ■ issue price

price to the investor of fund portions to draw know. It corresponds to the net asset value of a portion, plus the expenditure commission.

## ■ issues

1. questions.
2. problems.
3. points of disagreement and/or other assorted topics that can be brought up but are rarely disposed of satisfactorily.

## ■ IT investment management

an integrated approach to managing IT investments that provides for the continuous identification, selection, control, life-cycle management.

## ■ IT Strategic Planning (ITSP)

an ITIM-based planning methodology that looks at IT resources and projects as capital investments and forms a foundation for the selection, control and evaluation of IT resources and projects as part of a business-driven technology portfolio.

## ■ item

a non-specific term used to denote any product, including systems, subsystems, assemblies, subassemblies, units, sets, accessories, computer programs, computer software or parts.

## ■ item profile

data that describes the characteristics of an item. May include physical characteristics such as size and weight, transactional characteristics such as times sold/consumed and units sold/consumed or group characteristics such as sales channel, commodity, hazardous classification, etc. Item profiles are used in warehouse design and slotting.

## ■ jettison employees

the firing of one or more employees who will not be hired back.

## ■ job enlargement

adding tasks to a job to make it more interesting for the worker and/or to eliminate queues between workers. Some authors define both 'vertical job large enlargement' (which might add panning organising and inspecting his or her own work) and 'horizontal job enlargement' (which might add similar tasks). Some authors define the job enlargement as horizontal in nature you get more of your coworkers job. These same authors define job enrichment as vertical job enlargement you get more of your boss' job and get to decide which jobs you do first. See **job enrichment.**

## ■ job enrichment

adding more responsibility to a job. Job enlargement gives you more of your co-worker's job. Job enrichment gives you some of your boss's job. Note that the management literature does not have consistent definitions of the terms 'job enlargement and job enrichment'. See **job enlargement.**

## ■ job ready

1. a prospective employee with all the required skills.
2. older and more experienced workers.
3. retrained workers.

## ■ job rotation

the movement of workers between different jobs in an organisation. This policy can be an effective method of cross-training and can improve communication, increase process understanding and reduce stress and boredom. Job rotation can also prevents muscle fatigue and reduces work place injuries.

## ■ job shop

a factory (or department in a factory) that has a number of general-purpose machine and processes orders for customers. A pure job shop is always a 'make-to-order' process. Job shops typically offer fixed planned customer lead-times, have long queues and employ highly skilled workers.

## ■ job shop scheduling

the process of creating a schedule (a sequence with associated times) for jobs (orders) being processed in a job shop. See **job shop.**

**■ juran trilogy**

the interrelationship of three basic managerial processes with which to manage quality, quality control and quality improvement.

**■ Just-in-Time (JIT)**

a method of production and inventory cost control based on delivery of parts and supplies at the precise time they are needed in a production process.

**■ kaizen**

1. taken from the Japanese words kai and zen, where kai means change and zen means good. The popular meaning is continual improvement of all areas of a company not just quality.
2. Japanese term meaning continuous improvement involving everyone-managers and employees alike.

**■ kanban system**

a simple device that sends a pull signal. 'Kanban' is the Japanese word for sign. In the US, a kanban might be a card, a container or a square on a table or floor. An empty container gives a factory worker permission to work to fill the box. If a worker does not have an empty box to fill, the worker is 'blocked' from doing any more work and should be re-assigned somewhere else where their work is needed. A Kanban control system uses a signalling device to regulate JIT flows. Kanban means 'sign' or 'instruction card' in Japanese. The cards or containers make up the kanban pull system. The authority to produce or supply additional parts comes from downstream operations. A kanban is a card that is attached to a storage and transport container. It identifies the part number and container capacity, along with other information. A kanban system is a pull-system, in which the kanban is used to pull parts to the next production stage when they are needed. A MRP system (or any schedule-based system) is a push system, in which a detailed production schedule for each part is used to push parts to the next production stage when scheduled. The weakness of a push system (MRP) is that customer demand must be forecast and production lead times must be estimated. Bad guesses (forecasts or estimates) result in excess inventory and the longer the lead-time, the more room for error. The weakness of a pull system (kanban) is that following the JIT production philosophy is essential, especially concerning the elements of short set-up times and small lot sizes.

**■ key expectations**

the requirements concerning a specified product or service that a customer holds to be most important.

**■ kits, kitting**

grouping individual items together for future use. In a manufacturing context, 'kits' of parts are often put together in boxes and given to workers to assemble. In a distribution context, kits of parts are prepared to be packed and shipped. Kits have their own part numbers.

### ■ know-how

1. skill or capability derived from knowledge and experience.
2. the ability to cause a desired result. This may be the most valuable knowledge element of all. It is forward looking and predictive and reflects the person or organisations ability to act and achieve its goals.
This is built on another key knowledge element 'understanding' - what is, what was and why - that deals with knowing historic cause and effect and determining the current state of things.

### ■ knowledge

the combination of explicit data and information to which is added tacit expert opinion, skills and experience to result in a valuable asset which can be used to make key decisions. The essential factor in adding meaning to information.

### ■ knowledge assets (or intellectual assets)

those parts of an organisation's intangible assets that relate specifically to knowledge, such as know-how, best practices, intellectual property and the like. Knowledge assets are often divided into human (people, teams, networks and communities), structural (the codified knowledge that can be found in processes and procedures) and technological (the technologies that support knowledge sharing such as databases and intranets). By understanding the knowledge assets an organisation possesses, the organisation can improve its ability to use them to best effect and also to spot any gaps that may exist.

### ■ knowledge audit

a review of the knowledge required by an organisation, department or group in order to carry out its objectives effectively. It will include a needs analysis, information, competencies and communication audits and a review of interactions and knowledge flow. see **information audit.**

### ■ knowledge base

1. the fundamental body of knowledge available to the organisation.
2. an organised structure of information, which facilitates the storage of intelligence in order to be retrieved in support of a knowledge management process.

### ■ knowledge broker

a person who facilitates the creation, sharing and use of knowledge in an organisation. Many organisations have created knowledge broker roles such as 'knowledge co-ordinator'. The term knowledge broker is also sometimes used to describe companies or individuals that operate commercially as knowledge traders or provide knowledge-related services.

### ■ knowledge centre

a place where knowledge is gathered and stored and can be accessed and used by other people. It may be a physical place like a library, a 'virtual' place like an interactive website or an online discussion board or a place where people gather such as a café or an informal meeting room or discussion area created to encourage knowledge sharing.

■ **knowledge economy**

an economy in which knowledge plays a predominant part in the creation of wealth.

■ **Knowledge Enhanced Government (KEG)**

a government-wide policy framework for knowledge management led by the office of the e-Envoy.

■ **knowledge flows**

the ways in which knowledge moves around and in and out of, an organisation.

■ **knowledge harvesting**

a set of methods for making tacit knowledge more explicit - getting people's knowledge into documents, so that it can be more easily shared with others.

■ **knowledge interrogators**

person responsible for managing the content of organisational knowledge as well as its technology. Keep the database orderly, categorise and format documents and chucking the obsolete and connect the users with the information they seek.

■ **knowledge management**

1. the creation and subsequent management of an environment, which encourages knowledge to be created, shared, learnt, enhanced organised for the benefit of the organisation and its customers.
2. the systematic process of finding, selecting organising, distilling and presenting information in a way that improves an employee's comprehension in a specific area of interest.

■ **Knowledge Management Software (KMS)**

software that can store and manage unstructured information in a variety of electronic formats. The software may assist in knowledge capture, categorisation, deployment, inquiry, discovery or communication. Products include electronic document management systems.

■ **knowledge management solution**

strictly speaking, a solution to a knowledge management problem or the use of knowledge management techniques to solve an organisational problem. However, in practice a 'knowledge management solution' more often than not refers to a piece of knowledge management technology or software.

■ **knowledge management strategy**

a detailed plan outlining how an organisation intends to implement knowledge management principles and practices in order to achieve organisational objectives.

■ **knowledge management typology**

a framework that segments knowledge management into four key categories: intermediation, externalisation, internalisation and cognition.

## ■ knowledge manager

a role with developmental and operational responsibility for promoting and implementing knowledge management principles and practices.

## ■ knowledge mapping

1. a process to determine where knowledge assets are in an organisation and how knowledge flows operate in the organisation. Evaluating relationships between holders of knowledge will then illustrate the sources, flows, limitations and losses of knowledge that can be expected to occur.

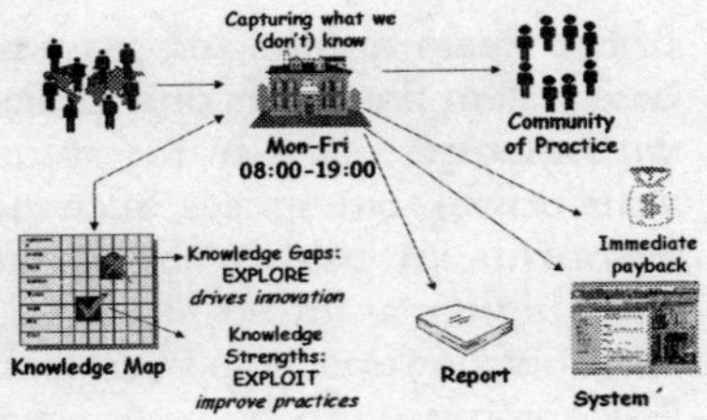


2. a process to determine the knowledge requirements of the organisation and its processes, its knowledge assets and knowledge flows. See **information audit.**

## ■ knowledge repository

a place to store and retrieve explicit knowledge. A low-tech knowledge repository could be a set of file folders. A high-tech knowledge repository might be based on a database platform.

## ■ knowledge worker

an employee whose role relies on his or her ability to find and use knowledge.

## ■ Knowledge-Centric Re-engineering - KCR:

the application of BPR and change enablement methodologies in support of enterprise wide KM, thereby effecting major cultural and process change that are fundamental to the management of the enterprise's competitive position.

## ■ knowledge-driven DSS

knowledge-driven DSS can suggest or recommend actions to managers. These DSS are person-computer systems with specialised problem-solving expertise. The 'expertise' consists of knowledge about a particular domain, understanding of problems within that domain and 'skill' at solving some of these problems. Tools used for building knowledge-driven DSS are sometimes called Intelligent Decision Support methods. Data mining tools can be used to create knowledge-driven DSS that have major data and knowledge components.

## ■ lag

a modification of a logical relationship, which directs a delay in the successor task. For example, in a finish-to-start dependency with a 10-day lag, the successor activity cannot start until 10 days after the predecessor has finished.

**■ land fund**

investment trusts, which put on their fortune mainly in shares of a certain country.

**■ land trusts**

non-profit organisations interested in the protection of natural resources and historic areas. Activities include public education, purchase and coordination of conservation easements and planning services.

**■ land value**

worth a property regarding the economic utilisation possibilities. The land value depends on the one hand on the situation and the underground condition, on the other hand of the technical and legal covering possibilities.

**■ laser scanner**

device that uses a moving laser to read bar codes. Devices can be portable hand-held units or fixed units.

**■ laser-guided**

guidance system used with AGVs that uses a rotating laser (mounted on top of the vehicle) to determine the vehicles location. Reflective targets need to be strategically placed along the vehicle's route. Must always maintain clear line-of-site to reflective targets for the system to work properly.

**■ last-in, first-out (LIFO)**

1. stock valuation. The method of valuing stocks that assumes that all issues or sales are charged at the most current cost but stocks are valued at the oldest cost available.
2. stock rotation. The method whereby the goods which the newest goods in stock are delivered (sold) and/or consumed first.

**■ Late Finish Date (LF)**

in the critical path method, the latest possible point in time that an activity may be completed without delaying a specified milestone (usually the finish date.)

**■ late of steam turbine and gas turbine systems**

of late steam turbine and gas turbine system financings one speaks with matures, already for some years existing enterprises. Such investments are usually connected with higher amounts invested, risky but however liquid and less. The enterprise can be sold faster or brought to the stock exchange.

**■ Late Start Date (LS)**

in the critical path method, the latest possible point in time that an activity may begin without delaying a specified milestone (usually the project date.)

**■ layoff**

1. a permanent firing of one or more employees.
2. a temporary firing where the employees may be hired again.

## ■ LCL

Lower Control Limit.

## ■ lead

in a project network diagram, a modification of a logical relationship, which allows an acceleration of the successor task. For example, in a finish-to-start dependency with a 10-day lead, the activity can start 10 days before the predecessor has finished.

## ■ lead time

amount of time required for an item to be available for use from the time it is ordered. Lead time should include purchase order processing time, vendor processing time, in transit time, receiving, inspection and any pre-pack times.

## ■ lead time syndrome

a perverse cycle whereby a supplier's planned lead times gets longer and longer. The cycle is as follows: a manufacture increases planned lead time (this could for almost any reason a vacation, a machine problem, a slight increase in demand, etc.) The customer learned about the increased lead time and immediately increases the order quantity to cover the demand. (Note that the customer's real demand has not changed.) The manufacturer sees the larger order quantity, assumes that demand is up and further increases planned lead times. This gets us back to step (a). The solution to the lead time syndrome is for customers to communicate their true demand to their suppliers to give their suppliers forward visibility of their true demand and for suppliers to work very hard to never increase their quoted lead times, even when the demand increases.

## ■ leader

prominent enterprise, which proves the best ecological and social achievement within its industry.

## ■ leadership

the way in which the project manager influences the project team to behave in a manner that will facilitate project goal achievement.

## ■ lead-time demand

forecasted demand during the lead-time period. For example, if your forecasted demand is 3 units per day and your lead time is 12 days, your lead-time demand would be 36 units.

## ■ lean manufacturing

alternate term used to describe the philosophies and techniques associated with Just-in-time (JIT) manufacturing.

## ■ leaner

1. a firm with fewer employees and/or less plant or equipment.
2. to produce the same amount with fewer people.

## ■ leapfrog development

development that occurs beyond the limits of existing development and creates areas of vacant land between areas of developed land.

## ■ learning curve (experience curve)

a mathematical model that relates the cost per unit (or labour time per unit) to the cumulative number of units produced. The learning curve equation is given by $y_n=y_1 n^b$, where $y_1$ is the cost/unit for the first unit produced, $y_n$ is the cost/unit for the n-th unit produced and b is the model parameter. The b parameter should be set to ln(k)/ln(2) for a 'k-percent learning curve'. Note that b is always negative. For example, an 80% learning has k=0.8 and b=ln(.8) /ln(2)=-0.32193. If $y_1$=100, the cost for the first 8 units is given by 100, 80, 70, 64, 60, 56, 53 and 51. (Note these values are rounded to the nearest integer.)

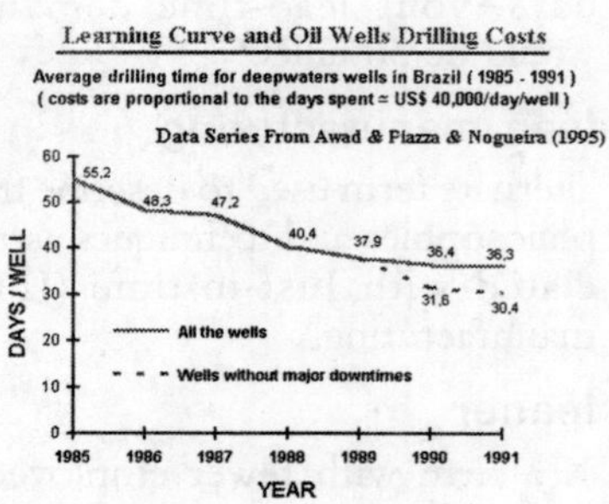


## ■ learning organisation

an organisation that views its future and subsequent competitive advantage based on continuous learning and adaptive behaviour. It develops a culture and processes to improve its ability to learn and share both at an individual and organisational level.

## ■ lessons learned

1. lessons learned are concise descriptions of knowledge derived from experiences that can be communicated through mechanisms such as storytelling, debriefing etc or summarised in databases. These lessons often reflect on 'what we did right', 'what we would do differently' and 'how we could improve our process and product to be more effective in the future'.
2. lessons learnt are concise and insightful descriptions of experiences, which may be communicated through mechanisms such as storytelling, debriefing, team learning, etc and/or summarised or abstracted in databases.

## ■ Level of Effort (LOE)

support-type activity (e.g., vendor or customer liaison) that does not readily lend itself to measurement of discrete accomplishment. It is generally characterised by a uniform rate of activity over a specific period.

## ■ lever force

see leverage.

## ■ leverage

to realise the inherently value of an asset, physical or knowledge-based, beyond what is currently exploited.

## ■ life cycle

1. the type of methodology to be used in project development, e.g. system development methodology, information engineering methodology or rapid application development methodology.

2. a generic term covering all phases of acquisition, operation and logistics support of an item, beginning with concept definition and continuing through disposal of the item.

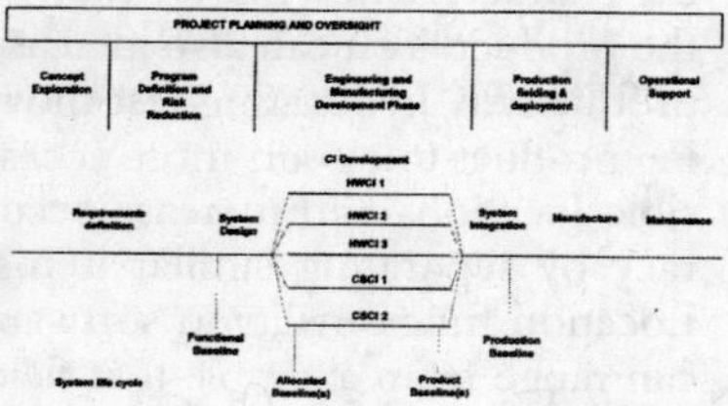


## ■ life-cycle cost

the overall estimated cost for a particular object over the time corresponding to the life of the object, including direct and indirect initial costs plus any periodic or continuing costs for operation and maintenance.

## ■ lights-out warehouse

describes fully-automated facilities. The idea being that if the facility requires no human operators, you can run it with no lights. Use of AS/RS units, AGVs, automated conveyors, robots, etc makes this possible.

## ■ limited rights

rights to use, duplicate or disclose technical data, in whole or in part, by or for the acquirer, with the express limitation that such data shall not without written permission of the party asserting limited rights, be: released or disclosed.

## ■ line manager

1. the manager of any group that actually makes a product or performs a service.
2. a functional manager.

## ■ linear programming

a mathematical model for optimal solution of resource allocation problems. A common model used in a model-driven DSS.

## ■ linear regression

a statistical method that fits a line to a set of historical data points in order to minimise the sum of the squared errors. This method is commonly used to find an approximate linear relationship between two or more variables.

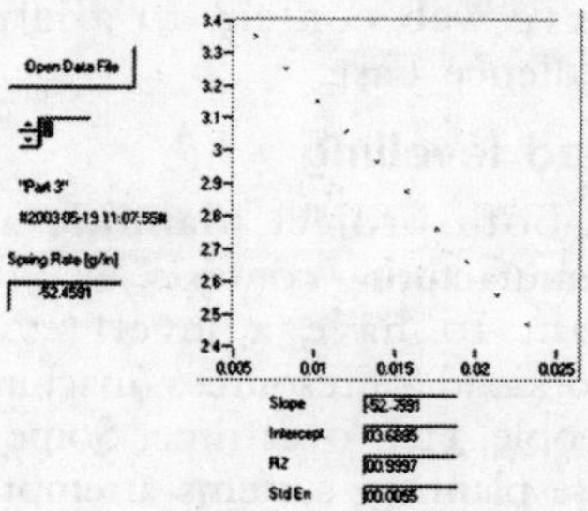


## ■ liquidity

with investment trust portions the portion owner is liquid, i.e., he can return its portions usually at any time. The fund companies are obligated to take portions back without terms of notice to the respective withdrawal price.

## ■ list of rhetorical questions

unanswered queries vaguely outline what is not being said.

## load

in manufacturing load is described as the amount of production scheduled against a plant or machine. In warehousing, load is described as the materials being handled by a piece of equipment. In transportation, it is described as the materials being transported.

## load balancing

a specialised function provided by third-party application providers. Load balancing software designed to distribute web content requests from a single URL accessed by an end user to any number of production servers. In this manner, multiple production servers can be used to serve web content to a larger audience base.

## load levelling

in both project planning and manufacturing contexts, we often want to have a level (even) workload for resources (machines, people, etc.) over time. Some finite planning systems attempt to create schedules that require about the same amount of a resource in every period. This is called level loading.

## locator system

locator systems are inventory-tracking systems that allow you to assign locations to your inventory to facilitate greater tracking and the ability to store product randomly. Prior to locator systems, warehouses needed to store product in some logical manner in order to be able to find it (stored in item number sequence, by vendor, by product description, etc.) By using locator systems you can increase space utilisation by slotting your product by matching the physical characteristics of the product to a location whose physical characteristics match that of the product. You can also increase productivity by locating fast moving product to closer, more accessible locations and increase accuracy by separating similar items. Location functionality in software can range from a simple text field attached to an item that notes a single location, to systems that allow multiple locations per item and track inventory quantities by location. Warehouse Management Systems (WMS) take locator systems to the next level by adding functionality to direct the movement between locations.

## logical relationship

a dependency between two project activities or between a project activity and a milestone.

## long haul

1. an extended period of time.
2. a period of time long enough to allow a good bit of uncertainty.
3. a year or more.

## long term

1. an extended period of time.
2. a period of time long enough to allow a good bit of uncertainty.
3. a year or more.

## long term of find

investment trust, which in obligations with one (remainder).

■ **long/short**

the strategies summarised under this term optimise net yield and risk by the combination of financial instruments. The purchase of a share, which suggests an increase in value (= long side), combined with the simultaneous sales of another share, by which a value lowering is expected (= short side).

■ **longitudinal flue space**

term used by fire codes to describe the space between the rows of back-to-back racking. Flue spaces allow the water from an overhead sprinkler system to reach lower levels of the rack. Normally a longitudinal flue space of at least 6 inches is required. It is important to note that the flue space is measured as the distance between the loads, not the distance between the racks.

■ **lot or batch**

one or more components or finished devices that consist of a single type, model, class, size, composition or software version that are manufactured under essentially the same conditions and that are intended to have uniform characteristics and quality within specified limits.

■ **lot size (order size, batch size)**

the quantity that is ordered. When we are dealing with suppliers, we typically call this the order size, when dealing with manufacturing orders placed on ones own factory, then it is called the lot size or batch size.

■ **Lot Tolerance Percent Defective (LTPD)**

the maximum level of percent defective acceptable in production lots.

■ **lowest replaceable item**

the lowest level component at which maintenance will be performed or discrete configuration control enforced. Note: sometimes lowest is known as the 'smallest' or 'Line' and 'Item' was termed 'unit' previously.

■ **LSL**

Lower Specification Limit.

■ **LTL**

Less-than-truckload. A small shipment that does not fill the truck or a shipment of insufficient weight to qualify for a truckload quantity discount.

■ **maintainability**

1. the probability that a failed system can be made operable in a specified interval or downtime.
2. ability of an item under stated conditions of use to be retained in or restored to, within a given period of time, a specified state in which it can perform its required functions when maintenance is performed under stated conditions and while using prescribed procedures and resources.

■ **major player**

a firm, union or other participant which is involved or has some influence.

■ **major review**

a formal demonstration and confirmation across the system that supports or constitutes a programme milestone event.

■ **make versus buy decision**

managers in manufacturing firms often have to decide between making a part (or product) and buying it from a supplier. These decisions require careful analysis of accounting data and often have strategic implications. One of the most difficult aspects of this decision is how to handle overhead. If you completely ignore overhead, the decisions will generally go in the direction of 'in-sourcing' if you fully allocate overhead, decisions will generally go in the direction of 'out-sourcing' and can lead the firm into the 'death-spiral' where the more you outsource, the more overhead you have, which leads you to more outsourcing. A company should never outsource a core competence.

■ **makes sense**

1. a logically correct assessment.
2. within the realm of possibilities.

■ **Make-to-Order (MTO)**

a process that produces products in response to a customer order. In other words, the firm does not keep any finished goods inventory. MTO processes typically produce products that are unique to the customers' requirements, but this is not always the case, it is possible to use a MTO process for standard products.

■ **Make-to-Stock (MTS)**

a process that produces standard products to be stored in inventory. These can be delivered quickly to the customer. The performance metric for MTS is the fill rate (unit, line or order fill rate).

■ **manage expectations**

1. limit enthusiasm.
2. prevent over hype
3. warn customers that their needs may not be satisfied.

■ **managed**

detailed measures of the software process and products quality are collected. Both the software process and products are quantitatively understood and controlled.

■ **management**

coordinated activities to direct and control an organisation.

■ **management reserve**

a separately planned quantity used to allow for future situations, which are impossible to predict (sometimes called 'unknown unknowns'). Management reserves may involve cost or schedule. Management reserves are intended to reduce the risk of missing cost or schedule objectives. Use of management reserve requires a change to the project's cost baseline.

■ **management style**

way, as for the reaching of the investment objective the investment decisions are met.

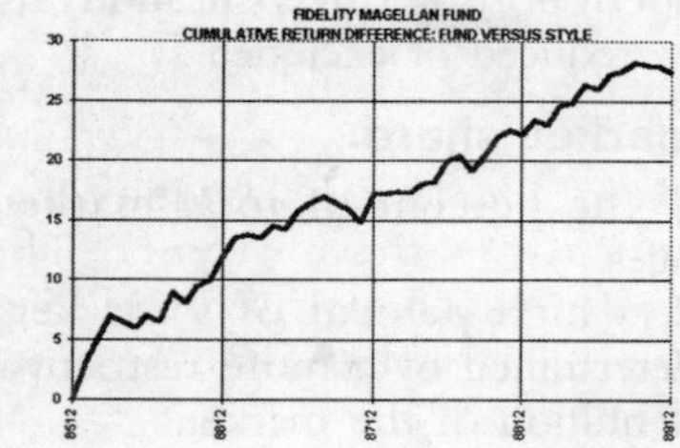


## ■ management system

system to establish policy and objectives and to achieve those objectives.

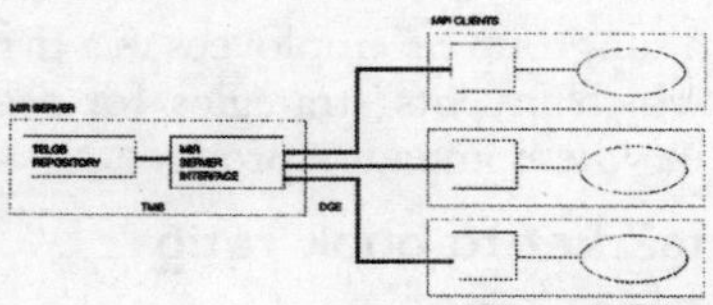


## ■ manufacturing cell

a manufacturing cell can be defined as a mini-production line dedicated to processing similar parts or products that require similar or identical operations. While a cell does not necessarily make the same parts repeatedly, it does make the same family of parts or products. The machines and fixtures within the cell are typically arranged so close to each other that there is no need to allow for storage between the operations or handling with hand trucks or pallet jacks. Cells offer a way to simplify production control and scheduling and shorten the manufacturing cycle time required to complete the product. They also reduce inventories and, therefore, manufacturing space required to satisfy production requirements.

## ■ Manufacturing Execution System (MES)

a Manufacturing Execution System (MES) provides real-time information on manufacturing operations from the time an order is started until it is completed in a factory. Unlike ERP and MRP systems, manufacturing execution systems do not plan order launch dates or order sizes, instead they focus on collecting data and planning the detailed operations after an order has been started. Functions include resource allocation and status, dispatching production orders, data collection/acquisition and quality management.

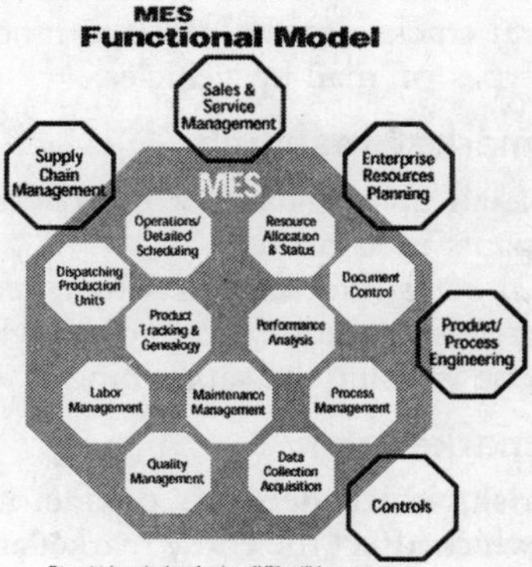


This model shows the eleven functions of MES and links to other systems different ways by product and need.

## ■ Manufacturing Resource Planning (MRP II)

a method for the effective planning of all the resources of a manufacturing company. Ideally it addresses operational planning in units, financial planning in money and has a simulation capability to answer what if questions. It is made up of a variety of functions, each linked together: business planning, master (or production) planning, master production scheduling, material requirements planning, capacity requirements planning and the execution systems for capacity and priority. Outputs from these systems would be integrated with financial reports such as the business plan, purchase commitment report, shipping budget, stock projections in money etc. Manufacturing resource planning is a direct outgrowth and extension of material requirements planning (MRP). For all practical purposes, ERP is just a new name for MRP II.

## ■ man-up.

term used to describe lift trucks designed to raise the operator with the load. Order selectors and turret trucks are the most common types of man-up vehicles.

## ■ market research

1. an investigation of the participants in a market.
2. get some idea of which way trends are headed to find out who else is doing the same thing.

## ■ market risk

risk, which depends on factors, which affect the entire market and not by portfolio diversification can be reduced or excluded.

## ■ market share

1. the percent of total market sales.
2. a high percent of a market, determined by a more restrictive definition of the market.

## ■ market value

market capitalisation = number of shares x share price. Used in the calculation of intellectual capital.

## ■ marketing department

a subgroup of employees in a firm which invents strategies for selling the company's products.

## ■ market-to-book ratio

common method of valuing knowledge intensive companies. Equal to (price per share X total number of shares outstanding) divided by book equity, which is the equity portion of a company's balance sheet.

**Market-to-Book Ratio for Foreign Investing Electric Utilities and Other Electric Utilities, 1987-1996**

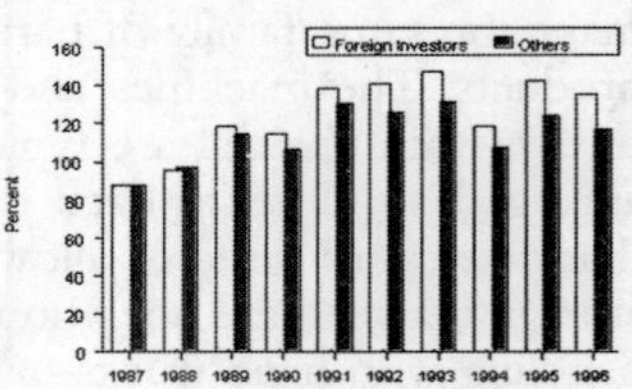


Note. Market-to-Book Ratio = Market Value of Common Shares as a Percent of Stockholders' Equity.
Source: Standard and Poors *Compustat*

## ■ mass customisation

producing customised products at nearly the same cost as mass-produced (standard) products. This is a strategy for producing products that are customised for a channel partner, a customer segment or an individual customer (personalisation) without sacrificing margin — ideally increasing margin.

### ■ Master Production Schedule (MPS)

MPS is a time-phased plan specifying how many and when the firm plans to build each end item. Example, the aggregate plan for a furniture company may specify the total volume of mattresses it plans to produce over the next month or next quarter. The MPS goes the next step down and identifies the exact size mattresses and their qualities and also states period by period (usually weekly) how many and when each of these mattresses types is needed. Further down this process is the MRP programme which calculates all raw materials, parts and supplies needed to make the mattress specified by the MPS.

### ■ master schedule

a comprehensive list of an approved project, containing schedule and progress statistics.

### ■ Material Requirements Planning (MRP)

a system to support manufacturing and fabrication organisations by the timely release of production and purchase orders using the production plan for finished goods to determine the materials required to make the product. Orders for dependent demand items are phased over time to ensure that the flow of raw materials and in-process inventories matches the production schedules for finished products. The three key inputs are the master production schedule, inventory status records and product structure records. See **MRP II.**

### ■ Material Review Board (MRB)

a standing committee that determines the disposition of items that have questionable quality.

### ■ materiel

a generic term covering systems, equipment, stores, supplies and spares, including related documentation, manuals, computer hardware and software.

### ■ matrix management

many employees report to more than one manager allowing each manager to have more employees reporting to him.

### ■ matrix organisation

any organisational structure in which the project manager shares responsibility with the functional managers for assigning priorities and for directing the work of individuals assigned to the project.

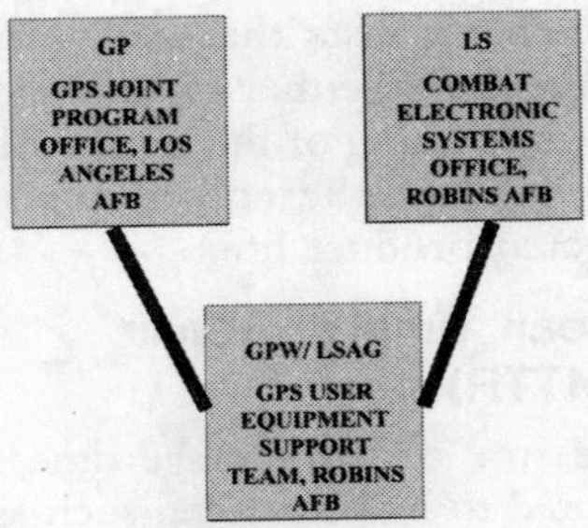

## Mean Absolute Deviation (MAD)

a measure of forecast error, where Et is the forecast error in period t and we have t observed values. See **forecast error.**

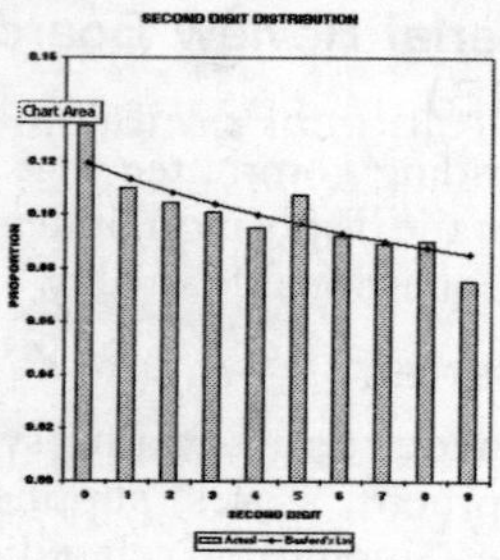


## Mean Absolute Percent Deviation (MAPD)

a measure of forecast error, where Et is the forecast error in period t, Dt is the actual demand in period t and we have t observed values. See **MAD, forecast error.**

## Mean Time Between Failure (MTBF)

the average time that a component is expected to work without failing. The MTBF is a good measure of the reliability of a product. The MTBF is often described as a 'bath-tub' curve, which suggests that most components fail either right away at the beginning of the product life or towards the end of the expected product life.

## Mean Time to Repair (MTTR)

measure of the average time required to fix something such as a machine. This is a measure of the complexity of a repair job.

## measured

1. small.
2. steady.
3. predictable.

## measurement control system

set of interrelated or interacting elements necessary to achieve metrological confirmation and continual control of measurement processes.

## measurement process

set of operations to determine the value of a quantity.

## measuring equipment

measuring instrument, software, measurement standard, reference material or auxiliary apparatus or combination thereof necessary to realise a measurement process.

## medium term bonds

plant forms at fixed interest with running times between two and eight years, spent by banks. For obligation funds, the medium term bonds are not applicable, since they are not certified to the official stock broking.

## memorandum of agreement

the document, which specifies agreements between involved parties relative to a specific interface. The MOA delineates responsibilities of each organisation and identifies formats and data elements required for a successful interface.

## ■ mentoring

mentoring is a one-to-one learning relationship in which a senior member of an organisation is assigned to support the development of a newer or more junior member by sharing his or her knowledge, experience and wisdom with them.

## ■ MES, Manufacturing Execution System

software systems designed to integrate with enterprise systems to enhance the shop-floor-control functionality that is usually inadequate in ERP systems. MES provides for shop floor scheduling, production and labour reporting, integration with computerised manufacturing systems such as automatic data collection and computerised machinery.

## ■ metadata

metadata or 'data about data' describes the content, quality, condition and other characteristics of data in order to facilitate efficient and effective searching of that data.

## ■ methodology

the processes, policies and guidelines that are included as part of the framework for project management.

*Methodology*

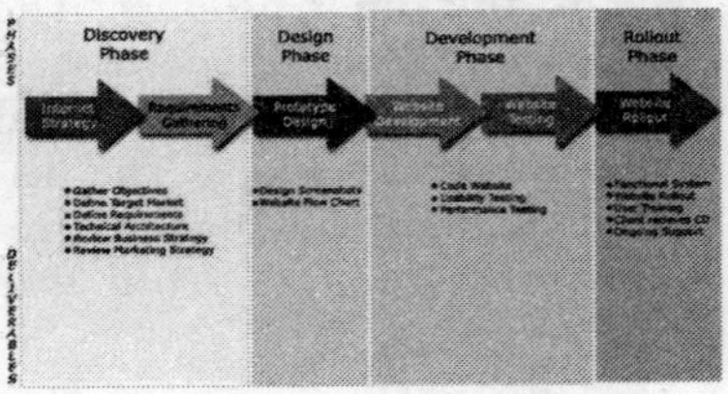


## ■ metrics

measures used to indicate progress or achievement.

## ■ metrological characteristic

distinguishing feature, which can influence the results of measurement.

## ■ metrological confirmation

set of operations required to ensure that measuring equipment conforms to the requirements for its intended use.

## ■ metrological function

function with organisational responsibility for defining and implementing the measurement control system.

## ■ mezzanine

a tiered structure within a building used to provide worker access to various levels. Mezzanines can be free-standing structures supported by posts and trusses or can be a series of walkways supported by storage equipment.

## ■ milestone

a significant event in the project, usually completion of a major deliverable.

## ■ milestone schedule

a summary-level schedule, which identifies the major milestones.

## ■ min/max inventory system

the min/max system (also known as an R,T system or S,s system) triggers an order when the inventory position falls below the reorder point (the 'min' or minimum). The order size is defined as the 'max' (maximum or target inventory) less the current inventory position. In other words, when you hit the minimum, you order enough to bring the inventory position up to the maximum. A special case of this is the S,S-1 system where orders are placed on a 'one-for-one' basis every time a unit is consumed, another is ordered. The S,S-1 policy is very practical for low demand items such as repair parts.

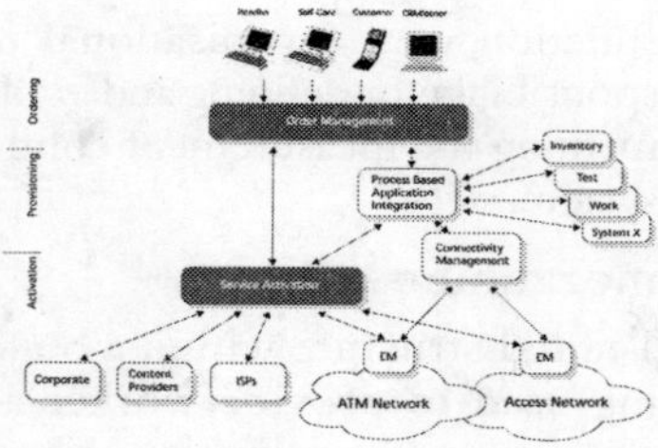


## ■ min-max

a simplistic inventory system in which a minimum quantity and maximum quantity are set for an item. When the quantity drops below min you order up to the max.

## ■ mission statement

a concise statement, usually one paragraph, summarising the purpose and goals of a project.

## ■ mitigate

dealing with a risk by developing strategies and actions for reducing (or eliminating) the impact, probability or both, of the risk to some acceptable level. It may also involve shifting the timeframe when action must be taken.

## ■ mitigation

taking steps to lessen risk by lowering the probability of a risk event's occurrence or reducing its effect, should it occur.

## ■ mitigation approach

the approach taken to deal with a risk. This can be to accept, research, watch or mitigate.

## ■ mitigation plan

an action plan for risks that are to be mitigated. It documents the strategies, actions, goals, schedule dates, tracking requirements and all other supporting information needed to carry out the mitigation strategy.

## ■ mix flexibility

the ability to increase the number of products in one facility and be profitable. (This is sometimes called product range.)

## ■ mixed model assembly

the practice of assembling more than one product during any period of time. For example, an assembly worker might see three units of product A, then two units of product B, then four units of product A, etc. The alternative to this policy is to make large batches of each product and then switch over to the other product. The advantage of mixed model assembly is that it reduces inventory and improves service levels. The disadvantage is that it requires frequent changeovers from one product to another and adds complexity to the manufacturing task.

**■ mixed use development**

development that is created in response to patterns of separate uses that are typical in suburban areas necessitating reliance on cars. Mixed use developments include residential, commercial and business accommodations in one area.

**■ model**

a representation of a set of components of a process, system or subject area. A model is generally developed for understanding, analysis, improvement and/or replacement of the process.

**■ model base**

a collection of pre-programmed quantitative models (e.g., statistical, financial, optimisation) organised as a single unit.

**■ model-driven DSS**

This type of DSS emphasises access to and manipulation of a model, e.g., statistical, financial, optimisation and/or simulation. Simple statistical and analytical tools provide the most elementary level of functionality. In general, model-driven DSS use complex financial, simulation, optimisation and/or rule (expert) models to provide decision support. Model-driven DSS use data and parameters provided by decision makers to aid decision makers in analysing a situation, but they are not usually data intensive, that is very large data bases are usually not need for model-driven DSS.

**■ modelling tools**

software programmes that help developers/users build mathematical models quickly. Spreadsheets and planning languages like IFPS are modelling tools.

**■ modular design (modularity)**

the basic idea underlying modular design is to organise a complex system (such as a large program, an electronic circuit or a mechanical device) as a set of distinct components that can be developed independently and then plugged together. Although this may appear a simple idea, experience shows that the effectiveness of the technique depends critically on the manner in which systems are divided into components and the mechanisms used to plug components together. Modularity is a general systems concept: it is a continuum describing the degree to which a system's components can be separated and recombined and it refers both to the tightness of coupling between components and the degree to which the 'rules' of the system architecture enable (or prohibit) the mixing and matching of components. Since all systems are characterised by some degree of coupling (whether loose or tight) between components and very few systems have components that are completely inseparable and cannot be recombined, almost all systems are, to some degree, modular.

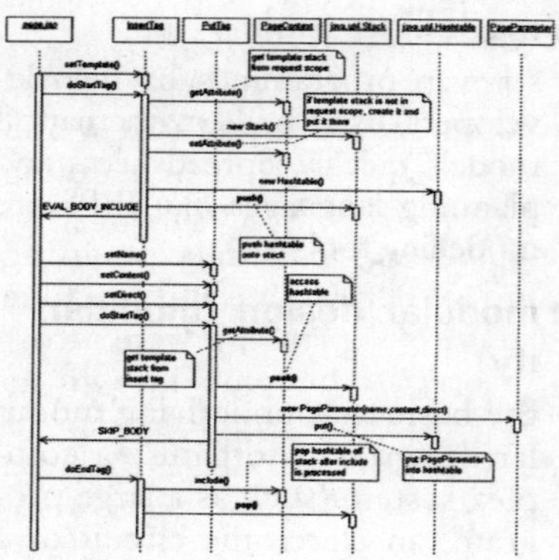

## ■ module

a self-contained part of a hardware item designed as a single replaceable unit, with a specific integral electronic function. It should require no installation other than mechanical mounting and completion of electrical connectors.

## ■ moment-of-truth

a moment of truth is the time that a firm 'touches' its customers. This is an opportunity for the firm's customers to find out the truth about the firm's employees and its character to find out 'who they really are'. This is a chance for the employees to show the customers that they really care about them. These are special moments and should be managed very carefully. When creating a process map, it is important to highlight the process steps that include the customer. A careful analysis of a typical service process often uncovers many more moments of truth than management truly appreciates a call for a quick question, a question posed to a salesperson, a contact regarding a billing problem, etc.

## ■ monitoring

the capture, analysis and reporting of project performance, usually as compared to plan.

## ■ Monte Carlo analysis

a schedule risk assessment technique that performs a project simulation many times in order to calculate a distribution of likely results.

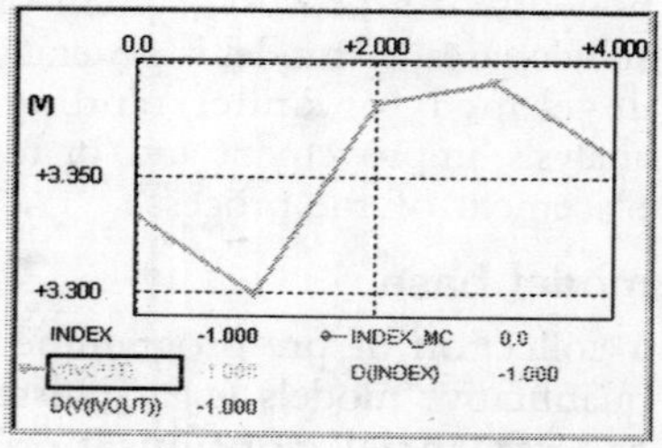


## ■ more competitive

1. to reduce costs by either firing employees.
2. reducing plant and equipment.
3. a lower price without less profits.

## ■ move on

1. take action.
2. put something behind.
3. go on to the next thing.

## ■ moving average

the average of the last N periods of data is said to be an 'N-period moving average'. This is sometimes used to make forecasts based on the most recent data. Exponential smoothing is a similar approach that applies weights to historical data with the weights declining geometrically with the age of the data. An N-period moving average is equivalent to simple exponential smoothed average with smoothing constant .

■ **MPS, Master Production Schedule**

production schedule specifying specific items, quantities and dates at which production is expected to take place.

■ **MRB**

Material Review Board.

■ **MRO (Maintenance, Repair, Operations)**

items that are purchased for a firm that are not used directly in the product. Examples include office supplies, cutting oil for machines, 3M sandpaper, etc. These items are generally not handled by the firm's ERP system, but are often significant expense items for many manufacturing firms.

■ **MRP generation**

term used to describe the running of the programmes that convert demand into planned orders. Depending on the operation, MRP generation may be run daily, weekly or even monthly. Since this processing requires a lot of system resources it is generally confined to off hours or weekend processing.

■ **MRP/MRP II, Manufacturing Resource Planning**

process for determining material, labour and machine requirements in a manufacturing environment. MRPII is the consolidation of Material Requirements Planning (MRP), Capacity Requirements Planning (CRP) and Master Production Scheduling (MPS). MRP was originally designed for materials planning only. When labour and machine (resources) planning were incorporated it became known as MRPII. Today the definition of MRPII is generally associated with MRP systems.

■ **MSA**

Measurement System Analysis.

■ **MTBF**

Mean Time Between Failures.

■ **multi billion dollar firm**

1. a business with sales of at least two billion dollars.

2. a firm with sales or assets of over a billion dollars.

3. any large firm.

■ **Multi-Dimensional Database (MDBS and MDBMS)**

a database that lets users analyse large amounts of data. An MDBS captures and presents data as arrays that can be arranged in multiple dimensions.

■ **multidisciplinary teamwork**

the timely and cooperative application of all appropriate disciplines in an open-communication, shared-information environment to effect people functioning as a team to achieve optimum solutions (people, product and process) satisfy customer needs, objectives and requirements.

Note: does not imply physically together.

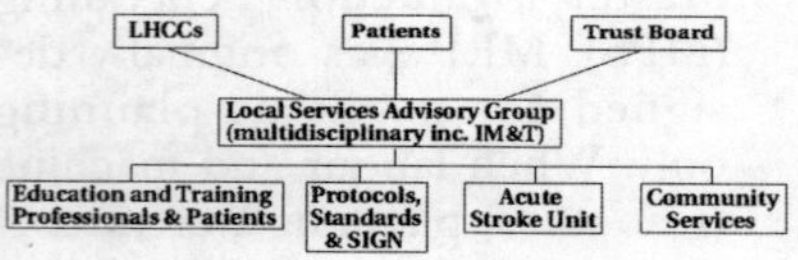


## ■ mushroomed

1. grew large quickly.
2. grew out of control.

## ■ near critical activity

an activity that has low total float.

## ■ negative comments

derogatory statements which are not used or appreciated by management.

## ■ negative declaration

giving a statement about what is not the case. The statement that something is not the case does not say what is the case. Example, Our president will not be fired. This does not imply the president will not leave the firm. He may retire, quit, pursue a better offer, change careers or be forced out.

## ■ negative inventory

an inventory system (computer) condition whereby the on-hand inventory balance is listed as a quantity less than zero.

## ■ network analysis

the process of identifying early/late start and finish dates for the uncompleted portions of project activities.

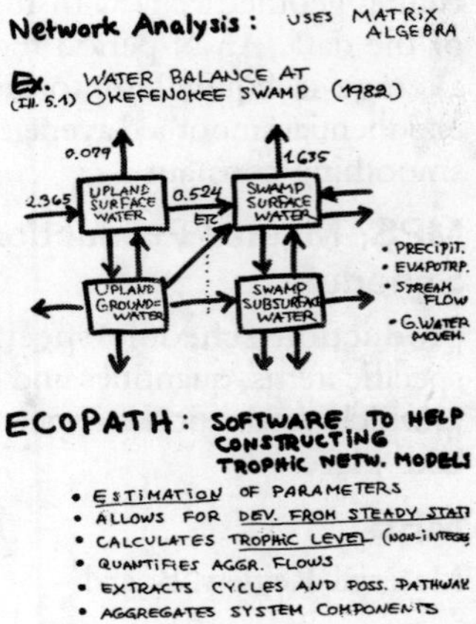


## ■ neural network

a form of artificial intelligence in which a computer simulates the way a human brain processes information.

## ■ newsvendor problem

a decision maker must decide how much to purchase, given the distribution of demand, the cost of under buying per unit (cu) and the cost of over buying per unit (co). The optimal order quantity is the demand associated with the critical ratio, which is defined as R=cu/(cu + co). In more mathematical terms, Q=F-1(R), where F-1(R) is the inverse of the cumulative distribution function. In a retail environment, cu is the sales price minus the unit cost (the gross margin) and co is the unit cost minus the salvage value. Solving the problem for a discrete distribution requires a simple search procedure. The newsvendor problem used to be called the 'newsboy' problem.

## ■ node

one of the defining points of a network. A junction point joined to some or all of the other dependency lines.

## ■ non conformance

1. product or material, which does not conform to the customer requirements or specifications.
2. the failure of a unit or product to conform to specified requirements.

## ■ non-contact methods

vision systems: a camera is used to take a video image of a part. The image is processed by software and electronic hardware to compare it against a reference template. The vision system determines the placement, size and shape of holes and the presence of part features. The snapshot of the image usually requires a strobe or high intensity light to produce an adequate part to background contrast. Laser-scan micrometers: these systems use reflected laser light to measure part dimensions. These systems are used to inspect single dimensions on highly repetitive work, such as intervals, diameters, widths, heights and linearity.

## ■ normal distribution.

term used in statistical analysis to describe a distribution of numbers in which the probability of an occurrence, if graphed, would follow the form of a bell shaped curve. This is the most popular distribution model for determining probability and has been found to work well in predicting demand variability based upon historical data.

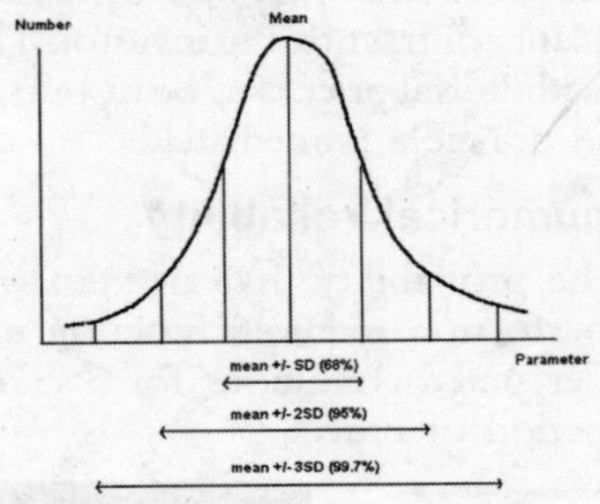


## ■ normal time

an industrial engineering term for the time observed from a time study. Step 1. The average time from a time study is collected. Step 2. Each person's average time is adjusted by the subjectively determined performance rating. The average of these times is called the normal time for the operation. Step 3. The normal time is adjusted for allowances to compute the standard time. See **standard time.**

## ■ normalisation

the process of reducing a complex data structure into its simplest, most stable structure. In general, the process entails the removal of redundant attributes, keys and relationships from a conceptual data model.

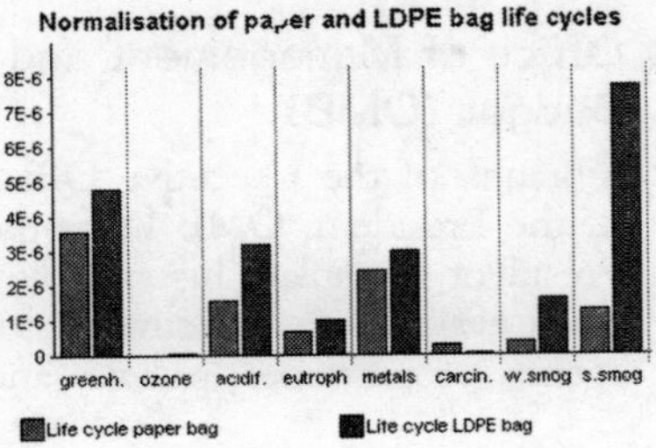

### ■ notice

in the investment trust business the revocation of the collective plant contract by the investor. The withdrawal price is to be disbursed in principle immediately.

### ■ numerical reliability

the probability that an item will perform a required function under stated conditions for a stated period of time.

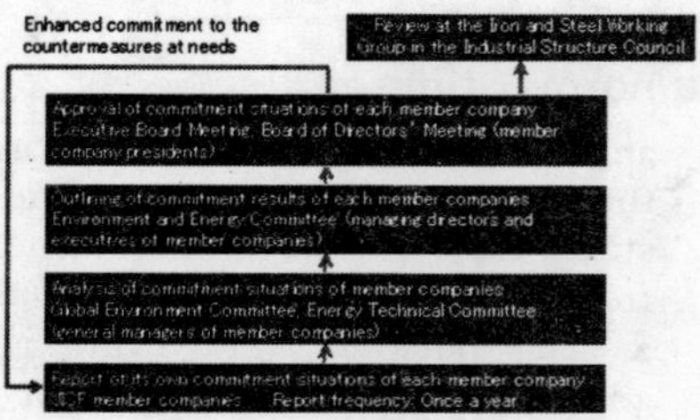


### ■ Numerically Controlled (NC) Machine

a machine that is under control of a computer, typically these are machines that cut and form metal. Comprised of a typical machine tool used to turn, drill or grind different types of parts and a computer that controls the sequence of processes performed by the machine.

### ■ objective evidence

data supporting the existence or verity of something.

### ■ Office of Management and Budget (OMB)

a branch of the Executive Office of the President. OMB helps the President formulate his spending plans, evaluates the effectiveness of agency programmes, policies and procedures, assesses competing funding demands among agencies and sets funding priorities. OMB ensures that agency reports, rules, testimony and proposed legislation are consistent with the President's budget and with Administration policies. In addition, OMB oversees and coordinates the Administration's procurement, financial management, information and regulatory policies. In each of these areas, OMB's role is to help improve administrative management, to develop better performance measures and coordinating mechanisms and to reduce any unnecessary burdens on the public.

### ■ Office of the Chief Financial and Chief Information Officer

an organisational unit in the Department whose primary responsibility is serving as the principal advisor to the Secretary of Education on all matters related to discretionary grant-making, co-operative agreements and procurement, as well as financial management, financial control and accounting.

### ■ office politics

the day to day manoeuvring to enhance one's position which can lead to favouritism.

### ■ on target

costs are close to projected costs and/or revenues are close to projected revenues.

### ■ one-piece flow

a policy of making only one part at a time (a batch size of one) before moving the part to the next step in the process. See **JIT and lean manufacturing.**

■ **ongoing support cost**

the periodic and continuing cost to operate and maintain the product or service delivered by the project.

■ **On-Line Analytical Processing (OLAP)**

software for manipulating multidimensional data from a variety of sources that has been stored in a data warehouse. The software can create various views and representations of the data. OLAP software provides fast, consistent, interactiveaccess to shared, multidimensional data.

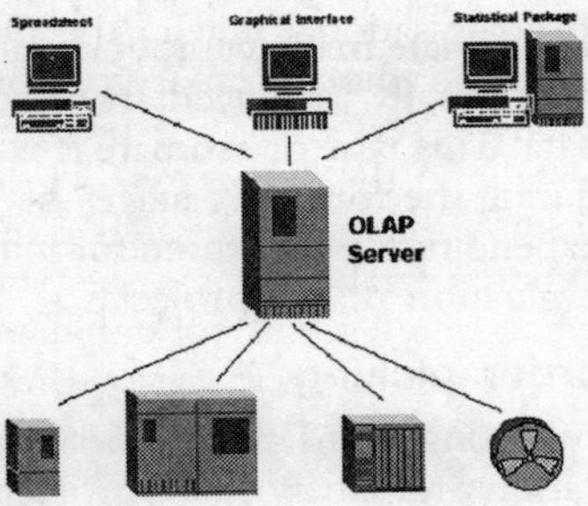


■ **on-time-delivery**

see service level.

■ **Operating Characteristic (OC) Curve**

an assessment of the probability of accepting a shipment, given the existing level of quality of the shipment. See **acceptance sampling.**

■ **operation**

at a general level, an operation is the overall work environment that includes the facility(s) and all activities that occur within it. When discussing MRP and related topics, an operation is a specific step that exists in the routing of a manufacturing process.

■ **operational or transaction database**

the database-of-record for a transaction-update system. The operational database is the source of data for the data warehouse. It contains detailed data used to run the day-to-day operations of the business. The data continually changes as updates are made and reflect the current value of the last transaction.

■ **operations strategy**

policies for using the firm's resources to support the business unit's strategy for gaining competitive advantage. These policies are usually defined in terms of the operations objectives of cost, quality, flexibility and service. Often firms can gain competitive strategic advantage by avoiding tradeoffs between these objectives.

■ **opportunity**

1. a problem which does not have a clear solution.
2. someone's assignment.

■ **opposite qualifiers**

when a description contradicts itself. Example, a small box, which is large on the inside.

**optical-guided**

guidance system that uses a special strip (taped or painted) on the floor to guide.

**optimise**

the decision strategy of choosing the alternative that gives the best or optimal overall value. A concept related to a specific capability in some model-driven DSS.

**optimising**

continuous process improvement is enabled by quantitative feedback from the process and from piloting innovative ideas and technologies.

**optional replenishment**

term used to describe the action of ordering or producing up to the max in a min-max system even though inventory has not reached the min. May be used to avoid down time on machines etc.

**order cost**

also known as purchase cost or set up cost order cost is the sum of the fixed costs that are incurred each time an item is ordered. These costs are not associated with the quantity ordered but primarily with physical activities required to process the order. For purchased items, these would include the cost to enter the purchase order and/or requisition, any approval steps, the cost to process the receipt, incoming inspection, invoice processing and vendor payment and in some cases a portion of the inbound freight may also be included in order cost. In manufacturing, the order cost would include the time to initiate the work order, time associated with picking and issuing components excluding time associated with counting and handling specific quantities, all production scheduling time, machine set up time and inspection time. Order cost is used as part of most cost-based order quantity/lot sizing calculations.

**order cycle**

also called replenishment cycle. Order cycle refers to the time between orders of a specific item. Most easily calculated by dividing the order quantity by the annual demand and multiplying by the number of days in the year.

**order of magnitude**

an estimate made without detailed data usually produced from cost data. This type of estimate is used during the formative stages of an expenditure programme for initial evaluation of the project.

**order picking**

collecting items from storage locations to satisfy a shop or customer order.

**order profile**

data describing the characteristics of inbound, outbound or internal orders (outbound is most common). Examples of characteristics incorporated into an order profile could include: line items per order, pieces per order, weight per order, cube per order, time of day, destination, shipment method order type, etc. Characteristics are often broken into logical groups such as breaking line items per order into groups of 1 line item, 2-4 line items, 5-10 line items, 11-25, 26+.

## ■ order qualifier, order winner

an order qualifier is a screening criterion that permits a firm's products to be considered as possible candidates for purchase. An order winner is a screening criterion that differentiates the products or service of one firm from another and often makes a critical difference in the buyer decision process.

## ■ organisation

1. group of people and facilities with an arrangement of responsibilities, authorities and relationships.
2. a unit within a company or other entity (e.g., Government agency or branch of service) within which many projects are managed as a whole. All projects within an organisation share a common top-level manager and common policies.

## ■ Organisational Breakdown Structure (OBS)

a depiction of the project organisation arranged to relate work packages to organisational units.

## ■ organisational capital

systematised and packaged competence, plus systems for leveraging the company's innovative strength and value-creating organisational capability.

## ■ organisational culture

in short, 'the way things are done in an organisation'. An organisation's culture is a mixture of its traditions, values, attitudes and behaviours. Different organisations can have very different cultures. In knowledge management, an organisation's culture is extremely important - if it is not based on qualities such as trust and openness, then knowledge management initiatives are unlikely to succeed.

## ■ organisational learning

the activity, by which knowledge is generated, captured and leveraged for the benefit of the organisation. The form of capturing the knowledge must be so that the knowledge can be replicated i.e. so the knowledge does not have to be re-learnt in isolation from the original learning.

## ■ organisational memory

the knowledge and understanding embedded in an organisation's people, processes and products or services, along with its traditions and values. Organisational memory can either assist or inhibit the organisation's progress.

## ■ organisational planning

identifying, documenting and assigning project roles, responsibilities and reporting relationships.

## ■ organisational structure

arrangement of responsibilities, authorities and relationships between people.

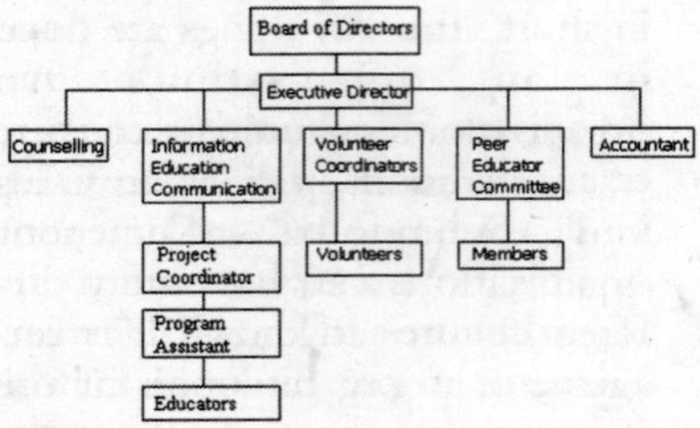


## ■ original

the current design activity document or digital data file(s) of a record.

## ■ out placement services

a bundle of services which can include: resume preparation, letter writing, interview training and job opportunity identification.

## ■ out sourced

1. use of resources not owned by the firm.
2. services provided to the firm by suppliers, consultants and temporary employees.

## ■ outcome

the ultimate, long-term, resulting effect—both expected and unexpected—of the customer's use or application of the organisation's outputs.

## ■ outside financing

corresponds to the commitments of the fund before liquidation taxes in per cent of the total fund assets.

## ■ outside operation

term describing a step in the manufacturing process that is performed by an outside vendor. System set-up for outside operations can get fairly complicated and generally requires linking a purchase order for the outside processing to a specific operation in the routing. The integration of the purchase order process and the work order process to ensure accounting, production planning and inventory management's needs are met can be confusing and is often problematic.

## ■ over time

1. during the next period of time.
2. in the future.

## ■ overall change control

co-ordinating changes across the entire project.

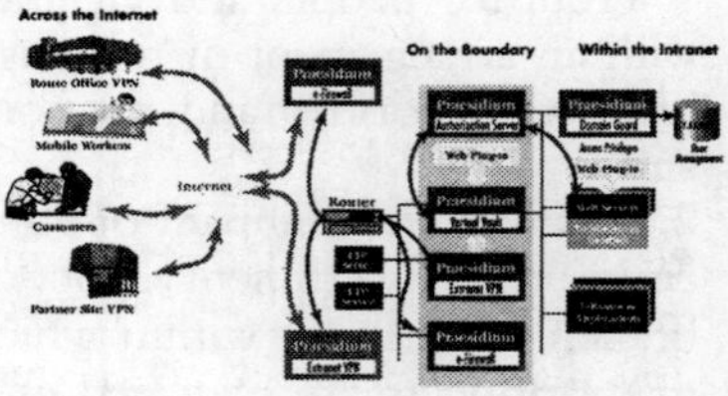


## ■ Overall Equipment Effectiveness (OEE)

OEE is a key metric for lean operations and is used extensively in TPM applications. OEE = (Availability rate) x (Performance rate) x (Yield rate). Availability rate is (Operating time less downtime)/(Total operating time) and reflects downtime losses due to changeovers, equipment failures and start-up losses. Performance rate is (Total output)/(Potential output a rated speed) and reflects speed loses due to idling and minor stoppages or reduced speed operation. Quality rate is (Good output)/(Total output) and is a function of defects and rework. There are six big losses. These are losses of quantity via defective products and losses of time due to decreased productivity from equipment breakdowns. (Affects the Availability rate.) Set-up and adjustment losses: these losses stem from defective units and downtime that may be incurred when equipment is adjusted to shift from producing one kind of product to another. (Affects the Availability rate.) Idling and minor stoppage losses: typically, these kinds of losses are relatively frequent. They result from brief periods of idleness when between units in a job or when easy-to-clear jams occur. (Affects the Performance rate.) Reduced speed losses: these losses occur when equipment is run at less than the design speed. Design speed may not be known. Materials or tooling may be off spec and require special treatment. There may be fear of running equipment if it is run too fast. (Affects the Performance rate.) Quality defects and rework: these are product related defects and corrections necessitated by malfunctioning equipment. (Affects the Quality rate.) Start-up losses: these are yield losses incurred during early production, i.e., from machine start-up to steady state. (Affects the quality rate.) Reasonable target values are Availability greater than 90%, Performance greater than 95% and Quality greater than 99%. The goal of measuring OEE is to improve the effectiveness of an equipment. Since equipment effectiveness affects shop floor employees more than any other group, it is appropriate for them to be involved in tracking OEE and in planning and implementing equipment improvements to reduce lost effectiveness. It is recommended that the operator collects the daily data about the equipment for use in the OEE calculation. Collecting this data will (1) teach the operator about the equipment (2) focus the cperator's attention on the losses. (3) grow a feeling of ownership of the equipment. The shift leader or line manager is often the one who will receive the daily operating data from the operator and process it to develop information about the OEE. Working hands on with the data will: (1) give the leader/manager basic facts and figures on the equipment. (2) Help the leader/manager give appropriate feedback to the operators and others involved in equipment improvement. (3) Allow the leader to keep management informed about equipment status and improvement results. However, managers should be careful to never use OEE to build inventory long before it is needed. Many firms find that they can improve both cost and quality if they can find a supplier that has a core competence in a particular area.

## ■ oversight committee

a body chartered by the Chief Information Officer, a Cabinet Secretary or a Agency Head to review and make recommenda tions regarding major IT projects within that Secretariat.

## ■ overview

a general description of the topic whose goal is not clarity.

## ■ pack-to-order

a customer's order is collected from standard components and packed into a box or some other shipping container. This is a very similar to 'assemble to order' except that no product assembly is required. It is also called 'pack to demand'. A country and language specific label is put on the box and shipped it to the distributor in the country.

## ■ pallet inverter

a type of stationary equipment used to transfer product between different types of pallets such as transferring from wood to plastic pallets or from pallets to slip-sheets. A load on a pallet is placed in the pallet inverter and the entire load is rotated 180 degrees allowing you to remove the original pallet and replace it with another.

## ■ paperless

when referring to processing in the warehouse (paperless picking, paperless receiving) or on the shop floor, paperless generally suggests that the direction of tasks and execution of transactions are conducted electronically without the use of paper documents. This is usually accomplished through the use of fixed or portable computers, bar code scanners, RFID readers, light-signalling technology (pick-to-light) or voice technology.

## ■ paradigm

an example, model, pattern or standard.

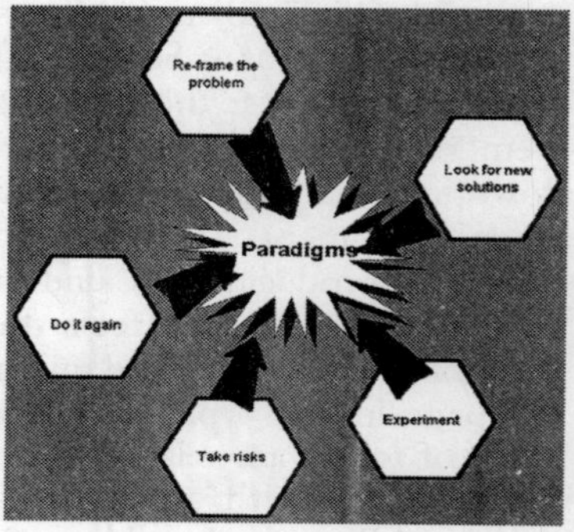


## ■ paradigm shift

1. a change in the well known typical example.

2. any major change in the generally accepted point of view.

## ■ parametric estimating

an estimating technique that uses a statistical relationship between historical data and other variables (e.g., square footage in construction, lines of code in software development) to calculate an estimate.

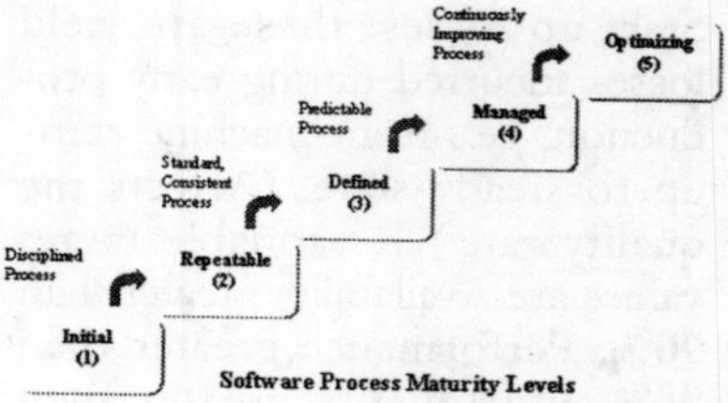


Software Process Maturity Levels

## ■ pare down

the firing of employees and/or the use of less plant and equipment.

## ■ Pareto chart

a histogram (bar chart) that helps identify and prioritise the most common sources of error or defects. The chart shows the problem frequencies and is sorted by from highest to lowest. See **Pareto's law.**

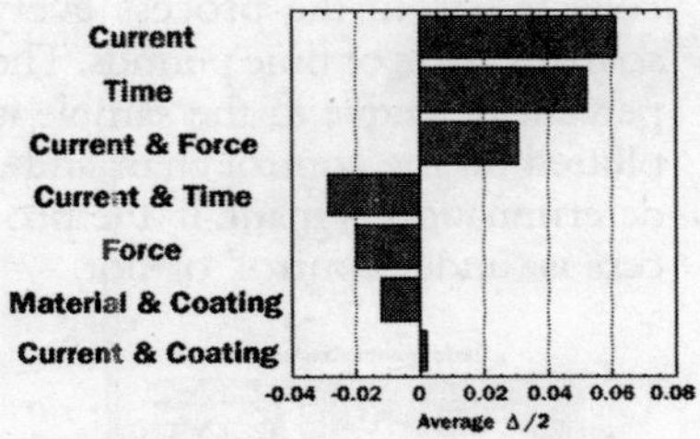


## ■ Pareto diagram

a histogram that ordered by frequency of occurrence, shows how many results were generated by each identified cause.

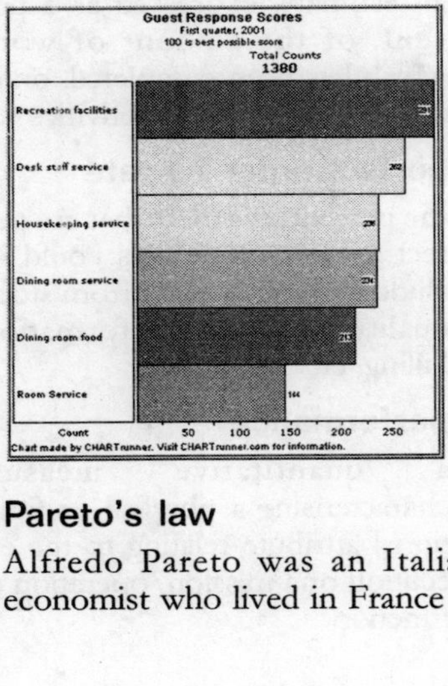


## ■ Pareto's law

Alfredo Pareto was an Italian economist who lived in France in the early 1900's. In studying the distribution of wealth in Milan, he found that 20% of the people earned 80% of the wealth. Pareto's Law is also known a the '80-20 rule', which tates that 80% of the value (or p oblems or whatever) is in the top 20% of the causes (items, people, etc.). Note that it may not be 80-20 ... it might be 80-10 or 90-20, etc. Pareto's Law can be observed in many, many situations such as inventory/value distribution (most of the value in an inventory is in just a few items), customer sales distributions (just a few customers give you most of your sales), quality control (most of the defects can be attributed to just a few problems), human relations (most of the problems in your life are caused by just a few people), etc. Pareto's Law can best be remembered by the phrase 'The trivial many and the important few'. The implication of Pareto's Law is that as a manager you need to find and manage the important few and ignore the trivial many hat do not matter that much.

## ■ Parkinson's law

work expands to fill the time allotted to it. (Work expands to fill the time allowed.)

## ■ parliamentary group

to understand in the investment trust business as the fraction of a fund portion.

## ■ part

one piece or two or more pieces joined together which are not normally subjected to disassembly without destruction or impairment of designed use (examples: gear, screws, transistors, capacitors, integrated circuits etc.)

**■ part or identifying number**

part or identifying number is an alpha-numeric designator which identifies parts, items or bulk materials that are covered by a specification.

**■ partner with**

a linkage between two firms.

**■ pass back to shareholders**

use money to either buy the firm's stock, pay dividends or in some other way increase payments to the stockholders.

**■ path**

a set of sequentially connected activities in a project network diagram.

**■ path convergence**

in mathematical analysis, the tendency of parallel paths of approximately equal duration to delay the completion of the milestone where they meet.

**■ paying fund**

investment trust, which pays the gained yields at its portion owners. Opposite: accumulating capital fund.

**■ payment**

the annual disbursement of the yields obtained by the fund to the shareholders. Opposite: accumulating capital.

**■ payment net yield**

the paid yield in relation to current market prices corresponds to the payment net yield.

**■ payroll orphans**

employees that were fired.

**■ p-chart**

a quality control chart that monitors the percent defective of the process. A sample of n parts is collected from the process every so many parts or time periods. The percent defective in the sample is plotted on the control chart and a determination is made if the process is 'under control' or not.

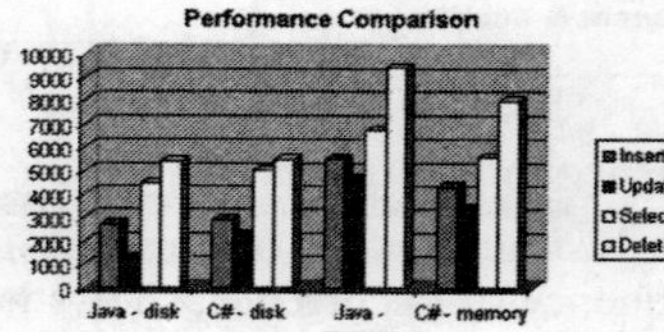


**■ Percent Complete (PC)**

an estimate, expressed as a percent, of the amount of work, which has been completed, on an activity or group of activities.

**■ perfect order fill rate**

the percent of orders that are perfect in every way. This could include on time or filled from stock, quality, packaging, information, billing, etc.

**■ performance**

a quantitative measure characterising a physical or functional attribute relating to the execution of a mission/operation or function.

## ■ performance gap

the gap between what customers and stakeholders expect and what each process and related sub processes produce in terms of quality, quantity, time and cost of services and products.

## ■ performance measurement

the process of developing measurable indicators that can be systematically tracked to assess progress made in achieving predetermined goals and using such indicators to assess progress in achieving these goals.

## ■ performance quality

the product design standard (specifications) set for the product and service attributes.

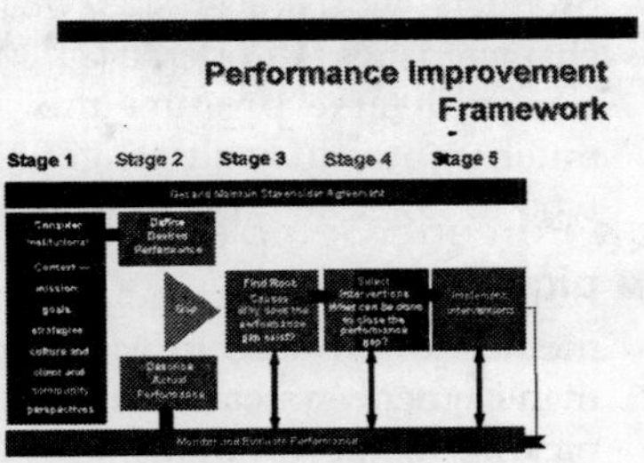


## ■ performance report

a report of the specific activities the recipient of a discretionary grant or cooperative agreement has performed during the budget or project period.

## ■ performance reporting

collecting and disseminating information about project performance to help ensure project progress.

## ■ performing organisation

the enterprise whose employees are most directly involved in doing the work of the project.

## ■ Period Order Quantity (POQ)

a simple lot sizing rule that defines the order quantity in terms of the periods' supply. POQ is implemented in MRP system simply by adding up the next POQ periods' of net requirements. The mathematically correct way to define the POQ is as the EOQ divided by the average demand per period.

## ■ periodic review system

an order-timing rule used for planning independent inventories. Every 'P' time periods, we place an order. Also known as a fixed-time period model, periodic system, fixed-order interval system or P-model. The system is 'time-triggered', rather than 'event-triggered' as the case of the order point model. The system is limited to placing orders at the end of a predetermined time period only the passage of time triggers the model. The system requires a larger average inventory than the order point system because it must also protect against stock-outs during the review period.

## ■ periods' supply

the concept of expressing an inventory quantity in terms of the periods of demand.

## ■ perpetual inventory system

an inventory control system where a 'real-time' record is kept of the amount of inventory for each item.

## ■ perspective

a point of view.

## ■ pert chart

a specific type of project network diagram.

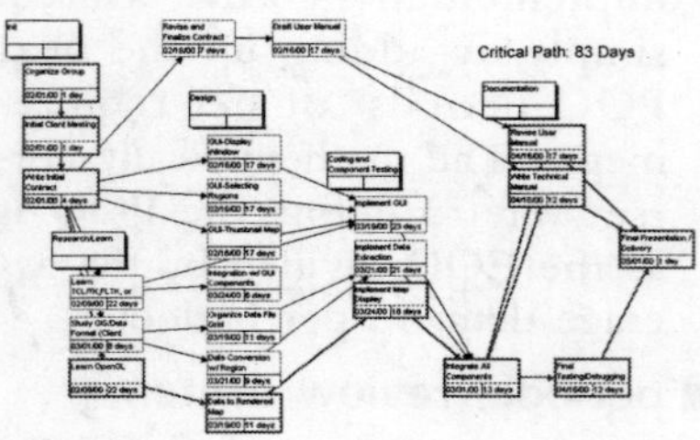


## ■ PFMEA

Process Failure Mode and Effects Analysis.

## ■ phantom bill of material

a bill of material coding and structuring technique used primarily for transient (non-stocked) sub-assemblies. A phantom bill of material represents an item that is physically built but rarely stocked before being used in the next level in the bill of material.

## ■ physical inventory

refers to the process of counting all inventory in a warehouse or plant. Operations are usually shut down during a physical inventory.

## ■ pick face

the primary location in a warehouse at which order picking, of less than pallet loads, is undertaken.

## ■ picking

the process of selecting items from a warehouse.

## ■ picking list

an output from an inventory control system designating those items, by part number, description and quantity, to be picked from stock to satisfy customer demand.

## ■ pick-to-carton

for parcel shippers, pick-to-carton logic uses item dimensions/weights to select the shipping carton prior to the order picking process. Items are then picked directly into the shipping carton. When picking is complete, dunnage is added and the carton sealed eliminating a formal packing operation. This logic works best when picking/packing products with similar size/weight characteristics. In operations with a very diverse product mix it's much more difficult to get this type of logic to work effectively.

## ■ pick-to-clear

method often used in warehouse management systems that directs picking to the locations with the smallest quantities on hand.

## ■ pick-to-light

pick-to light systems consist of lights and LED displays for each pick location. The system uses software to light the next pick and display the quantity to pick. Pick-to-light systems have the advantage of not only increasing accuracy, but also increasing productivity. Since hardware is required for each pick location, pick-to-light systems are easier to cost justify where very high picks per SKU occur. Carton flow rack and horizontal carousels are good applications for pick to light. In batch picking, put-to-light is also incorporated into the cart or rack that holds the cartons or totes that you are picking into. The light will designate which order you should be placing the picked items in.

**■ ping**

1. discuss.
2. mention.
3. verify.
4. notify.

**■ pinwheel or pin wheeling**

refers to a method for loading trailers where you alter the direction of every other pallet. Basically you use pin wheeling to load more pallets on a trailer when the depth of the pallet is longer than half the trailer width, but the depth plus the width is less than the trailer width. You can also use it as a productivity/ space utilisation compromise or to reduce load shifting when loading pallets where the depth of the pallet is less than half the trailer width.

**■ pipeline inventory**

the products, which are currently being moved from one location to another.

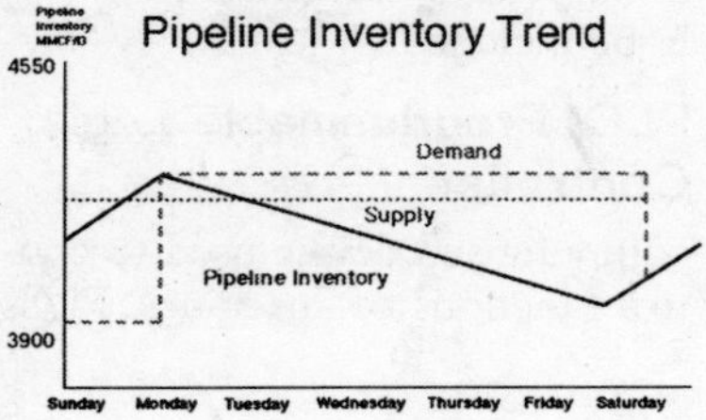


**■ pivot**

changing the dimensional orientation of a display or report.

**■ plan**

an intended future course of action.

**■ planned order**

term used within MRP and DRP systems for system-generated planned order quantities. Planned orders only exist within the computer system and serve multiple functions. One function is to notify the materials/planner or buyer to produce or order materials, which is done by converting a planned order into an purchase order, shop order or transfer order. Another function is used by the MRP or DRP system to show demand, which is used by subsequent MRP and DRP programmes to generate additional planned orders. (MRP/DRP systems sometimes run several programmes in a specific sequence to generate all planned orders, one programme may convert forecasts or customer orders into planned orders which creates the demand. The next programme uses this demand to create additional planned orders).

**■ Planned Unit Development (PUD)**

PUDs are areas that are planned and developed as one entity, by a single group. Planned unit developments usually include a variety of uses, including different housing types of varying densities, open space and commercial uses.

Project planning and density is calculated for the entire development rather than individual lots.

**■ planning**

a managerial function concerned with making forecasts, formulating outlines of things to do and identifying methods to accomplish them. Planning is anticipatory decision making.

**■ Planning Commission**

an appointed public body with duties that include preparation of a comprehensive plan, zoning and subdivision ordinances and capital improvement programmes. Members are appointed by the governing body and are residents of the community who are qualified to make decisions on community growth and development.

**■ planogram**

a plan for retail space allocation designed to maximise the return on investment for the retail space. A good planogram allows inexperienced employees to properly maintain shelf stock and appearance. The benefits of a planogram system include better control of inventory investments, improved inventory turnover, reduction in labour cost, more satisfied customers, increased sales and increased profit.

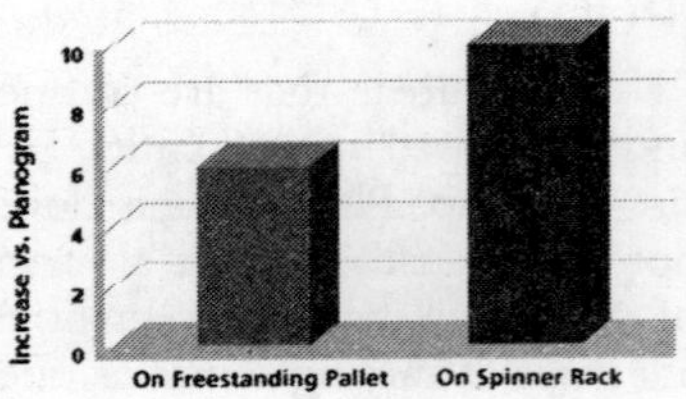


**■ plant currency**

currency, in which an investment trust transacts its plants. Not to confound with the reference currency and the money of account.

**■ plant horizon**

the time, for which an investor wants to invest a part of its fortune.

**■ plant instruments**

the different plant categories, e.g., shares, obligations etc.

**■ plant principles**

the plant principles characterise and specify the fund. The investor receives information about the securities, the plant currency, held in the portfolio, the geographical range of the plants.

**■ platform strategy**

a new product development strategy that plans new products around a small number of basic product designs (platforms) that allow many different final products with differing features, functions and prices. This strategy is well known in the automotive industry where a platform is often a chassis/drive-train combination upon which many different models are built.

**■ play a role**

1. take part in.
2. have some influence on.
3. be included.

**■ PLC, Programmable Logic Controller**

computerised device used to control functions of machines. PLCs are used in automation of manufacturing equipment and material handling equipment such as automated conveyor systems.

■ **Point of Sale (POS)**

a data collection device where the product are sold, usually a scanning and cash register device in a retail store. POS data is a rich source of data that can be used to inform the entire supply chain.

■ **poka-yoke**

a Japanese word for a 'foolproof device' or 'avoid mistakes'. Poka-yoke principles teach us to design products that cannot be assembled in the incorrect way and processes that are easy to do in the correct way and hard to do in the wrong way. See **Failure Model Effects Analysis (FMEA).**

■ **policy**

are general statements of direction and purpose designed to promote the co-ordinated planning, practical acquisition, effective development and efficient use of information technology resources.

■ **population**

the universe of data under investigation from which a sample will be taken.

■ **pop-up sorter**

sorting equipment integrated into conveyor to move materials off of conveyor at fixed points. Pop-up sorters are installed in fixed positions and may consist of a series of wheel or small belts that are normally located slightly below the conveyor rollers. The wheels or belts are momentarily raised (pop-up) to enable diverting materials off of the conveyor.

■ **portion**

demand of the individual investor in relation to the fund line on relative participation in fortunes and yield of the investment trust.

■ **portion light**

security-moderate documentation of the portion by a document of an investment trust in a document.

■ **position**

the firms point of view which usually changes over time.

■ **position a product**

1. an attempt to convince customers that this product will satisfy their desires.
2. to differentiate a product from competitors products.

■ **positive comments**

1. an upbeat view.
2. optimistic statements.

■ **positive tax benefits**

a reduction in tax payments.

■ **post implementation report**

documents of the successes and failures of a project and suggest follow up actions. It provides a historical record of the planned and actual budget and schedule. Other selected metrics on the project can also be collected, based upon state organisation procedures. The report also contains recommendations for other projects of similar size and scope.

## post-award performance conference

the first major discussion between the department and some grantees after a new award has been made. The conference generally focuses on the proposed project outcomes as stated in the grantee's approved application and on the ways in which project progress will be assessed.

## Post-Implementation Review (PIR)

an evaluation tool that compares the conditions before the implementation of a project (as identified in the business case) with the actual results achieved by the project.

## postponement

a manufacturing / distribution strategy where specific operations associated with a product are delayed until just prior to shipping. Storing product in a generic state and then applying custom labels or packaging before shipping is an example of postponement.

## postponement principle

it is best to keep products standardised as long as you can in the process to minimise complexity and inventories. The advantage is that standardised products can be made a lower cost and that you do not want to inventory an enormous variety of products. This is foundational principle for mass customisation. This is sometimes called the 'maximum delay' principle. See **mass customisation.**

## Precedence Diagramming Method (PDM)

a network diagramming technique in which activities are represented by boxes (or nodes). Activities are linked by precedence relationships to show the sequence in which the activities are to be performed.

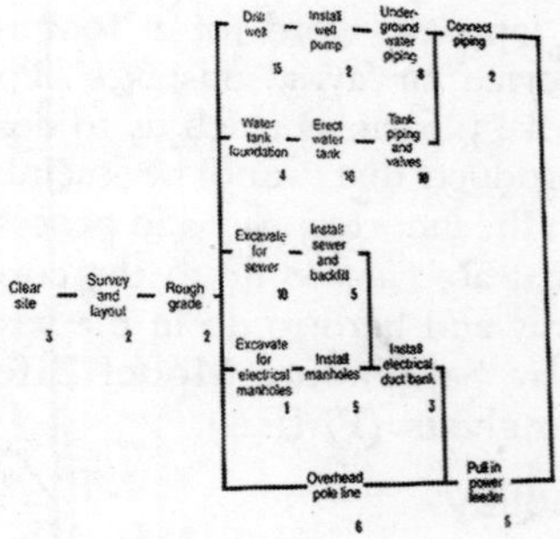


## precedence relationship

the term used in the precedence diagramming method for a logical relationship. In current usage, however, precedence relationship, logical relationship and dependency are widely used interchangeably regardless of the diagramming method in use.

## predecessor activity

1. in the arrow diagramming method, the activity that enters a node.
2. in the precedence diagramming method, the 'from' activity.

## predictive maintenance

predictive maintenance is the practice of monitoring a machine with a measuring device that can anticipate and predict when it is likely to fail. This is often based on vibration. Maintenance is then scheduled based on feedback from this measuring device. See **preventive maintenance.**

### ■ pre-event trigger

a call-out to an external programme prior to an action completing within the server application. The pre-event trigger supplies the external programme the information it needs to properly execute the external programme and return completion status information back to the calling server process.

### ■ prevention

a future-oriented strategy that improves quality by directing analysis and action toward correcting the production process. Prevention is consistent with a philosophy of never-ending improvement.

### ■ preventive action

action to eliminate the cause of a potential nonconformity or other undesirable potential situation.

### ■ preventive maintenance

preventive (or preventative maintenance) is the practice of checking and repairing a machine on a scheduled basis before it fails. The schedule is usually based on some historical information on the time between failures for the population of machines. The machine operators often perform it. The opposite of preventive maintenance is emergency maintenance, where the maintenance is done after the machine fails. In the practice of dentistry, preventive maintenance is your annual check-up and cleaning and emergency maintenance is the emergency trip to the dentist when you have a toothache.

### ■ print-to-order

a printing process that has very small printing batch sizes, typically equal to a customer order size. Print to order is made possible by new printing technologies.

### ■ priority

the imposed sequences desired with respect to the scheduling of activities within previously imposed constraints.

### ■ proactive

a step taken before something happens.

### ■ probability

the likelihood the risk will occur. Probability is one of the three attributes of risk.

### ■ procedure

1. a collection of steps that the organisation is responsible for implementing to ensure that policies and process requirements are met. The agency may use guidelines to develop these procedures.
2. specified way to carry out an activity or a process.
3. a series of activities carried out to accomplish a task or operation.

## ■ process

1. the combination of people, machine and equipment, raw materials, methods and environment that produces a given product or service.
2. set of interrelated or interacting activities, which transforms inputs into outputs.

## ■ process capability

the measured, built-in reproducibility (consistency) of the product turned out by the process. Such a determination is made using statistical methods, not wishful thinking. The statistically determined pattern or distribution can only then be compared to specification limits to decide if a process can consistently deliver product within those parameters.

## ■ process control

see Statistical Process Control (SPC).

## ■ Process Failure Mode and Effects Analysis (PFMEA)

an analytical technique used by a manufacturing responsible engineer/team as a means to assure that, to the extent possible, potential failure modes and their associated causes/mechanisms have been considered and addressed.

## ■ process flow chart (process map)

a diagram showing the logical flow of entities through a process. Ideally, the process map should show the queues and delays because these often represent 80% of the total process flow time. Process maps should also highlight handoffs (because this is where information is likely to be lost), moments of truth (this is where the process touches the customer) and failure points (this is where the process is likely to fail).

**ROLES IN THE MHB PROCESS**

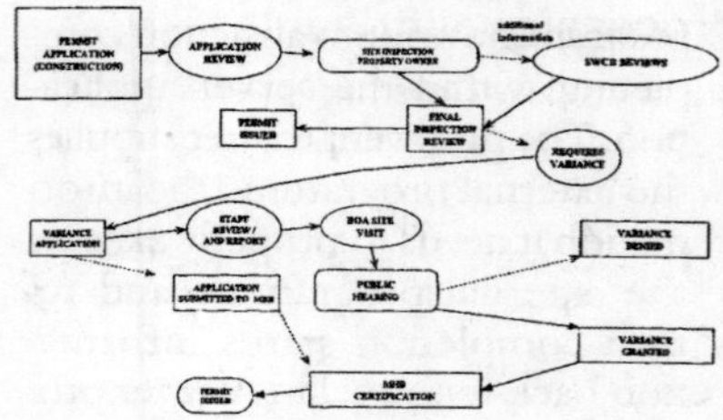


## ■ process improvement team

includes experienced employees from different departments who solve problems and improve work processes that go across-function l lines.

## ■ process layout

an approach for organising the physical configuration of a facility so that work-centres are grouped by process, rather than organised to match the requirements of a particular product. A process layout will have all of the grinding machines together, all of the lathes together, etc. A process layout is appropriate for a 'job shop' where the routing sequence for products is almost completely unpredictable. See **product layout.**

## ■ process manufacturing

type of manufacturing where a product is produced or transformed through mixing, chemical reactions, etc. Examples of process manufacturing would be refining crude oil into gasoline, extracting copper from ore, combining materials to make paint. Process as opposed to discrete manufacturing. Also see **discrete manufacturing.**

## ■ process quality audit

an analysis of elements of a process and appraisal of completeness, correctness of conditions and probable effectiveness.

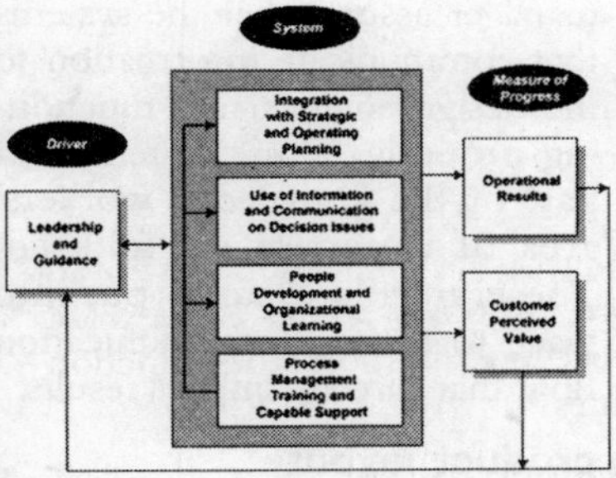


## ■ process validation

establishing by objective evidence that a process consistently produces a result or product meeting its predetermined specifications.

## ■ procurement

the procedures for obtaining goods or services, including all activities from the planning steps and preparation and processing of a requisition, through receipt and acceptance of delivery and processing of a final invoice for payment.

## ■ procurement cost

the total estimated cost of the goods or services being purchased.

## ■ product

general terms used to define the result of a project delivered to a customer.

## ■ Product Data Management (PDM)

software for product development. The best PDM systems are web-based collaborate applications for product development that allow enterprises to integrate business processes and product data with dispersed divisions, partners and customers. The challenge is to maximise the time-to-market benefits of concurrent engineering while maintaining control of your data and distributing it automatically to the people who need it - when they need it. The way PDM systems cope with this challenge is that master data is held only once in a secure 'vault' where its integrity can be assured and all changes to it monitored, controlled and recorded. Duplicate reference copies of the master data, on the other hand, can be distributed freely, to users in various departments for design, analysis and approval. The new data is then released back into the vault. When a 'change' is made to data, what actually happens is that a modified copy of the data, signed and dated, is stored in the vault alongside the old data, which remains in its original form as permanent record. This is the simple principle behind more advanced PDM systems.

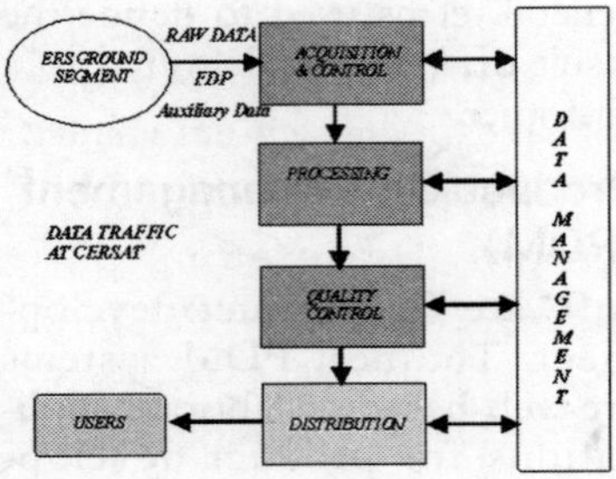


## ■ product description statement

a non-formal, high-level document that describes the characteristics of the product/process to be created.

## ■ product design quality

the degree to which the product design contributes to the creation of a high quality product. Product design quality is the output of the knowledge workers who generally work in marketing, design, development, quality assurance and operations. Quality historically originated in a task-oriented manufacturing environment. The challenge is how to integrate a quality philosophy into the knowledge work areas of marketing, design and development. Existing quality tools traditionally used in production settings may not work in this environment or may require serious adaptation. The approach to quality must adapt to be successful in the knowledge/professional environment. The approach to communication is a vital element in this environment. The knowledge workers' manager needs to have sufficient technical expertise to be seen as competent by the knowledge worker in their area of expertise. The manager manages outcomes, not the process details. A design engineer is already trained how to analyse designs by various boundary conditions, hand calculations, FEA or other means. The outcome should be a design report (folder) with drawings, technical specifications, producability requirements and supporting analysis reports. In order to assure the quality of the creative process, the manager assures that the systems that communicate information to the design engineer are functioning properly. Thus, systems not part of the knowledge workers' area of expertise are audited. These are the systems put into place to manage communication flow that directly impact results.

## ■ product layout

an approach to organised the physical configuration of a facility that is driven by the steps required to build a particular product. See **process layout.**

## ■ product liability or service liability

a generic term used to describe the onus on a producer or others to make restitution for loss related to personal injury, property damage or other harm caused by a product or service.

## ■ product quality audit

a quantitative assessment of conformance to required product characteristics.

### ■ product structure

see bill of material.

### ■ production plan

generally used to describe a long-term plan of what will be produced at a family level.

### ■ production planning (production plan)

see aggregate planning.

### ■ productive value

this is computed from the current renting incomes and a real estate-specific interest rate. To rents must appropriately and in the long term appear available, in order to flow completely into the computation. Main interest during the evaluation of net yield real estate properties is with the productive value.

### ■ productivity

a ratio of an output measure divided by an input measure (e.g., hamburgers created per hour). Is a measure of how well a country, industry, business unit, person or machine is using its resources. It is a relative measure. Productivity can be compared to another company or to itself over time. Total factor productivity is measured in monetary units. Partial factor productivity is measured in individual inputs, with labour being the most common.

### ■ Programme Determination Letter (PDL)

an official written notice from an authorised Department of Education management official to an audited grantee that sets forth the Department's decision on findings in an audit report, including all necessary actions and repayment of funds for which the grantee is responsible.

### ■ program generator

program generators are software programmes that generally provide graphical user interfaces and tools that allow a user to create a programme without having to write actual computer code. Currently these programmes are more frequently referred to as 'development tools' and are usually designed to write code for specific applications such as data-collection programmes for portable computers. While a user does not need to be a programmer to use this software, the user does need to have a higher level of technical skills than that of most standard software users.

### ■ programme office

a sub-unit of a Principal Office that conducts the daily work of administering the Department's discretionary grant and cooperative agreement programmes, including the review and ranking of applications.

### ■ programme

a group of related projects managed in a co-ordinated way. Programmes usually include an element of ongoing activity.

### ■ Programme Evaluation and Review Technique (PERT)

an event-oriented network analysis technique used to estimate project duration when there is a high degree of uncertainty with the individual activity duration estimates. PERT applies the critical path method to a weighted average duration estimate.

## ■ programme manager

1. a person responsible for the management and co-ordination of a group of related projects.
2. the role at a high enough level in an organisation that the primary focus is the long-term vitality of the organisation, rather than the short-term project and contractual concerns and pressures. In general, a senior manager for engineering would have responsibility for multiple projects.

## ■ progress analysis

the evaluation of progress against the approved schedule and the determination of its impact. For cost, this is the development of performance indices.

Analysis Process

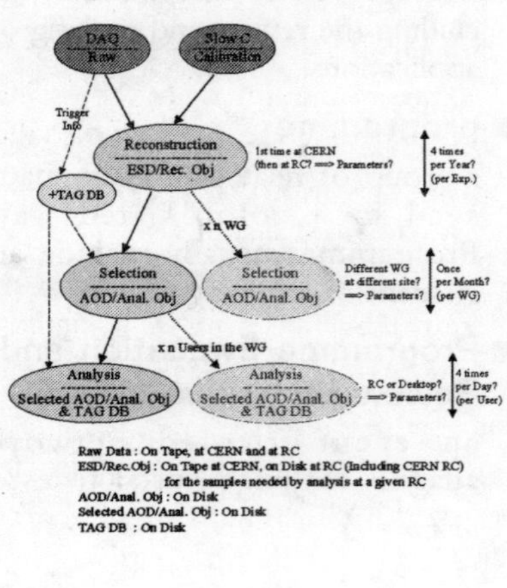


## ■ project

1. a temporary endeavour undertaken to deliver a unique product or service.
2. unique process, consisting of a set of coordinated and controlled activities with start and finish dates, undertaken to achieve an objective conforming to specific requirements, including the constraints of time, cost and resources.

## ■ project administration

making project plan modifications may result from such things as: new estimates of work still to be done, changes in scope/function lity of end-product(s), resour e changes, unforeseen circumstan es. It includes monitoring the - various execution phase activities, monitoring risks, status reporting and reviewing/authorising project changes as needed.

## ■ project business objective

a desired result produced by a project that answers or resolves a business problem.

## ■ project charter

a document issued by senior management that provides the project manager with the authority to apply organisational resources to project activities.

## ■ project communications management

a subset of project management that includes the processes required to ensure proper collection and dissemination of project information. It consists of communications planning information distribution, performance reporting and administrative closure.

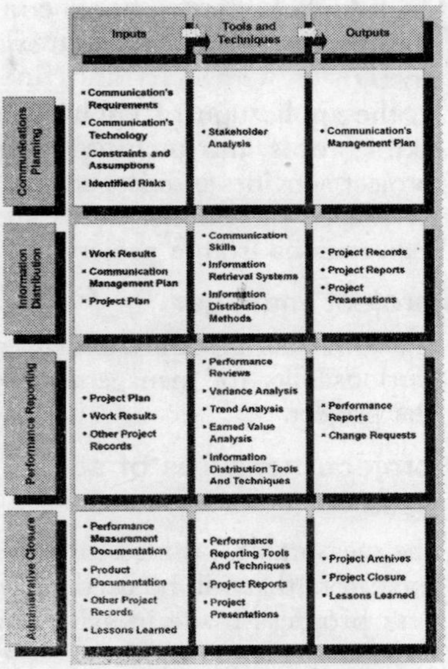


## ■ Project Concept Document (PCD)

the document that is the foundation for making a decision to initiate a project. It describes the project purpose and presents a preliminary business case for pursuing the project. It gives decision makers the opportunity to determine project viability.

## ■ project cost

the total cost to provide the business driven, technology-based product or service. The costs include the hardware, software, services, installation, management, maintenance, support, training and internal staffing costs planned for the project. Internal staffing costs are the apportioned salaries and benefits of the project team members.

## ■ project cost management

a subset of project management that includes the processes required to ensure that the project is completed within the approved budget. It consists of resource planning, cost estimating, cost budgeting and cost control.

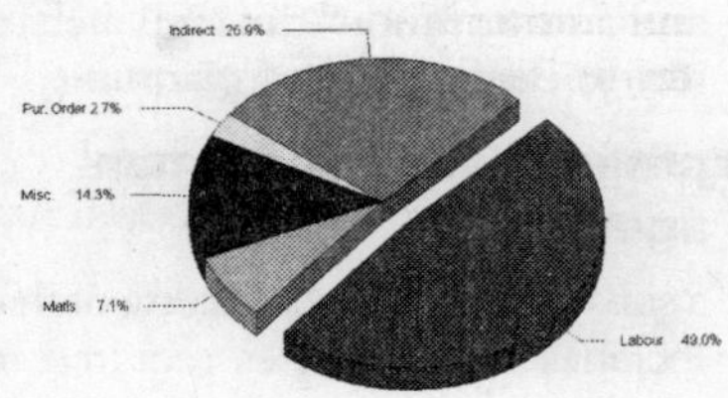


## ■ project description

an initial, high-level statement describing the purpose, benefits, customer(s), general approach to development and characteristics of a product or service required by the organisation.

## ■ project duration

the elapsed time from project start date through to project finish date.

## ■ project human resource management

a subset of project management that includes the processes required to make the most effective use of the people involved with the project. It consists of organisational planning, staff acquisition and team development.

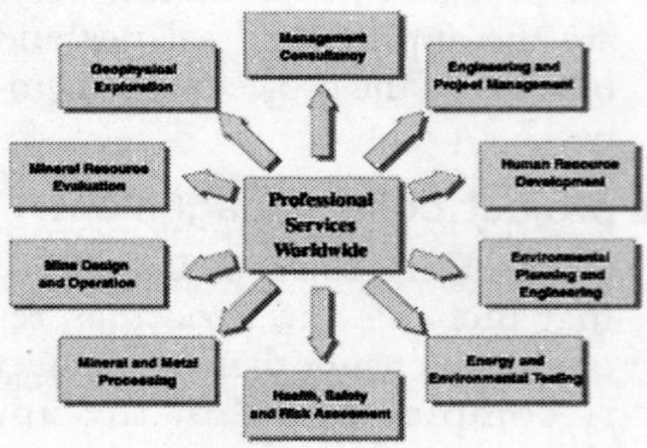


### ■ project initiation

the conceptual development phase of a project. A process that leads to approval of the project concept and authorisation (through a charter) to begin detailed planning.

### ■ project integration management

a subset of project management that includes the processes required to ensure that the various elements of the project are properly co-ordinated. It consists of project plan development, project plan execution and overall change control.

FUNCTIONAL SCHEMATIC

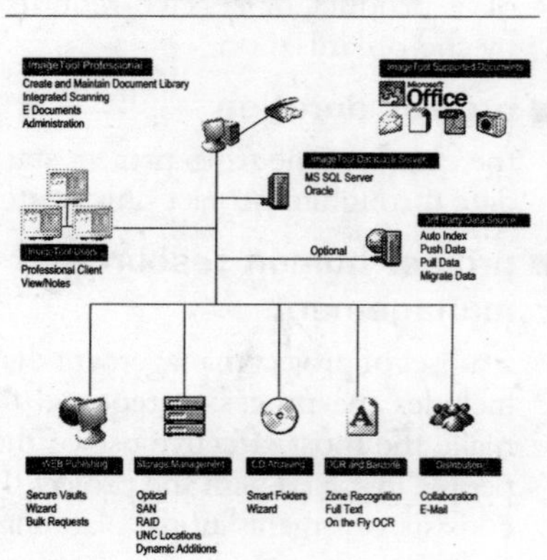


### ■ project management

1. the planning organising, scheduling, directing and controlling of a one-time activity to meet or exceed stakeholder-defined constraints on scope, schedule and cost.
2. the application of knowledge, skills, tools and techniques to project activities in order to meet or exceed stakeholder needs and expectations from a project.

### ■ project manager

the individual appointed and given responsibility for management of the project.

### ■ project measures of success

the measurable, business-oriented indicators that will be used to assess progress made in achieving planned project objectives.

### ■ project network diagram

any schematic display of the logical relationships of project activities. The diagram is always drawn from left to right to reflect project chronology. Often incorrectly referred to as a 'PERT chart'.

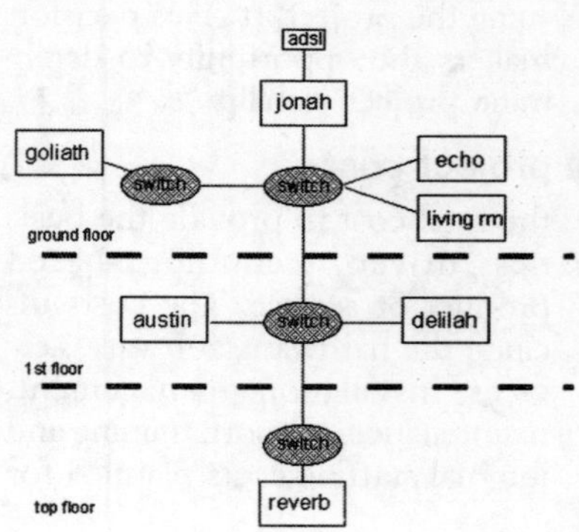

## ■ project oversight

a process that employs a variety of quality control, inspection, test measurement and other observation processes to ensure that planned project objectives are achieved in accordance with an approved plan. Project oversight includes both technical and management oversight. Project oversight is usually done by an independent entity (separate from the project team) trained or experienced in a variety of management and technical review methods.

## ■ project period

the total amount of time (sometimes several years) during which the Department authorises a grantee to complete the approved work of the project described in the application. Project periods of more than one year are divided into budget periods. Sometimes referred to as 'performance period.'

## ■ project phase

a collection of logically related project activities, usually culminating in the completion of a major deliverable.

## ■ project plan

a formal, approved document used to guide both project execution and project control. The primary uses of the project plan are to document planning assumptions, decisions and project baselines, facilitate communication among stakeholders and, essentially describe how the project will be executed and controlled.

## ■ project procurement management

a subset of project management that includes the processes required to acquire goods and services from outside the performing organisation. It consists of procurement planning, solicitation planning, solicitation, source selection, contract administration and contract closeout.

## ■ project quality management

a subset of project management that includes the processes required to ensure that the project will satisfy the needs for which it was undertaken. It consists of quality planning, quality assurance and quality control.

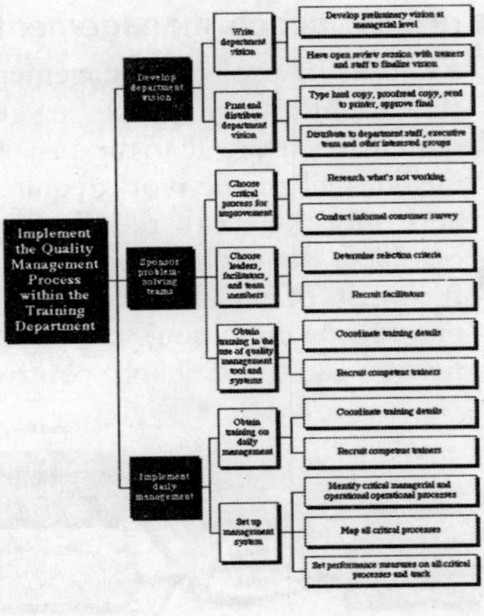


## ■ project risk management

a subset of project management that includes the processes concerned with identifying, analysing and responding to project risk. It consists of risk identification, risk quantification, risk response development and risk response control.

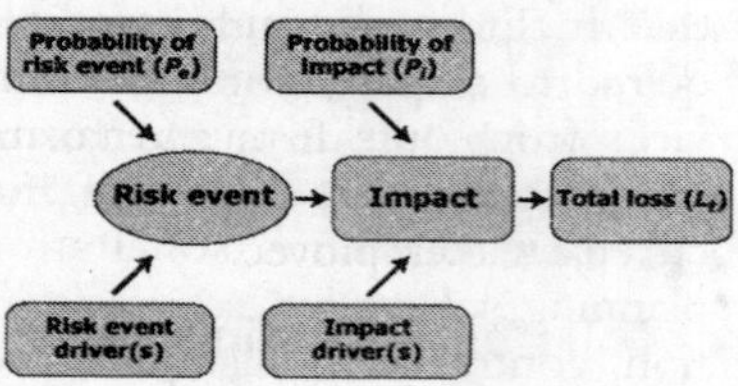


■ **project schedule**

the planned dates for performing activities and meeting milestones.

■ **project scope**

the sum of the products and services to be provided as a project. It establishes the limits of a project. The project scope defines who, what, where, when and why for a project.

■ **project scope management**

a subset of project management that includes the processes required to ensure that the project includes all of the work required and only the work required, to complete the project successfully. It consists of initiation, scope planning, scope definition, scope verification and scope change control.

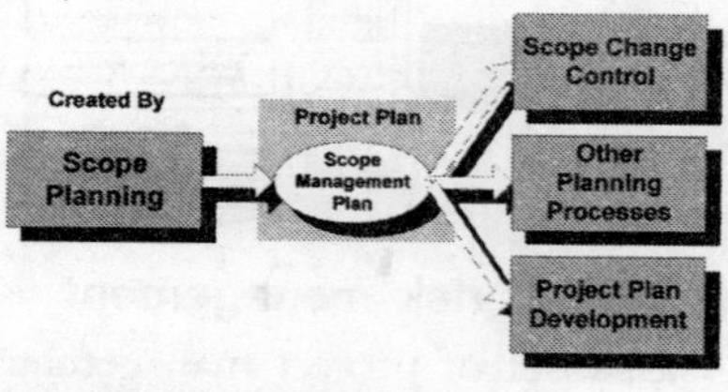


■ **project sponsor**

an individual, usually part of the organisation management team, who makes the business case for the project. This individual usually has the authority to define project goals, secure resources and resolve organisational and priority conflicts.

■ **project team members**

the individuals that report either part time or full time to the project manager and are responsible for the completion of project tasks.

■ **project time management**

a subset of project management that includes the processes required to ensure timely completion of the project. It consists of activity definition and activity sequencing, activity duration estimating schedule development and schedule control.

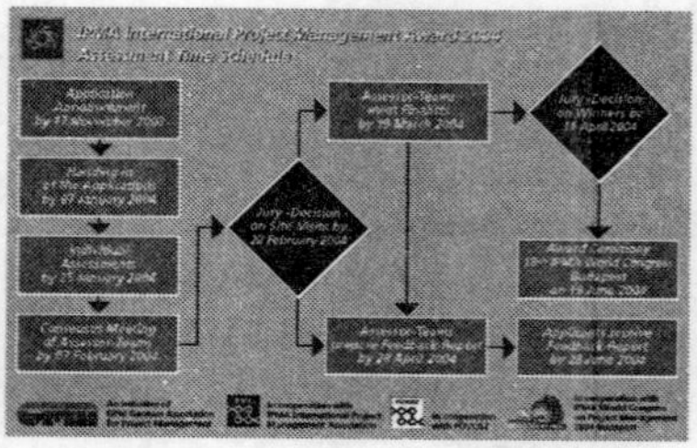

■ **project transition checklist**

a document that ensures that the activities of the planning phase have been finished, reviewed and signed off so that the project may move from the planning phase into the execution phase.

■ **projectised organisation**

any organisational structure in which the project manager has full authority to assign priorities and to direct the work of individuals assigned to the project.

### proof by example

the listing of supportive anecdotal evidence. Giving cases where something has happened does not prove the line of reasoning. Anecdotal evidence can be interesting but rarely reliable.

### proprietary specification

a specification that restricts the acceptable product(s) or service(s) to that of one or more manufacturer(s) or vendor(s). A common example would be the use of a 'brand name' specification that would exclude consideration of proposed 'equals'. Although all sole source specifications are proprietary, all proprietary specifications are not sole source. Proprietary items may be available from several distributors through competitive bidding.

### prototyping

a strategy in system development in which a scaled down system or portion of a system is constructed in a short time, tested and improved in several iterations. A prototype is an initial version of a system that is quickly developed to test the effectiveness of the overall design being used to solve a particular problem. Prototyping is similar to the Evolutionary (Iterative) Design Process. It is sometimes termed rapid prototyping and is similar to Rapid Application Development (RAD).

### provide an employee benefit

give employees something of value. Some are paid for by the firm, the employee or both. Some are paid by the firm and taxable to the employee. Some are chosen by the employee.

### public broadcasting services

public telecommunications are non-commercial educational or cultural radio and television programmes and related instructional or informational material that may be transmitted by means of electronic communications.

### public warehouse

a public warehouse is a business that provides short or long-term storage to a variety of businesses, usually on a month-to-month basis. A public warehouse will generally use their own equipment and staff, however, agreements may be made where the client either buys or subsidises equipment. Public warehouse fees are usually a combination of storage fees (per pallet or actual sq. footage) and transaction fees (inbound and outbound). Public warehouses are most often used to supplement space requirements of a private warehouse.

### purchase of development rights

programmes through which local governments may purchase development rights and dedicate the land for conservation easements, protecting it as open space or agricultural areas.

## ■ purchase order

a document used to approve, track and process purchased items. A purchase order is used to communicate a purchase to a supplier. It is also used as an authorisation to purchase. A purchase order will state quantities, costs and delivery dates. The purchase order is also used to process and track receipts and supplier invoices/payments associated with the purchase.

## ■ purchasing lead-time

the time between the release and receipt of a purchase order from a supplier. This is also known as the replenishment lead-time. See **lead time.**

## ■ push for

1. recommend.
2. suggest to management.

## ■ push versus pull systems

all production and inventory control systems deal with fundamentally only two decision variables when to order and how much to order. It is easiest to understand 'push' and 'pull' systems for managing these two variables in a logistics context. Suppose, for example that we have a factory supplying two regional warehouses. With a push system, the people (and the computer) at the factory decide when and how much to ship to each of the two warehouses based of forecasted demand and inventory position information. With a pull system, we disaggregate the problem so that people (and the computer) at each warehouse decide when and how much to order from the factory based on their need. (Of course, the factory might not have the inventory, so some of these orders might not be filled.)

## ■ push-back rack

racking system that incorporates a carriage or other sliding device to allow you to feed multiple pallets into the same location 'pushing back' the previous pallet.

## ■ put forward

assert something as factual.

## ■ put off of work

the firing of employees who may be hired back again.

## ■ put-to-light

technology similar to pick-to-light, however, the light modules are used do direct which tote, bin or carton, the item is to be picked into, rather than directing which locations to pick from.

## ■ QFD

Quality Function Deployment.

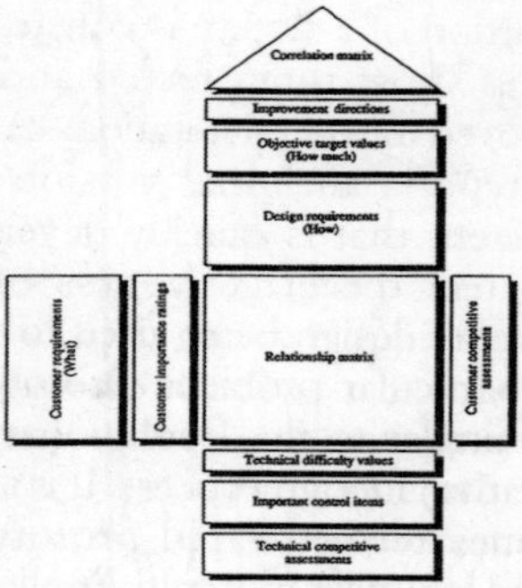


**Basic elements of a QFD 1 chart.**

**■ QMS**

Quality Management System.

**■ QSR**

Quality System Requirements.

**■ qualification process**

process to demonstrate the ability to fulfil specified requirements.

**■ qualification testing**

testing performed to demonstrate to the acquirer that a CSCI, HWCI, system or subsystem meets its specified requirements.

**■ quality**

1. the totality of features and characteristics of a product or service that bear on its ability to satisfy stated or implied needs.
2. degree to which a set of inherent (existing) characteristics fulfils requirements.

**■ quality assurance**

1. all those planned or systematic actions necessary to provide adequate confidence that a product or service will satisfy given requirements for quality.
2. part of quality management focused on providing confidence that quality requirements will be fulfilled.

**■ quality audit**

a systematic and independent examination and evaluation to determine whether quality activities and results comply with planned arrangements and whether these arrangements are implemented effectively and are suitable to achieve objectives.

**■ quality characteristic**

inherent characteristic of a product, process or system related to a requirement.

**■ quality circle**

a small group of employees organised to solve work-related problems, often voluntarily, usually not chaired by a department manager.

**■ quality control**

1. the operational techniques and the activities used to fulfil requirements of quality.
2. part of quality management focused on fulfilling quality requirements.

**■ quality engineering**

that branch of engineering which deals with the principles and practice of product and service quality assurance and control.

**■ Quality Function Deployment (QFD)**

a method for ensuring that the customer has a voice in the design specification of a product. QFD uses inter-functional teams from manufacturing, engineering and marketing. The process begins with market research, studying and listening to customers to define their needs and then breaking these needs down into categories called customer requirements. Requirements are then weighted based on their importance to the customer. Customers are asked to rate the firm's products against competitor's products. This process assists the firm in determining what the customer values and how the customer rates the product compared to a competitor's product. QFD results in a better focus on customer's needs and product characteristics in need of improvement.

**■ quality improvement**

part of quality management focused on increasing the ability to fulfil quality requirements.

**■ quality initiative**

a formal effort by an organisation to improve the quality of its products and services, usually involves top management development of a mission statement and long-term strategy.

**■ quality loop, quality spiral**

conceptual model of interacting activities that influence the quality of a product or service in the various stages ranging from the identification of needs to the assessment of whether these needs have been satisfied.

**■ quality management**

1. a collection of quality policies, plans, procedures, specifications and requirements is attained through quality assurance (managerial) and quality control (technical).
2. the aspect of the overall business management function that determines and implements the quality policy.

**■ quality management system**

management system to direct and control an organisation with regard to quality.

**■ quality manual**

document specifying the quality management system of an organisation.

**■ quality measure**

a quantitative measure of the features and characteristics of a product or service.

**■ quality objective**

something sought or aimed for, related to quality.

**■ quality plan**

a document setting out the specific quality practices, resources and activities relevant to a particular product, process, service, contract or project.

**■ quality plan audit**

see quality system audit.

**■ quality planning**

1. identifying which quality standards are relevant to the project and determining how to satisfy them.
2. a structured process for defining the methods (i.e., measurements, tests) that will be used in the production of a specific product or family of products (i.e., parts, materials).

**■ quality policy**

1. the overall intentions and direction of an organisation as regards quality as formally expressed by top management.
2. overall intentions and direction of an organisation related to quality as formally expressed by top management.

■ **quality surveillance**

the continuing monitoring and verification of the status of procedures, methods, conditions, products, processes and services and analysis of records in relation to stated references to ensure that requirements for quality are being met.

■ **quality system**

the organisational structure, responsibilities, procedures, processes and resources for implementing quality management.

■ **quality system audit**

a documented activity performed to verify, by examination and evaluation of objective evidence, that applicable elements of the quality system are suitable and have been developed, documented and effectively implemented in accordance with specified requirements.

■ **quality system review**

a formal evaluation by management of the status and adequacy of the quality system in relation to quality policy and/or new objectives resulting from changing circumstances.

■ **queue time**

amount of time a job waits at an operation prior to set up or processing. Part of manufacturing lead time.

■ **queuing theory**

a branch of mathematics that deals with understanding systems with customers (orders, calls, etc.) arriving and being served by one or more servers. The time between arrivals and/or the service times could be random variables. Queuing theory models are usually concerned with estimating the steady state performance of the system such as the utilisation, the mean time in queue, the mean time in system, the mean number in queue and the mean number in system. Queuing theory is sometimes called 'stochastic processes'. Queuing theory models are sometimes good tools for understanding capacity issues, but are limited by the assumption that the mean arrival rate and the mean service rate do not change over time.

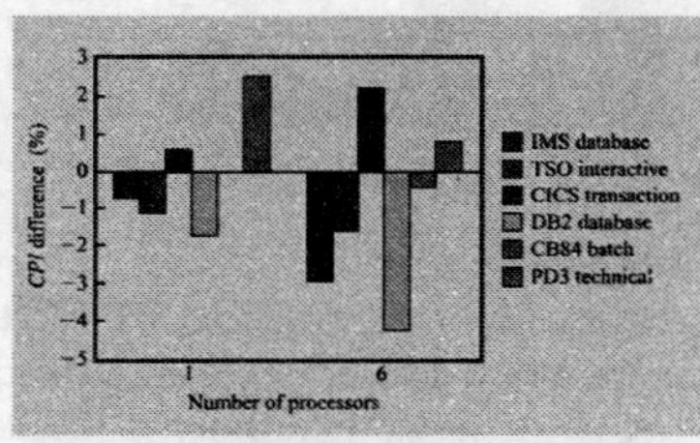


Figure

**Difference between *CPI* of ES/9000 system and that of model, for various applications running on a uniprocessor and 6-way multiprocessor.**

■ **quick win**

an initiative or a solution that yields rapid positive results.

■ **rational decision behaviour**

behaviour that is goal-oriented in reaching a decision. Behaviour is guided by the consequences likely to result from the selection of a given alternative. A decision maker believes based upon analysis that a chosen alternative will result in achieving one or more desired objectives. Rational decision behaviour should be supported by DSS.

## ■ r-chart

a quality control chart that monitors the range (variability) of the process. A sample of n parts is collected from the process every so many parts or time periods. The range (maximum minus minimum) of the sample is plotted on the control chart and a determination is made if the process is 'under control' or not.

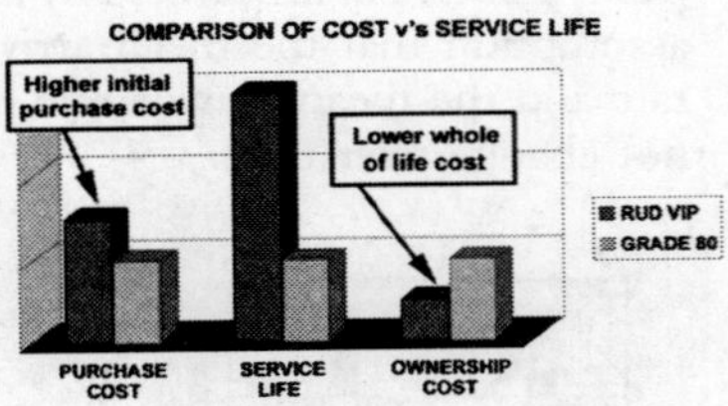


## ■ reaction plan

the action specified by a control plan when nonconforming product or process instability is identified.

## ■ record

a group of data values consisting of one value for each of a prescribed set of relational fields, an occurrence of a record type.

## ■ records management

every organisation creates records, whether in paper, film, electronic record or some other format. Records management helps an organisation to make sure it is creating and maintaining an adequate documentary record of its functions, policies, decisions, procedures and essential transactions. It then helps the organisation to decide which ones to keep and which ones to destroy and how best to organise them all. Hence it involves processes relating to the generation, receipt, processing, storage, retrieval, distribution, usage and retirement of an organisation's records.

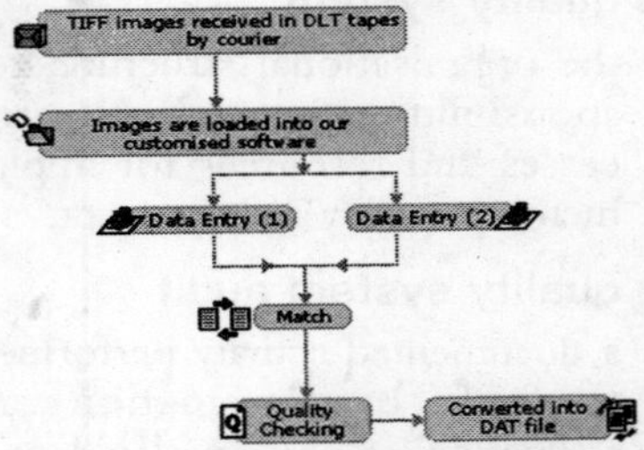


## ■ referenced documents

management and design activity standards, drawings, specifications or other documents referenced on drawings or lists or other technical documents.

## ■ registrar

a company that conducts quality system assessments to the quality system requirements.

## ■ regrade

alteration of the grade of a nonconforming product in order to make it conform to requirements differing from the original ones.

## ■ relative quality

degree of excellence of a product or service.

## ■ release

permission to proceed to the next stage of a process.

### reliability

1. the probability that an item will continue to function at customer expectation levels at a measurement point, under specified environmental and duty cycle conditions.
2. the ability of an item to perform a required function under stated conditions.

### reluctant

not willing to do something but still open to ideas.

### Remaining Duration (RDU)

the time needed to complete an activity.

### remanufacturing

remanufacturing is the process of repairing, refurbishing and/or disassembling products into reusable components. Remanufacturing is being driven by both economic and environmental rational. In some countries, remanufacturing is required by law.

### reorder point (order point) system

an approach for managing independent demand items that releases an order when the inventory position hits a certain level called the reorder point. An order point system is generally a continuous review system based on perpetual inventory records. The equation for the reorder point is R=dL+SS, where d is the average demand per period, L is the planned lead time and SS is the safety stock in units. The safety stock should be set to SS=kL0.7ód, where ód is the standard deviation of the demand per period and k is the safety factor. The safety factor should be either based on a target service level or on the economics of a stock out. The determination of the proper safety factor is beyond the scope of this document.

### repair

action taken on nonconforming product so that the product will fulfil the intended usage although the product may not conform to the original requirements.

### repeatable

basic project management processes are established to track cost, schedule and functionality. The necessary process discipline is in place to repeat earlier successes on projects with similar applications.

### requirement

1. a characteristic that a system, HWCI or CSCI must possess in order to be acceptable to the acquirer.
2. a mandatory statement in a standard or another portion of the contract.
3. a statement or set of statements that define what the user(s) of a product want that product to do. Generally, it defines what capabilities a product needs to have, based on the needs of the users.

### requirements document

a formal document that consists of a statement or set of statements that define product functions and capabilities as set by the end user.

■ **reserve**

a provision in the project plan to mitigate cost and/or schedule risk. Often used with a modifier (e.g., management reserve, contingency reserve) to provide further detail on what types of risk are meant to be mitigated. The specific meaning of the modified term varies by application area.

■ **resource**

something that is ready for use or that can be drawn upon for aid or to take care of a need.

■ **resource levelling**

any form of network analysis in which scheduling decisions (start and finish dates) are driven by resource management concerns (e.g., limited resource availability or difficult-to-manage changes in resource levels.)

■ **resource loading profiles**

detailed staffing plan including number of personnel by type over time.

■ **resource planning**

determining what resources (people, equipment, materials) are needed in what quantities to perform project activities.

■ **resource-limited schedule**

projects schedule whose start and finish dates reflect expected resource availability. The final project schedule should always be resource-limited.

■ **response development**

defining enhancement steps for opportunities and mitigation steps for threats.

■ **response time**

the time between a request for service and the time the service actually begins. In the field service context, the travel time is not considered a part of the response time.

■ **Responsibility Assignment Matrix (RAM)**

a structure which relates the project organisation structure to the work breakdown structure to help ensure that each element of the project's scope of work is assigned to a responsible individual.

■ **responsiveness**

1. the amount of delay before any action is taken.
2. an action taken that need not be informative or definitive.

■ **responsiveness to change**

changes to system and programme requirements in response to directed changes by the procuring activity or problem solutions identified shall be evaluated for total programme impact with respect to performance, cost and schedules.

■ **restructuring**

1. the firing of employees and the reorganisation of those remaining.
2. some reductions in plant and equipment.

■ **result variables**

in a model-driven DSS a result variable shows the consequences of changing decision variables. Result variable are also referred to as dependent variables.

■ **retainage**

a portion of a contract payment that is held until contract completion in order to ensure full performance of the contract terms.

■ **rethink**

1. to review a position or policy.
2. a possible change in the firm's position or policy.
3. a new position or policy.

■ **Return on Investment (ROI)**

1. a figure of merit used to help make capital investment decisions. ROI is calculated by considering the annual benefit divided by the investment amount.
2. an estimate of the financial benefit (the return) on money spent (the investment) on a particular initiative.

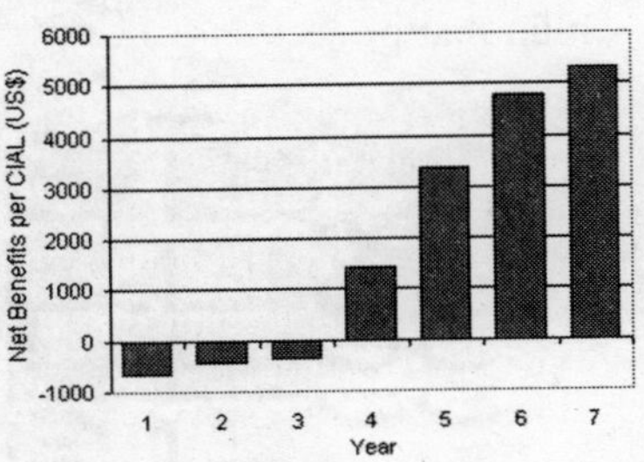


■ **revenue sharing**

revenue sharing programmes redistribute a tax base without changing boundaries. Growth in the property tax base is redistributed with special attention to below average areas.

■ **reverse logistics**

the management of the return flow for products, salvage and or waste from the customer to either safe disposal or reuse, often via the manufacturer or distributor. The materials could be either hazardous or non-hazardous. Reverse logistics involves managing movement of goods and related information, from the points of consumption towards upstream facilities in a manufacturing or service system. These reverse flows are common in a variety of industries, such as consumer goods, reusable components and packaging material. Returned items can be directly reused, repaired, recycled, remanufactured or disposed. Recently, integration of the forward and reverse logistics activities attracted considerable attention, resulting in a growing body of literature on closed-loop supply chains.

■ **review**

activity undertaken to determine the suitability, adequacy and effectiveness of the subject matter to achieve established objectives.

■ **rework**

action taken on a nonconforming product so that it will fulfil the specified requirements before it is released for distribution.

■ **right questions**

1. current unanswered questions which may impact a decision.

2. questions that will not be answered at the present time.

## ■ right sized

the firing of employees and/or the reduction of plant and equipment.

## ■ risk

any component that affects the project being completed on time and within budget. It is the possibility of suffering a loss. In a development project, the loss describes the impact to the project, which could be in the form of diminished quality of the end product, increased costs, delayed completion or failure.

## ■ risk analysis

a technique to identify and assess factors that may jeopardise the success of a project or achieving a goal. The technique also helps define preventive measures to reduce the probability of these factors from occurring and identify countermeasures to successfully deal with these constraints when they develop.

## ■ risk assessment

review, examination and judgment of whether or not the identified - risks are acceptable. Initial risk assessment is used as a tool o determine project oversight requirements.

## ■ risk control

involves executing the risk management plan in order to respond to risk events over the course of the project.

## ■ risk event

a discrete occurrence that may adversely or favourably affect the project.

## ■ risk identification

determining which risk events are likely to affect the project.

## ■ risk management

1. the process of identifying, analysing and responding to risk factors throughout the life of a project and in the best interests of its objectives.
2. an organised process to identify what can go wrong, to quantify and access associated risks and to implement/control the appropriate approach for preventing or handling each risk identified.

## ■ risk management plan

a formal plan or documentation of the risk management practice (processes, methods and tools) to be used for a specific project. This directs and manages the activities used to perform risk management within that project.

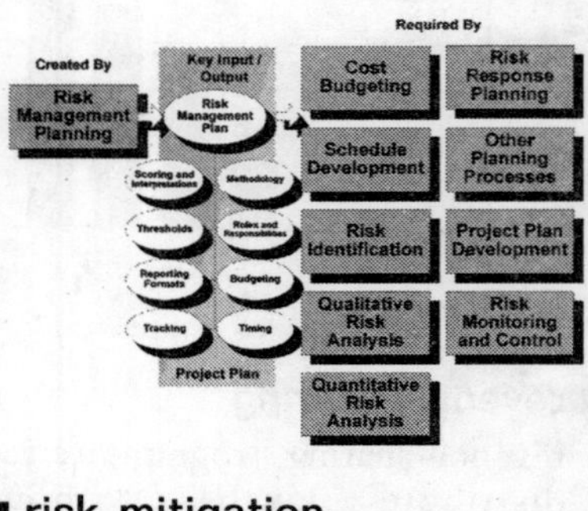


## ■ risk mitigation

the act of revising the project's scope, budget, schedule or quality, in order to reduce uncertainty on the project.

■ **risk quantification**

evaluating the probability of risk event occurrence and effect.

■ **risk response control**

responding to changes in risk over the course of the project.

■ **risk statement (also known as statement of risk)**

a description of the current conditions that may lead to a loss or a description of the loss or consequence.

■ **rough-cut capacity**

used to determine estimated load on key pieces of equipment or resources. May use production plan or master production schedule. Rough-cut capacity is used as a check to verify that manufacturing resources are adequate to execute the production plan.

■ **routing**

used in conjunction with the bill of material in manufacturing operations. While the BOM contains the material requirements, the routing will contain the specific steps required to produce the finished items. Each step in the routing is called an operation, each operation generally consists of machine and labour requirements.

■ **rule**

a formal way of specifying a recommendation, directive or strategy, expressed as 'if' premise 'then' conclusion.

■ **rules of thumb**

shortcuts to solutions to new problems that resemble problems previously solved by experienced workers.

■ **running time**

time interval from the emission to the maturity and/or for the premature repayment of an obligation. Not to confound with the duration.

■ **runs**

the patterns in a control chart within which a number of points line up on only one side of the central line.

■ **runtime**

the time required to produce a single part or product. The total runtime for an order is the batch size times the runtime.

■ **sacrifice**

the firing of employees and/or the reduction of plant and equipment.

■ **safety**

the expectation that a system does not, under defined conditions lead to a state in which human life is endangered.

■ **safety lead time**

safety lead time is a way to represent your safety stock as a number of days demand. Safety lead time can be beneficial when you want to 'pad' your lead-time to compensate for supplier variability, transportation variability or internal process variability. For example, if can take 2 or 3 days to get incoming materials processed through your receiving process, you may want to set your safety lead time to 2 or 3 days. This will calculate the requested dates for your purchase orders 2 or 3 days earlier than actual need. This is much cleaner than adding the 2 to 3 days to the suppliers lead time (which can be confusing when the supplier's stated lead-time is different from what is in your system).

## ■ safety stock

the average inventory on hand when an order is received. In an independent demand inventory system, the safety stock should be a function of the standard deviation of the demand during the replenishment lead time.

## ■ Sales and Operations Planning (S&OP)

S&OP is a horizontal communications process in which key managers from sales and operations meet frequently to develop realistic plans and promise dates for new orders. Sales and operations planning is the set of vital communications and decision-making processes for developing a company game plan that balances market demand with resource capability. A working sales and operations planning process provides a way to draw out functionally conflicting objectives and resolve them so as to develop a true manufacturing/marketing contract, integrate all functions of the business by developing a 'single set of numbers' from which all other plans and schedules can be developed and provide a forum for evaluating company performance. Any good general manager can harmonise his company through a process called 'Sales and Operations Planning', in which he meets with his top managers on a regular and frequent basis to update plans for all departments. The plans take into account projections made by the sales and marketing departments, the resources available from manufacturing, engineering, purchasing and finance and are directed toward hitting the company's objectives. Sales and operations planning is done on an 'aggregate' or 'family' level and covers a sufficient span of time to make sure that the necessary resources are available. The approved aggregate plans drive the individual departmental plans. Each month or more frequently if the market conditions are volatile the representatives meet again to determine whether the overall company plan is on course and to adjust for changes in the marketplace and changes or problems within the company.

## ■ sales department

the subgroup of people in a firm, which executes the marketing departments strategies. This group frequently values incentives and rewards.

## ■ salvage value

the value of an item when it is scrapped instead of sold. Both retailers and manufacturers can usually find a salvage firm or discounter to buy obsolete inventory.

**■ sample**
one or more individual events or measurements selected from the output of a process for purposes of identifying characteristics and performance of the whole.

**■ satisfice**
to obtain an outcome that is good enough. Satisficing action can be contrasted with maximising action, which seeks the biggest or with optimising action, which seeks the best. In recent decades doubts have arisen about the view that in all rational decision-making the agent seeks the best result. Instead, it is argued, it is often rational to seek to satisfice.

**■ scalability**
the ability to scale hardware and software to support larger or smaller volumes of data and more or less users. The ability to increase or decrease size or capability in cost-effective increments with minimal impact on the unit cost of business and the procurement of additional services.

**■ schedule development**
analysing activity sequences, activity durations and resource requirements to create the project schedule.

**■ Schedule Performance Index (SPI)**
the ratio of work performed to work scheduled.

**■ Schedule Variance (SV)**
1. any difference between the scheduled completion of an activity and the actual completion of that activity.
2. in earned value.

**■ schema**
a conceptual structure of how a digital asset shall be organised.

**■ scope**
the sum of the products and services to be provided as a project.

**■ scope change**
any change to the project scope. A scope change usually requires an adjustment to the project cost or schedule.

**■ scope creep**
any increase in the project scope (products and services described by the project) that happens incrementally and is subtle in recognition.

**■ scope definition**
decomposing the major deliverables into smaller, more manageable components to provide better control.

**■ scope planning**
developing a written scope statement that includes the project justification, the major deliverables and the project objectives.

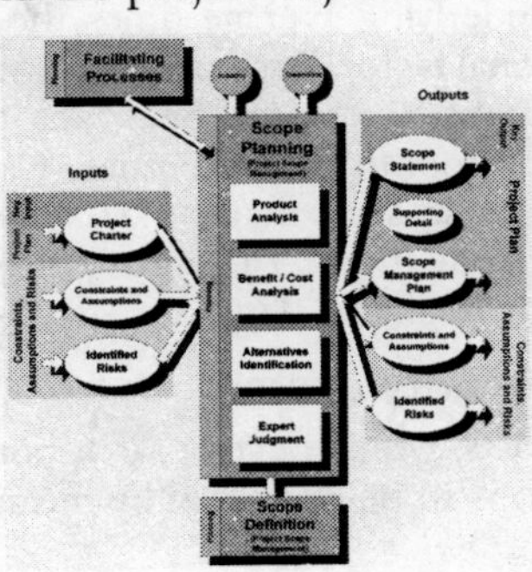

## ■ scope verification

ensuring that all identified project deliverables have been completed satisfactorily.

## ■ scrap

the number units of products or raw material that are defective and cannot be sold or reworked to product saleable product. Material outside of specifications and possessing characteristics that make rework impractical.

## ■ s-curve

graphic display of cumulative costs, labour hours or other quantities, plotted against time. The name derives from the S-like shape of the curve (flatter at the beginning and end, steeper in the middle) produced on a project that starts slowly, accelerates and then tails off.

## ■ search cost

the cost of finding a supplier that can provide a satisfactory product at an acceptable price.

## ■ seasonal factor

many forecasting models apply a multiplicative seasonal factor. The forecast, therefore, is equal to the underlying average times the seasonal factor. For example, a retailer might have a seasonal factor for the month of December (Christmas season) that is 4.0, whereas for the month of January, the factor might be 0.6.

## ■ security costs

costs, which develop, if a portfolio is to be protected by means of dynamic. With portfolios with dynamic security primarily purchase and sales costs develop with the shift of funds between the core portfolio and the opportunity portfolio. In the case of a static security the costs can arise with the purchase of derivatives instruments.

## ■ security fund

investment trusts, which give the possibility to the investors to participate on the positive development of the financial markets but against unfavourable market fluctuations.

## ■ semi-structured decisions

decisions in which some aspect of the problem are structured and others are unstructured. Structured means clearly defined and well-understood.

## ■ sensitivity analysis

running a decision model several times with different inputs so a modeller can analyse the alternative results.

## ■ sequence-dependent set up time

the time to changeover from producing one product to another is dependent upon the order in which the products are produced. For example, a paint manufacturing process might be easy to changeover from white to yellow, but very difficult to changeover from black to white. The optimal sequence to the sequence-dependent set up problem can be found by solving the famous 'travelling salesperson problem'.

■ **service factor**

factor used as a multiplier with the standard deviation to calculate a specific quantity to meet the specified service level.

■ **service failure**

when a service provider (such a barber) does not provide satisfactory service (e.g., a very bad haircut), the service episode is considered a 'service failure'. The best service organisations pay a great deal of attention to these and try very hard to recover the customers before they become 'terrorists' and give a bad report to large number of potential customers.

■ **service guarantee**

a set of two promises offered to customers before they buy a service. The first promise is the level of service provided. The second promise is what the provider will do if the first promise is not kept. Advantages include helping to retain customers who are about to defect (and give bad reports about the firm), helps the organisation to learn from its mistakes and to improve its service offerings, provides some opportunity to advertise service quality. A service g arantee often has more impact on the operations of a firm than it - does for advertising. A service guara tee is a promise relating to the intangible attributes of the service (e.g., timeliness, results, satisfaction, etc.), whereas a product warranty is on the physical attributes of the product (durability, physical performance, etc.). However, from a legal standpoint, they are both considered warranties.

■ **service recovery**

resorting customers to a strong positive relationship with the firm after they have been experienced a service failure. The six steps to service recovery are listen, apologise and show empathy, ask the 'recovery' question 'What can we do to completely satisfy you?' fix the problem quickly - prioritise customers and escalate if needed, offer symbolic atonement, follow-up to make sure that the relationship is fixed.

■ **services**

any activities performed by an independent contractor wherein the service rendered does not consist primarily of acquisition of equipment or materials or the rental of equipment, materials and supplies.

■ **servqual**

a service quality instrument that measures the gap between customer expectations and perceptions after a service encounter. The instrument was created by Parasuraman, Zeithaml and Berry (1988) and has been used in numerous service industries. The servqual instrument is organised around five dimensions of customer service: Tangibles - physical facilities, equipment and appearance of personnel Reliability - ability to perform the promised service dependably and accurately Responsiveness - willingness to help customers and provide prompt service Assurance - competence, courtesy, credibility and security Empathy - access, communication and understanding. The instrument has been criticised in a number of different research papers for a number of different reason, but continues to be popular in many industries. One of the main criticisms is that service quality may not be a function of the gap between expectation and service but is a function of the value that is delivered to the customer.

## ■ set up cost (changeover cost order cost)

the marginal cost of a set up. This generally includes the labour and the materials cost associated with the scrap generated by the set up. Allocated overhead (fixed costs) should not be included as a part of the set up cost. The cost of a set up at a bottleneck (constrained) resource should include the opportunity cost of entire system. The cost of a set up at a non-bottleneck resource should be only the marginal cost of the labour and materials.

## ■ set up reduction methods

for many processes, the key to process improvement is to reduce the set up time and cost. One of the key methods for doing this is to move the set up time to 'external' set up time. An external set up is done to prepare a job for a machine while the machine is still running.

## ■ seven tools of quality

quality improvement tools that include the histogram, Pareto chart, check sheet, control chart, cause-and-effect diagram, flowchart and scatter diagram.

## ■ share

security, which confirms a portion right by a document at a corporation. As a partner, the shareholder has membership rights (right to vote, right of information) and real property rights (right to portion of the profit, subscription right).

## ■ share fund

investment trusts, which invest their fortune mainly in shares.

## ■ shop floor control

shop floor control (also known as production activity control) involves all of the activities required to monitor the process of moving an order through a factory, from order release to order completion. SFC systems often involve information systems to communicate the status of shop orders and work centres. Major functions of shop-floor control include: assigning priority of each shop order, maintaining WIP quantity information, conveying shop-order status information to the office, providing actual output data for capacity control purposes, providing quantity by location by shop order for WIP inventory and accounting purposes, measuring efficiency, utilisation and productivity of manpower and machines.

## ■ short term

1. a short period of time.
2. a period of time short enough to give reasonable.

3. assurance of stability.

### ■ silo

an individual group within an organisation, such as a department or unit. The term is often used to suggest that such groups tend to be inward-looking, in that they do not take into account what other similar groups are doing or how their work affects other such groups.

### ■ Single Minute Exchange of Dies (SMED)

the reduction in die set-up time to less than one minute. This is the time from the last good part for one order to the first good part of the next order. A single minute is not required, but is used as a reference.

### ■ single point of contact

a service quality principle that suggests that a customer should have to talk to only one person for the delivery of a service. The opposite of this happens in many service organisations when a customer waits a long time in queue only to be told by the unfriendly service worker that they have to go see someone else and never builds any relationship with any service worker and no service worker ever takes any 'ownership' of the customer's needs. Advantages of the single point of contact principle include the firm builds a closer relationship with the customer, the customer does have to wait in multiple queues, much less information is lost in the 'handoffs' between multiple service workers, the job design is more satisfying for the service worker because they get to 'own' the entire set of the customer's needs.

### ■ single source and sole source supplier

with a single source supplier the firm has only one supplier for a part, but has other suppliers who are qualified to provide the part. With a sole source supplier, the firm has one and only one source capable of supplying the part. A sole source supply is basically a monopoly situation and can be very dangerous for the customer. However, in some situations a sole source relationship is unavoidable.

### ■ single-loop learning (or adaptive learning)

single-loop learning involves using knowledge to solve specific problems based on existing assumptions and often based on what has worked in the past. In contrast, double-loop learning goes a step further and questions existing assumptions in order to create new insights.

### ■ sit down across a table

1. have a possible confrontational meeting.
2. a meeting where some work is planned.

### ■ situation

a development that is hard to explain away.

### ■ six sigma

six sigma has at least three different meanings depending upon the context. Six Sigma is the structured application of the tools and techniques of total quality management on a project basis to achieve strategic business results. Six sigma is a management philosophy. Six sigma is a customer based approach realising that defects are expensive. Fewer defects mean lower costs and improved customer loyalty. The lowest cost, high value producer is the most competitive provider of goods and services. Six sigma is a way to achieve strategic business results. Six sigma is six sigma is a statistic. Six sigma processes produce less than 3-4 defects or mistakes per million opportunities. Many successful six sigma projects do not achieve a 3.4 ppm (parts per million) or less defect rate (or 99.99966% good). That just indicates that there is still opportunity. Six sigma is that six sigma is a process. To implement the six sigma management philosophy and achieve the six sigma level of 3.4 defects per million opportunities or less there is a process that is used. The six sigma process includes five steps define, measure, analyse, improve and control. Note that six sigma is not a set of new or unknown tools. Six sigma tools and techniques all are found in total quality management. Six sigma is the application of the tools on selected important projects at the appropriate time. Six Sigma training programmes develop leaders in the following three categories: master black belts who have completed numerous projects and train other black belts, black belts who are team leaders with between four to eight weeks of training and green belts who are team members with between two and four weeks of training.

## ■ skills directory

see expertise directory.

## ■ SKU, Stock Keeping Unit

referring to a specific item in a specific unit of measure. For example, if you distributed thirty-weight motor oil in both quarts and gallons you would maintain the inventory as two SKUs even though they are both thirty-weight motor oil.

## ■ slack

term used in PERT for float.

## ■ SMWT

Self-Managed Work Teams.

## ■ socialisation

the process of sharing tacit knowledge by bringing people together to discuss things, share experiences or work together.

## ■ society type

this investment trust has its own juridical personality. The portions are issued in the form of shares. The investor becomes shareholder and possesses both fortune and membership rights.

## ■ specification

the document that prescribes the requirements with which the product or service has to conform.

## ■ specification documents

documents that provide specific information about the project deliverable characteristics.

## ■ spin off

the sale of a part of a firm to new shareholders or to an outside firm.

## ■ spreadsheet

in the accounting world a spreadsheet was and is a large sheet of paper that lays everything out for a businessperson. It spreads or shows all of the costs, income, taxes, etc. on a single sheet of paper for a manager to look at when making a decision. An electronic spreadsheet organises information into columns and rows. The data can then be 'added up' by a formula to give a total or sum. The spreadsheet can summarise information from many sources and present the information in a format to help a decision maker see the financial 'big picture' for the company.

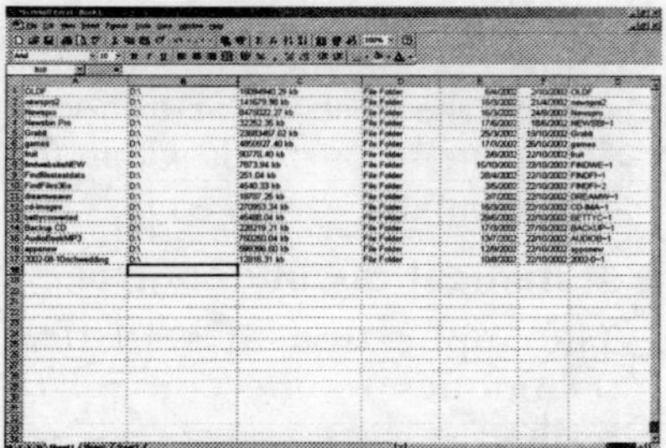

squeaky wheel gets the grease
a vital employee can get a raise by asking for it.

## ■ stage-gate process

in project management and in new product development, a stage-gate (or simply a gate) is a step (sometimes called a milestone) where the merits and progress of the project are evaluated before further progress is allowed. A gate involves a review that often results in a 'go/ no go' decision for the project. Examples include freezing product designs, updating projected costs to completion and gaining customer acceptance prior to funding full tooling or scale-up. See **project management.**

A process typically used in projects where significant investment is being made, such as capital improvements or new product development programs. Stage-gate processes are especially useful when the level of investment increases with subsequent decision points. The process is composed of stages and gates, hence the name. A stage is the time between gates, typically with activities and deliverables. A gate is a decision point where the merits and progress of the project are evaluated before further progress is allowed.

## ■ stakeholder

1. individuals and organisations that are involved in or may be affected by project activities.

2. an individual or group of individuals with a common interest in the performance of the supplier

organisation and the environment in which it operates.

## standard

mandatory requirements employed and enforced to prescribe a disciplined uniform approach to software development, that is, mandatory conventions and practices are in fact standards.

## standard deviation

a measure of the variability of a random variable. The sample standard deviation is the square root of the sample variance and is defined by: The first expression is known as the definitional form, the second expression is known as the 'computational form' because it is easier for computing purposes. The population standard deviation should have n instead of in the denominator.

## standardisation

ensuring the workers perform tasks consistently in the same manner, usually to ensure safety, productivity and quality.

## standards

are specific and where applicable, technical documents containing directives and mandatory specifications governing the management, development and use of information technology resources.

## starving

a process is 'starved' if it runs out of input materials to process. This is very bad for the bottleneck process because it will reduce the output of the entire system. Starving a non-bottleneck process generally has few consequences for the overall output of the system. Starving at a non-bottleneck process signals that we should use that worker somewhere else in the process. Starving at a bottleneck resource occurs because of a disruption at an upstream process or simply because of poor planning and improper priorities.

## state agency or agency

any agency, institution, board, bureau, commission, council or instrumentality of state government in the executive branch listed in the appropriation act.

## Statement of Work (SOW)

a narrative description of products or services to be supplied under contract.

## statements of desires

a statement that something is hoped for does not imply any action is to be taken to ensure the desired outcome. Example: I want us all to be happy with our compensation.

## statistical control

the condition describing a process from which all special causes have been removed, evidenced on a control chart by the absence of points beyond the control limits and by the absence of non-random patterns or trends within the control limits.

## statistical quality control

The application of statistical techniques to the control of quality.

■ **status reports**

a report containing information on a specific project, indicating if the project is ahead of schedule, on schedule or behind schedule in relation to the project plan.

■ **stay on task**

continue on a path toward an objective and not get distracted.

■ **stick to your knitting**

staying with your main lines of business while other lines of business may suffer cutbacks in employees and/or plant and equipment.

■ **story telling**

1. a technique employed in knowledge management environments to describe complicated issues, explain events, communicate lessons learnt or bring about cultural change. The technique is based on established processes of constructing stories to communicate information, learning and values.
2. the use of stories in organisations as a way of sharing knowledge and helping learning. Stories can be very powerful communication tools and may be used to describe complicated issues, explain events, communicate lessons learned or bring about cultural change.

■ **strategic decision**

a major choice, usually about market.

■ **strategic planning**

a decision-making process in which decisions are made about establishing organisational purposes/mission, determining objectives, selecting strategies and setting policies.

■ **strong market**

price is rising due to a large or rising demand.

■ **structural capital**

1. assets not directly related to the presence of employees' what stays behind when employees go home - including databases, customer lists, manuals, trademarks and organisational structures.
2. an organisation's 'captured knowledge' such as best practices, processes, information systems, databases etc. Often described as the knowledge that remains in the organisation 'after the employees have gone home for the night'. Structural capital is one component of intellectual capital.

■ **structured decisions**

standard or repetitive decisions situations for which solution techniques are already available (also sometimes called routine or programmed decisions). The structural elements in the situation, e.g. alternatives, criteria, environmental conditions, are known, defined and understood.

■ **style**

term used to denote differences in design or appearance.

■ **subcontractor**

an individual, partnership, corporation or an association that contracts with an organisation (i.e., the prime contractor) to design, develop and/or manufacture one or more products.

**■ substantial progress**

a level of achievement that a grantee must make in its project during a specified period of time (e.g., budget period, performance period), which produces measurable and verifiable evidence that the activities undertaken have attained a preponderance of project goals and objectives during the period.

**■ substantive**

reality as seen by an unbiased observer and not just the official view of the management.

**■ subsystem**

an element of a system that, in itself may constitute a system.

**■ successful meeting**

1. productive discussion.
2. an uneventful meeting.
3. a concluded meeting.

**■ supplemental capabilities**

those that add value to core capabilities but that could be imitated.

**■ supplier**

1. organisation or person that provides a product.
2. any person or group inside or outside the organisation that produces a product or service. Suppliers improve quality by identifying customer expectations and adjusting work processes so that products and services meet or exceed those expectations.

**■ supplier qualification and certification**

a customer 'qualifies' a supplier when it has been determined that the supplier is capable of providing a part. A supplier becomes 'certified' when it has delivered parts with perfect quality over a pre-specified time period (say six months). At that point, inspection is no longer needed. In some cases, the two firms share the savings.

**■ suppliers**

the term 'suppliers' includes contractors, sub-contractors, vendors, developers, sellers or any other term used to identify the source from which products or services are obtained.

**■ supply chain management**

the central idea of supply chain management is to apply total system approach to managing the flow of information, materials and services from raw material suppliers through factories and warehouses to the end customers. The result of this should be lower total system cost (lower inventory, higher quality) and higher service levels. However, the benefits of such changes need to be shared between the players in the supply chain.

**■ surplused**

the firing of employees and/or the reduction of plant and equipment.

**■ suspend operations**

1. the temporary interruption of normal business activity.

2. the permanent closing of an office or plant.

**■ sustainable development**

development with the goal of preserving environmental quality, natural resources and liveability for present and future generations. Sustainable initiatives work to ensure efficient use of resources.

**■ switching cost**

the customer's cost of switching from one supplier to another. It is often in the supplier's best interests to increase the customer's switching costs so that the customer does not defect to the competition the first time that the competition offers a small price decrease.

**■ switching gears**

1. changing the pace.
2. changing the topic.

**■ synergy**

1. a common attribute.
2. the combination of two things could produce more with fewer employees and/or plant and equipment.

**■ synthesis**

the translation of input requirements (including performance, function and interface) into possible solutions (resources and techniques) satisfying those inputs. Defines a physical architecture of people, product and process solutions for logical groupings of requirements (performance, functions and interface) and their designs for those solutions.

**■ system**

set of interrelated or interacting elements.

**■ tacit knowledge**

highly personalised knowledge that is hard to formalise and communicate. Tacit knowledge consists of know-how, mental models, beliefs and perspectives largely based of experience.

**■ tailoring**

the tailoring of requirements is the responsibility of the acquirer (customer), suggested tailoring may be provided by prospective and selected developers (prior to contract agreement).

**■ take a position**

1. have an opinion.
2. have a point of view.

**■ take care of your concerns**

1. to overcome objections and/or questions.
2. explanations suffice in place of answers.

**■ take charge of**

1. to take responsibility for an activity.
2. to guide the activity.

**■ take questions**

1. listen to questions from one or more people.
2. some response may be offered to each question but none is promised.

**■ takt time**

daily demand rate divided by the number of working hours in the day. This is really just the cycle time required to meet the demand rate.

■ **tardiness**

an order is said to be 'tardy' if it is past the due date (or due time). Tardiness is zero if the order is on-time or is early. Average tardiness is a common measure, but should be used with caution because it only considers orders that are tardy. For example, a firm has hundreds of orders that are tardy with an average of 2 days. The firm dramatically improves its on-time performance for nearly all orders. However, it now has two orders that are tardy with an average tardiness of 4 days.

■ **target standard**

the target design standards for prototype systems, toward which work during the development phase is directed in regard to prototypes.

■ **task**

1. a sequence of instructions treated as a basic unit of work.
2. a well-defined unit of work in the software process that provides management with a visible checkpoint into the status of the project. Tasks have readiness criteria (preconditions) and completion criteria (post conditions).

■ **task force**

a group of employees given the responsibility to research some aspect of a firm's business.

■ **task interleaving**

term used in describing functionality of warehouse management systems to mix tasks to reduce travel time. Sending a forklift driver to put away a pallet on his way to his next pick is an example of task interleaving.

■ **tax increment financing**

a programme designed to leverage private investment for economic development projects in a manner that enhances the benefits accrued to the public interest.

■ **taxonomy**

a high level device constructed to enable the user to get an understanding of and to navigate round, the intellectual capital of the enterprise.

■ **team**

a collection of people, often drawn from diverse but related groups, assigned to perform a well-defined function for an organisation or a project. Team members may be part-time participants of the team and have other primary responsibilities.

■ **team member**

the individuals, reporting either part time or full time to the project manager, who are responsible for some aspect of the project's activities.

■ **team player**

someone who goes along with policies and gets along with others.

■ **technical data**

recorded information, regardless of medium or characteristics, of a scientific or technical nature. It may, for example document research, experimental, developmental or engineering work or be usable or used to define a design or process or to acquire, support, maintain or operate materiel. Technical data does not include computer software or financial, administrative, cost and pricing and management data or other information incidental to contract administration.

■ **technical effort**

a technical effort is any activity that influences system performance by defining, designing or executing a task, requirement or procedure.

■ **technical expert (in an audit)**

person who provides specific knowledge of or expertise on the subject to be audited.

■ **technical performance measurement**

the continuing prediction and demonstration of the degree of anticipated or actual achievement of selected technical objectives. It includes an analysis of any differences among the 'achievement to date', 'current estimate' and the specification requirement. 'Achievement to date' is the value of a technical parameter estimated or measured in a particular test and/or analysis. 'Current Estimate' is the value of a technical parameter predicted to be achieved at the end of the contract within existing resources.

■ **technical programme planning and control**

the management of those design, development, test and evaluation tasks required to progress from an operational need to the deployment and operation of the system by the user.

■ **technical specifications**

specifications that establish the material and performance requirements of goods and services.

■ **technique**

a method of performing an analysis.

■ **technological capability**

term used to encompass the system of activities, physical systems, skills and knowledge bases, managerial systems of education and reward and values that create a special advantage for a company or line of business.

■ **technology infrastructure**

means telecommunications, automated data processing, word processing and management information systems and related information, equipment, goods and services.

■ **technology investments**

assets such as business-driven applications, data, facilities, IT human resources, infrastructure, services, operations and processes used to support the flow or processing of information for business activities.

**technology portfolio**

a management tool comprised of essential information about technology investments, structured to facilitate the evaluation of investment alternatives in support of an agency's overall strategic business plan.

**termination**

the firing of an employee who will not be hired back.

**test**

determination of one or more characteristics according to a procedure.

**test requirement**

the stimulus, measurement, power, loads and any special test equipment or procedure essential to validate proper operation of a device or some predetermined design control or product specification definition.

**testable**

a requirement or set of requirements is considered to be testable if an objective and feasible test can be designed to determine whether each requirement has been met.

**the planned lead time**

(or planned customer lead time) is usually a fixed quantity, which may be conditioned on some attribute of the order (quantity, complexity, routing, materials, size, etc.). For example, a firm might offer a two-week lead time for standard products and a three-week lead time for non-standard products. The service level for respond-to-order systems is measured in terms of on-time delivery (OTD). OTD is the percent of orders received (or shipped) within the promise date (or request date). Ideally, a firm should compute OTD based on the customer request date. The promise date may or may not satisfy the customer's requirements. Most firms find this difficult to implement and therefore use only the promise date. This is complicated by the fact that the promise date can be 'updated' as the situation changes. In other words, it is possible that the promise date is updated (e.g., revised, manipulated) so that orders are rarely late. Ideally, a firm should compute OTD from the customer's perspective. Therefore, firms should measure OTD based on the customer receipt date rather than the ship date. However, most firms do not have access to the customer receipt date information and therefore measure OTD against their shipping dates — and then hold their distribution/transportation partners responsible for their portion of the customer lead time. OTD can be improved by either setting a very long planned customer to make safer promises (e.g., promise 20 weeks instead of two weeks) or reducing the mean and/or variance of the manufacturing lead time. The first alternative can have a negative impact on the demand. The second alternative requires Six Sigma thinking to reduce the mean and variability of the customer lead time.

## ■ Theory of Constraints

the Theory of Constraints (TOC) is a management philosophy developed by Dr. Eliyahu M. Goldratt, an Israeli physicist. TOC recognises that there are very few critical areas, resources or policies that truly block the organisation from moving forward. As Goldratt states, 'a chain is only as strong as its weakest link'. This is really an application of Pareto's Law to process management and process improvement. The concepts are consistent with managerial eco omics that teach that the se up cost for a bottleneck resource is the opportunity cost of the lo t gross margin and that the op ortunity cost for a non-bottl eneck resource is nearly zero. S e throughput accounting, drum-buffer-rope. According to TOC, if performance is to be improved, an organisation must identify its constraints, exploit the constraints in the short run and in the longer term, find ways to overcome the constraints (limited resources.) His theory of constraints is composed of the following: Identify the system constrains — No improvement is possible unless the constraint or weakest link is found. Decide how to exploit the system constraints — Make the constraints as effective as possible. Subordinate everything else to that decision — Align every other part of the system to support the constraints, even if this reduces the efficiency of non-constraint resources. Elevate the system constraints. (If output is still inadequate, acquire more of this resource so it no longer is a constraint. If, in the previous steps, the constraints have been broken, go back to Step 1, but do not let inertia become the system constraint. (After this constraint problem is solved, go back to the beginning and start over. This is a continuous process of improvement: identifying constraints, breaking them and then identifying the new ones that result.) Underlying Goldratt's work is the notion of synchronous manufacturing, which refers to the entire production process working in harmony to achieve the profit goal of the firm. When manufacturing is truly synchronised, its emphasis is on total system performance, not on localised measures such as labour or machine utilisation. This leads to the whole goal of the firm, which is to make money. In operations terms, this is accomplished through increasing throughput, reducing inventory and maintaining or reducing operating expenses. The 'constraint' is the bottleneck, which is any resource that has capacity less than the market demand. Alternatively, the process that has the lowest average processing rate for producing end products. (Remember a constraint or bottleneck, can be a machine, a process, a regulation, a person, etc.) Ways to manage the constraint: in Art's words from his presentation -Identify the constraint (where is the largest queue? What process has the least idle time?) -Manage the constraint to protect it from being idle or wasting capacity. (Reduce set up times, increase lot sizes, inspect before the constraint) -Manage other processes so the constraint is never starved (everything else has small lot sizes, do not overproduce, move people to balance the flow) -Find additional capacity (work more hrs, use alternative routings, buy more capacity, subcontract)

### ■ throughput accounting

accounting principles based on the Theory of Constraints. See **Theor of Constraints.** Throughput is the r te at which an organisation gen erates money through sales. Goldratt defines throughput as the difference between sales revenue nd unit-level variable costs such as aterials and power. Cost is the mo t important driver for our oper tions decisions, yet costs are- unreliable due to arbitrary allo ation of overhead, even with Activity Based Costing. Since the goal of the firm is to make money, operations can help this through three items of throughput accounting: Inventory (I), operating expenses (OE) and throughput (T) Inventory = materials cost and other truly variable costs with no overhead Operating expenses = overhead and labour cost (the things that turn 'I' into 'T') Throughput rate = revenue materials cost out of pocket selling costs. When we apply throughput accounting to the bottleneck (constraint), we must look at key performance measurements: output, set up time (average set up time by product and total set up time per period), downtime (planned and emergency) and yield rate. We focus on the constraint because it can have the biggest impact on our throughput accounting measures (I, T, OE), which in turn affect the goal, which is making money for the firm.

### ■ tight supply and demand

a rising price due to both a high demand and a low supply.

### ■ time fence

period of time prior to the scheduled production date beyond which changes can be made without significant adverse effects.

### ■ time-based competition

a strategy to shorten customer lead times in order to segment the demand to target the time-sensitive (and price-insensitive) customers, reduce finished goods inventory cost, drive out non-value activities.

### ■ timeframe

the period when action is required to mitigate the risk. Timeframe is one of the three attributes of risk.

### ■ timely

at a time anywhere near when it is needed.

### ■ time-outs

time-outs are conditional tasks that execute when a certain task has not been completed for a given period of time. Time-outs are typically used in conjunction with workflow approvals.

### ■ time-phased order point

an extension of the reorder point system that uses a demand

forecast to plan when the inventory position will hit the safety stock level. An order is then planned to arrive at that time. The start date for the order is planned to be 'L' time units earlier, where 'L' is the planned lead time.

■ **time-scaled network diagram**

any project network diagram drawn in such a way that the positioning and length of the activit represents its duration. Essetially, the diagram is a bar chart that includes network logic.

■ **title sponsor**

the firm after which something is named. Firms frequently attach their name to buildings, stadiums, tournaments and other structures and events.

■ **TL 9000**

requirements for suppliers to the telecommunications industry.

■ **TMS, Transportation Management System**

category of operations software that may include products for shipment manifesting, rate shopping, routing, fleet management, yard management, carrier management, freight cost management.

■ **top line**

gross revenues to a firm.

■ **top management**

person or group of people who directs and controls an organisation at the highest level.

■ **total cost**

the sum of all cost (fixed and variable) for a particular item or activity over a specified period.

■ **Total Cost of Ownership (TCO)**

a calculation of the fully burdened cost of owning a component. The calculation helps consumers and enterprise managers assess both direct and indirect costs and benefits related to the purchase of IT components. For the business purchase of a computer, the fully burdened costs can also include such things as service and support, networking, security, user training and software licensing.

■ **Total Quality Control (TQM)**

a management approach advocating the involvement of all employees in the continuous improvement process-not-just quality c ntrol specialists.

■ **Total Quality Management (TQM)**

an approach for improving quality that involves all areas of an organisation, sales, engineering, manufacturing, purchasing, etc. with

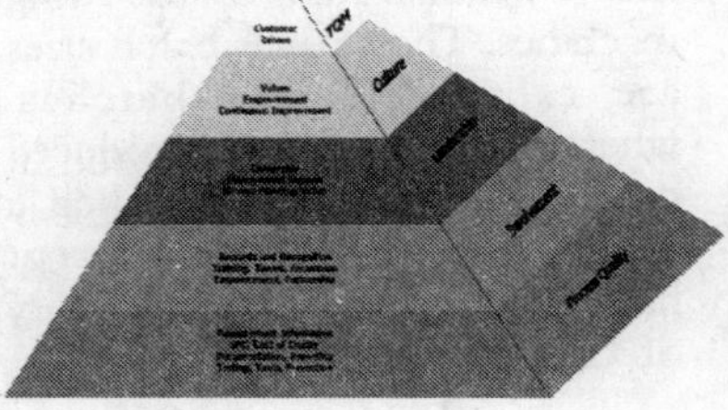

a focus on employee participation and customer satisfaction. TQM can involve a wide variety of quality control and improvement tools.

**■ total risk**

see risk.

**■ traceability**

the ability to trace the history, application or location of an item or activity and like items or activities by means of recorded identification.

**■ track the project**

keep management informed of progress made. Management may feel that the project may not be completed on time.

**■ trade-off study**

an objective evaluation of alternative requirements, architectures, design approaches or solutions using identical ground rules and criteria.

**■ transaction cost**

the cost of processing one transaction. In a supply chain management context, this is the cost of processing one purchase order.

**■ transfer batch**

when a batch is produced on one machine, smaller batches can be moved (transferred) to following machines. The smaller batch sizes are called 'transfer batches' whereas the larger batch produced on the first machine is called a 'production batch'. This concept has been promoted in the 'Theory of Constraints'.

**■ tremendous contribution**

1. great help in the accomplishment.
2. help from someone who may have been one of many in a group.

**■ trend (for forecasting)**

the average rate of increase for the demand. This will be the slope of a demand. One simple way to estimate this is with simple linear regression.

**■ trigger**

thresholds for indicators that specify when an action, such as implementing a contingency plan, may need to be taken.

**■ trim costs**

the firing of employees and/or the reduction of plant and equipment with a minimum reduction in production.

**■ trim fat**

the firing of employees and/or the reduction of plant and equipment. These were non productive inputs.

**■ two-bin system**

a two-bin inventory system is a very simple visual 'reorder point' system with the main bin used for normal inventory. The reserve bin is only opened when the main bin is empty. When the reserve bin (the reorder point) is opened, an order is placed. It is a good idea to put a lock on the reserve bin in order to make sure that the ordering discipline is enforced.

■ **unclassified**
not attracting a security classification but control may be required for other reasons. Therefore official information of a unclassified nature should not be disclosed without formal departmental/ programme approval.

■ **Under Ministry Control (UK)**
the point when the responsibility for authorising changes to a design, defined as modifications, is transferred to a government controlled committee.

■ **unit load**
material handling term that describes any configuration of materials that allow it to be moved by material handling equipment as a single unit. While smaller manually handled configurations could be considered unit loads, the term generally defines larger configurations that would be moved by a lift truck such as palletised loads, crates, bales, etc.

■ **unit of measure**
the standard unit of an item used in the stock account and to construct order quantities.

■ **unstructured decisions**
this type of decision situation is complex and no standard solutions exist for resolving the situation. Some or all of the structural elements of the decision situation are undefined, ill-defined or unknown. For example, goals may be poorly defined, alternatives may be incomplete or non-comparable, choice criteria may be hard to measure or difficult to link to goals.

■ **utilisation**
the percent of the possible work time that a resource is busy. Utilisation is often a bad goal.

■ **vacuous reasoning**
when a non explanative statement is given as a reason. Example: Since this is this year, our sales are good.

■ **validation**
1. the evaluation of a product at the end of the development lifecycle to ensure that it not only complies with the requirements and the specific criteria set forth by the customer, but performs exactly as expected.
2. confirmation by examination and provision of objective evidence that the particular requirements for a specific intended use can be consistently fulfilled.

■ **value add**
1. benefit.
2. help.

■ **value chain**
a concept developed by Michael Porter to illustrate an organisation's value-creating ability and expressed as flow.

■ **value engineering**
the systematic application of recognised techniques by a m lti-disciplined team to identi y the function of a product or service, establish a worth for that function, generate alternatives through the use of creative thinking and pro-

vide the needed functions to accomplish the original purpose of the project, reliably and at the lowest life-cycle cost without sacrificing safety, necessary quality and environmental attributes of the project. Engineering with the purpose of simplifying products and processes by achieving equivalent or better performance at a lower cost. An approach of redesigning parts to try to get the same function at less cost.

## ■ value proposition

the logical link between action and payoff that knowledge management must create to be effective. Customer intimacy, product-to-market excellence and operational excellence are examples.

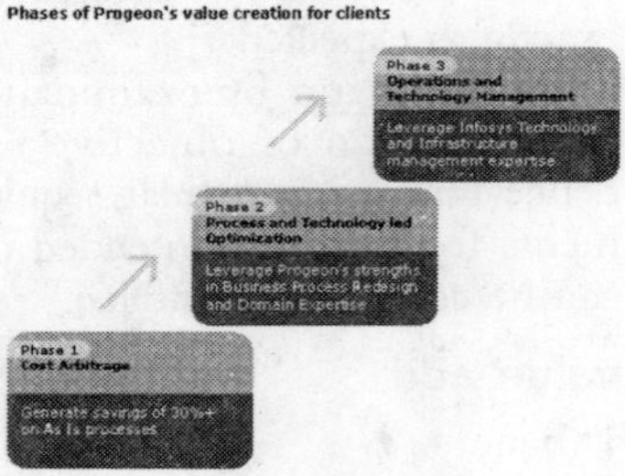


## ■ value proposition

this how you have positioned your product in the market. For example, if you are offering a very low priced product that has few features, then your firm is trying to 'proposition' your customers based on price and not on features. A statement of differentiated and timely value of a product or service, which meets a need or solves a problem for an individual customer or group of customers. It consists of a package of benefits from which a customer is persuaded that he/she derives greater value than from a competitor's offering. In an economic sense, the value proposition is the sum of features divided by the life-cycle cost.

## ■ values

an expression of beliefs that will express and serve the cause, i.e. in the ultimate sense what will help to survive.

## ■ variables

those characteristics of a part that can be measured. Examples are length in millimetres, resistance in ohms, closing effort of a door in kilograms and the torque of a nut in foot pounds.

## ■ variation

the inevitable difference among individual outputs of a process. The sources of variation can be grouped into two major classes: common causes and special causes.

## ■ vendor

a manufacturer or supplier of an item.

## ■ Vendor Managed Inventory (VMI)

in the VMI process, the vendor assumes responsibility for managing the replenishment of stock. Rather than a customer submitting orders, the vendor will replenish stock as needed. This is sometimes referred to as supplier-managed inventory (SMI) or co-managed inventory.

## ■ verification
the process of determining whether or not the products of a given phase of a project fulfil the established requirements.

## ■ verification function
tasks, actions and activities to be performed to evaluate progress and effectiveness of the evolving system (people, product and process) solutions and to measure compliance with requirements. Analysis, (including simulation) demonstration, test and inspection are verification approaches used to evaluate, risk, people, product and process capabilities, compliance with requirements and proof of concept.

## ■ vertical integration
when a firm owns its sources of supply and/or its channel of distribution, it is said to be 'vertically integrated'.

## ■ vesting period
1. the number of years before an employee owns his employer paid benefit.
2. the percent owned by the employee that grows over the entire period. This increase is rarely steady and can be from 0 to 10 years or more.

## ■ viable
able to last for a least a while.

## ■ virtual (virtual team)
'virtual' is a term used to describe something that exists or is brought together via electronic networks, rather than existing in a single physical place. For example, a 'virtual team' is a team whose members are not located together and who utilise electronic networks for communication, collaboration and work processes.

## ■ virtual organisation
an organisation without permanent facilities, e.g., building and without many permanent employees. It relies on contractual relationships with suppliers, distributors and a contingent workforce.

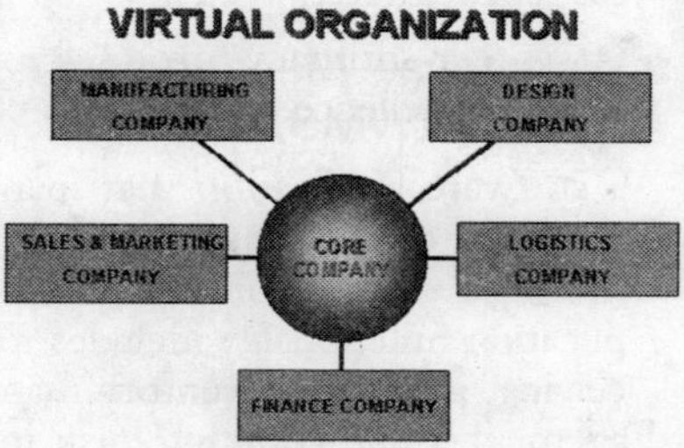


## ■ virtual team
a team whose members are not co-located and who utilise electronic networks for communication, collaboration and work processes.

## ■ voice of the customer
customer feedback both positive and negative including likes, dislikes, problems and suggestions.

## ■ voice of the process
statistical data that is feedback to the people in the process to make decisions about the process stability and/or capability as a tool for continual improvement.

**volume flexibility**

the ability to increase or decrease the production rate and be profitable.

**waiver**

written authorisation to use or release a quantity of material, components or stores already manufactured but not conforming to the specified requirements.

**want you to feel**

1. ask you to believe.
2. a desire to be believed with little evidence offered.

**Warehouse Management System (WMS)**

a software application that manages the operations of a warehouse or distribution centre. Application functionality includes receiving, put away, inventory management, cycle counting, task interleaving, wave planning order allocation order picking, replenishment, packing, shipping, labour management and automated material-handling equipment interfaces. Some systems use bar codes and/or radio frequency technology to provide accurate information in real time.

**waterfall**

this term is used in project management and new product development to suggest that a set of steps is not started until the previous set of steps is complete. The opposite of this is concurrent engineering. See **project management.**

**weak market**

price is falling due to a low demand.

**well behaved price**

1. stable price.
2. a price that is little changed.
3. a price, which is not falling or rising over time.

**well positioned**

1. desired by customers.
2. a claim to satisfy customer's needs.

**white pages**

in knowledge management terms a white pages is a structured directory of people within an organisation, usually in electronic form. It is often the basis for an expertise directory.

**whittle a department away**

1. slowly close a part of a firm.
2. to gradually fire all the employees in a section of the firm.

**wider context**

1. a broader point of view.
2. looking at other related topics.

**WIP, Work-In-Process**

generally describes inventory that is currently being processed in an operation or inventory that has been processed through one operation and are awaiting another operation. WIP is actually an inventory account that represents the value of materials, labour and overhead that has been issued to manufacturing but has not yet produced a stockable item. Depending on how your accounting and inventory systems are set up, it may also include components picked for production usage or finished products awaiting final inspection.

**■ work breakdown structure**

a product-oriented listing, in family tree order, of the hardware, software, services and other work tasks which completely defines a product or programme. The listing results from project engineering during the development and production of a materiel item. A WBS relates the elements of work to be accomplished to each other and to the end product.

**■ work environment**

set of conditions under which work is performed.

**■ work package**

a deliverable at the lowest level of the work breakdown structure, when that deliverable may be assigned to another project manager to plan and execute. This may be accomplished through the use of a subproject where the work package may be further decomposed into activities.

**■ work partnership**

a mutually beneficial work relationship between internal and external customers and suppliers.

**■ work process**

a series of work steps that produce a particular product or service for the customer.

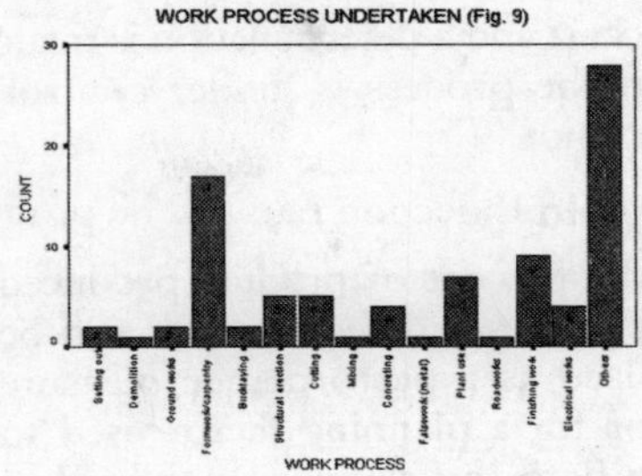


**■ work to make it happen**

1. do all that is necessary to obtain the desired result.
2. do what little may be needed to be done.
3. do nothing to prevent the desired result.

**■ workaround**

a response to a negative risk event. Distinguished from contingency plan in that a workaround is not planned before occurrence of the risk event.

**■ workflow**

the logical sequence of activities to achieve an outcome.

**■ x-bar chart**

a quality control chart that monitors the mean of the process. A sample of n parts is collected from the process every so many parts or time periods. The mean of the sample is plotted on the control

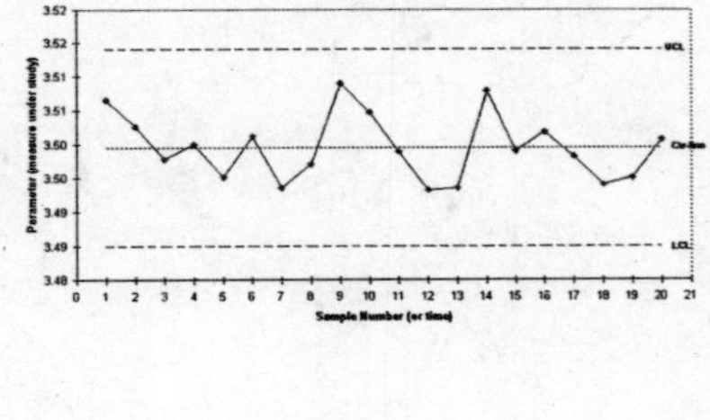

chart and a determination is made if the process is 'under control' or not.

## ■ yield

the percent of product produced that is not defective. This can be used as a performance measure or for a planning factor used to inflate the required production start quantity.

## ■ yield management

for many capital-intensive businesses such as airlines, theatres, stadiums and utilities, the goal is to maximise revenue because nearly all costs are fixed. Yield management is an approach to maximising revenue given that the capacity-related costs are relatively fixed. Yield management systems change prices and capacity allocations over time as the date of the event approaches. For example, it is said that airlines change their prices 60,000 per day. Note that the goal is not to maximise utilisation (although that is usually the result), the goal is to maximise revenue per unit of resource. This is sometimes also called 'revenue management' or 'perishable asset resource management'.

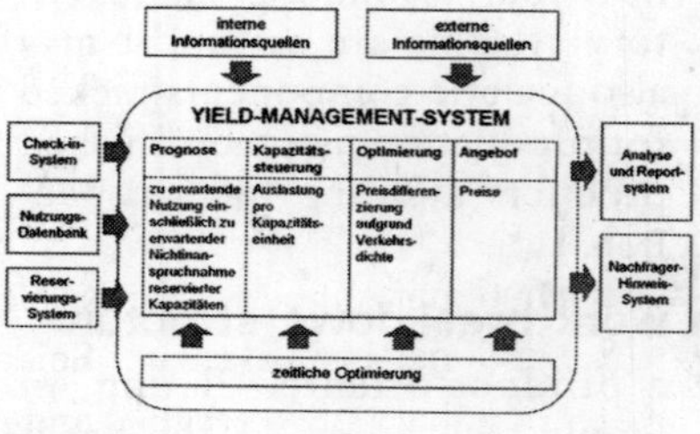


## ■ zero defects

the quality concept of zero tolerance for defects.

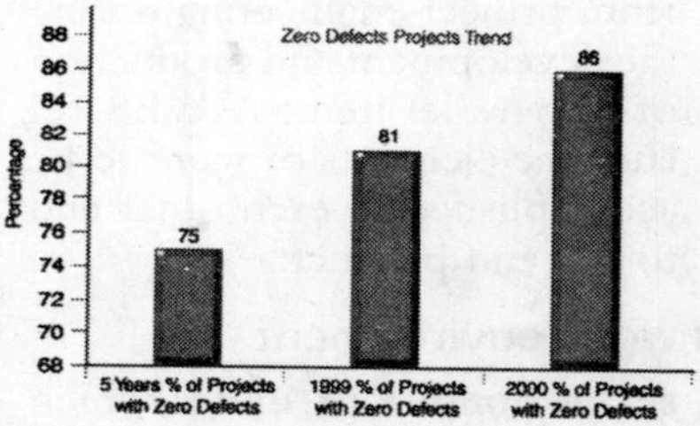


## ■ zero inventory

this is a name used by some to describe a JIT inventory system.

## ■ zone picking

order picking method where a warehouse is divided into several pick zones order pickers are assigned to a specific zone and only pick the items in that zone orders are moved from one zone to the next (usually on conveyor systems) as they are picked (also known as 'pick-and-pass').

**Other Books on**

# LOTUS ILLUSTRATED DICTIONARIES

| | |
|---|---|
| 1. Dictionary of New Words (New) | 125/- |
| 2. Dictionary of Veterinary Sciences (New) | 125/- |
| 3. Dictionary of Synonyms and Antonyms (New) | 150/- |
| 4. Dictionary of Idioms and Phrases (New) | 150/- |
| 5. First English Dictionary | 125/- |
| 6. Astronomy | 125/- |
| 7. Agriculture | 125/- |
| 8. Anthropology | 125/- |
| 9. Archaeology | 125/- |
| 10. Architecture | 125/- |
| 11. Art | 125/- |
| 12. Banking Finance & Accounting | 125/- |
| 13. Bio-Chemistry | 125/- |
| 14. Business Administration | 125/- |
| 15. Bio-Technology | 125/- |
| 16. Biology | 125/- |
| 17. Botany | 125/- |
| 18. Culture | 125/- |
| 19. Chemical Engg. | 125/- |
| 20. Chemistry | 125/- |
| 21. Civil Engineering | 125/- |
| 22. Computer Science | 125/- |
| 23. Commerce | 125/- |
| 24. Cooking & Food | 125/- |
| 25. Ecology | 125/- |
| 26. Economics | 125/- |
| 27. Education | 125/- |
| 28. Electrical Engineering | 125/- |
| 29. Electronic & Telecommunication | 125/- |
| 30. Environmental Studies | 125/- |
| 31. Festival | 125/- |
| 32. Geography | 125/- |

| | |
|---|---|
| 33. Geology | 125/- |
| 34. Genetic Engineering | 125/- |
| 35. Health & Nutrition | 125/- |
| 36. History | 125/- |
| 37. Import and Export | 125/- |
| 38. Information System Management | 125/- |
| 39. Internet | 125/- |
| 40. IT | 125/- |
| 41. Inorganic Chemistry | 125/- |
| 42. Law | 125/- |
| 43. Library & Information Science | 125/- |
| 44. Literature | 125/- |
| 45. Management | 125/- |
| 46. Mathematics | 125/- |
| 47. Marketing & Sales | 125/- |
| 48. Mass Communication | 125/- |
| 49. Mechanical Engg. | 125/- |
| 50. Medical | 125/- |
| 51. Music | 125/- |
| 52. Organic Chemistry | 125/- |
| 53. Philosophy | 125/- |
| 54. Physical Education | 125/- |
| 55. Physics | 125/- |
| 56. Psychology | 125/- |
| 57. Science | 125/- |
| 58. Sex | 125/- |
| 59. Sociology | 125/- |
| 60. Sports | 125/- |
| 61. Textile | 125/- |
| 62. Zoology | 125/- |

Lotus PRESS

Unit No. 220, Second Floor, 4735/22,
Prakash Deep Building, Ansari Road, Darya Ganj,
New Delhi - 110002, Ph.: 32903912, 23280047, 09811594448
E-mail: lotuspress1984@gmail.com, www.lotuspress.co.in